SOCIAL WORK

To all those who struggle to make our world
a more inclusive and peaceful place

SOCIAL WORK

Theory and practice for a changing profession

Lena Dominelli

polity

First published in 2004 by Polity Press
Reprinted 2004, 2005

Polity Press
65 Bridge Street
Cambridge CB2 1UR, UK

Polity Press
350 Main Street
Malden, MA 02148, USA

A catalogue record for this book is available from the British Library.

Library of Congress Cataloging-in-Publication Data

Dominelli, Lena.
    Social work : theory and practice for a changing profession / Lena Dominelli.
        p. cm.
Includes bibliographical references and index.
    ISBN 0–7456–2382–4 (hb : alk. paper) – ISBN 0–7456–2383–2 (pb : alk. paper)
1. Social service. 2. Social policy. 3. Social workers. 4. Sociology. I. Title.

HV40.D6562 2004
361.3–dc21   2003014517

Typeset in 10.5 on 12 pt Palatino
by Graphicraft Limited, Hong Kong
Printed and bound in Great Britain by
TJ International, Padstow, Cornwall

For further information on Polity, visit our website: www.polity.co.uk

CONTENTS

ABBREVIATIONS

BASW	British Association of Social Workers
CCA	National Health Service and Community Care Act 1990
CCETSW	Central Council for Education and Training in Social Work
CDPs	Community Development Projects
CJA	Criminal Justice Act 1991
CJCS	Criminal Justice and Court Services Act 2000
CJS	criminal justice system
COS	Charity Organization Society
CQSW	Certificate of Qualification in Social Work
CSS	Certificate in Social Services
DHSS	Department of Health and Social Security
DipSW	Diploma in Social Work
DPS	Diploma in Probation Studies
FGC	family group conference
FMI	Financial Management Initiative
GSCC	General Social Care Council
IASSW	International Association of Schools of Social Work
IFSW	International Federation of Social Workers
NALGO	National Association of Local Government Officers
NSI	Next Steps Initiative
NVQ	National Vocational Qualification
PFI	Private Finance Initiative
PPP	Public–Private Partnership
PSR	pre-sentencing reports
QAA	Quality Assurance Agency

SCIE	Social Care Institute for Excellence
TOPSS	Training Organization for the Personal Social Services
YJB	Youth Justice Board
YOT	Young Offenders Team
YTSs	Youth Training Schemes

ACKNOWLEDGEMENTS

Writing a book is an adventure shared with others – people whose ideas, opinions and behaviours influence the thinking that informs what is written and the readers whose interpretation of what is said and the value attached to it determine the success or failure of that particular intervention in creating new discourses or affirming existing ones. I cannot name all these contributors to my work – the men and women clients, practitioners and policymakers who agreed to be interviewed by me – but I thank you all for shaping my thinking and challenging me to maintain reflexivity as a way of growing and expanding my views of life. Thank you for your insights and generosity. Then there are specific individuals who are too numerous to mention by name. These include my colleagues in the Department of Social Work Studies at the University of Southampton, the School of Social Work at the University of Victoria and the International Association of Schools of Social Work. Thank you all for your good-natured discussions with me. Special thanks go to Maria, Rita and Nicola for their unending hospitality and support. To my parents for their boundless wisdom, I say, 'thank you from the bottom of my heart' and hope that you will find your values reflected in this work. And to Nicholas and David, who were always there despite my moments of despair, I humbly acknowledge my debt of love.

Lena Dominelli

INTRODUCTION

Introduction

Social work is a troubled and troubling profession. Its role and place in the professional firmament of the twenty-first century are hotly contested. Challenges to its current organizational structures and purpose are emanating from several sources: policymakers disillusioned by its failure to control deviant populations and respond adequately to human need; other professionals, particularly those in the health arena, who find social work's remit vague and its helping stance antagonistic to theirs; 'clients'[1] who complain about its oppressive and coercive dimensions; managers who seek to curb professional autonomy; practitioners who endeavour to provide appropriate forms of practice in unconducive contexts that are exacerbated by an inadequate resource base, high staff mobility and overwhelming caseloads; and social work educators who struggle to theorize its position in a demanding globalizing environment and contribute to the development of new forms of practice. Each of these stakeholders has a legitimate perspective and shifting sets of concerns that have to be addressed if social work is not to be dismembered by the forces of change that are reconfiguring its professional boundaries and questioning its existing ways of working and knowledge base.

Understanding the nature of the changes that are reframing social work locally, nationally and internationally is crucial if social work is to survive as a discipline and practice making a worthwhile contribution to human well-being. Responding to this becomes a challenge that requires social work educators and practitioners to rethink their approach to social work to develop theories and forms of practice that can use the profession's existing strengths, particularly its capacity for critical, reflexive practice, to move in directions that are consistent with a value base rooted in promoting human rights and social justice in and through practice. A key context for practice is a globalizing one in which what have been taken as the fixed borders of the nation-state, which have hitherto bounded social work as a discipline responding to parochial matters, have become a leaking sieve as global forces shape the local while in turn being reframed in and through the local. Increased social interaction within and across borders combines with technological developments to bring home the message that people live in an interdependent world where events in one locality carry considerable implications for what happens in another, with attendant consequences for residents. Engaging with others to reformulate practice requires contextualization at the local, national and international levels.

In this book, I take the reader on a journey that explores the complex, interactive and multi-layered contexts of practice to unpack its professional depths, examine the dynamics underpinning particular approaches to social work and highlight their strengths and weaknesses. I do this in the hopes of contributing to client empowerment by encouraging practitioners to become the best they can be: that is, practitioners who can respond to the contemporary demands of practice and work within an egalitarian, human rights-based framework to promote the well-being of clients as active citizens. To meet this aim, I embed practice in a partnership rooted in the principles of solidarity and reciprocity to link individual growth with social support and development. An individual becomes a person by interacting with others, whose own humanity and agency are (re)affirmed in the process. Responses to human well-being are negotiated and welfare needs met (or not) through these interactions.

A critical, reflexive approach to practice highlights the transferable elements of knowledge and skills that practitioners gain in their work with specific client groups and settings. It helps to refocus their theoretical and conceptual thinking in ways that transcend the limitations of particular ways of working to facilitate innovation and a wider understanding of issues and how to address them. A broadened comprehension of the intricate dynamics of practice also reveals the importance of responding to postmodern critiques of identity and difference, not least because these attributes are so ingrained in individual consciousness and agency, but also because social work's value base promotes social justice and human well-being. It also assists practitioners in developing a critical perspective that does not paralyse them in the chaos of intersecting sets of social divisions, each of which demands solutions that eliminate oppression and hardship or decrease their confidence in their capacity to deal with these effectively. The insights so gained will help practitioners in improving their practice regardless of the setting or client groups to whom they relate at any given time. Social workers will have to make these perceptions their own and adapt them to the specificities of their situation through further reflection and action.

Rethinking social work: Interrogating practice in an uncertain and difficult clime

Social work is suffering a crisis of confidence as it faces constant attacks from policymakers, practitioners, clients, academics and the lay public. These question its professional integrity and failure to deliver on its promises to protect vulnerable people, control deviant populations and improve the life circumstances of society's most disadvantaged individuals. In a globalizing world in which the nation-state is being restructured to promote the interests of global capital and neo-liberal ideologies, social work practitioners find themselves in the contradictory position of having to justify their existence as professionals explicitly charged with improving the quality of people's lives at both individual and collective levels while being subjected to the 'new managerialism' (Clarke and Newman, 1997) and asked to do more with less by becoming increasingly efficient and effective in rationing their chosen interventions at the same time as demand for their services is rising dramatically (Teeple, 1995; Ralph, Regimbald and St-Amand, 1997). These factors create an uncertain and difficult clime within which practitioners are obliged to respond to human need while reformulating their thinking about practice and how they do it.

While social workers are being publicly castigated for failing to do their job, particularly in the area of child welfare, the boundaries of practice are being reconfigured. Other professionals, especially those in health care, psychiatry and psychology, have assumed control of many of social work's constituent parts and the borders between the different professions have become increasingly blurred and contested. Additionally, many of social work's clients are turning to self-help groups to meet their needs as they begin to demand a greater say in the type of services available and more control over how these are accessed and run. At the same time, as they raise their voices and demand to be heard, clients have begun to challenge the validity of expert knowledge as *the* determining knowledge that not only defines how their problems are constructed and given meaning, but also affirms what options might solve them. Government is also assisting these developments through social policies and legislation that encroach on social work's terrain while introducing new arenas where its work is being promoted. For example, in Britain, the personal advisers working in Job Centres and community workers linked to Sure Start and other community regeneration initiatives are doing social work. In these ways, the contours of social work are being both appropriated and extended and the boundaries of the profession are becoming more fluid and less certain than previously.

The specific nature of the disenchantment with its practitioners varies from country to country, as might be expected in a locality-based profession like social work. The possibilities for initiating real changes in the circumstances in which people live seem greater in low-income countries where social workers sit alongside clients to address structural inequalities by mobilizing local populations in community-based actions (Kaseke, 1994; Healy, 2001). In Britain, even the term 'social work' is in danger of disappearing from public pronouncements as political discourses in this field pro-mote the label of 'social care' in its place. This replacement signals more than a semantic shift. It signifies the deprofessionalization of practice in a particularly Fordist simplification of social work's complexities by embodying these in the notion of competence-based practice that is being foisted upon practitioners through public policies and legislative fiat.

The attempt to assert Fordist principles in practice is paralleled by that of (re)affirming the importance of empiricist knowledge, a move best typified in the rush to evidence-based practice (Sheldon, 2000; Trinder, 2000) that takes uncritically the view that there is only one possible way of collecting and verifying evidence. This is a primarily positivist approach reflected in the dominance of risk assessments as the key tool for intervention strategies (Cowburn and Dominelli, 2001). By ignoring experiential evidence, empiricist approaches to evidence-based practice devalue the richness and complexity of human interactions and the dialogical features that arise through the exercise of agency between participating parties. Thus, the resulting 'evidence' can often be a simplistic caricature that is used to create a fictive narrative which can be easily repro-duced as expert knowledge signifying *the* 'truth'.

The competing focus on experiential evidence exposes the contested nature of knowledge (Belenky et al., 1997) and indicates that there are many knowledge-producing narratives that have to be taken into account. This alternative approach helps to unmask the reality that what passes as empirical evidence is little more than the systematic collection of anecdotal narratives that become treated as data through the power of research and the ability of the researcher to create a consistent story by analysing accumulated materials through a particular lens. This becomes posited as *the* accepted truth with a power of representation that lasts as long as other people, whether or not involved in the research, find it credible.

What counts as evidence has a highly subjective element to it. This subjectivity is central in (re)defining relationships between individuals and groups and their external world and affects their consciousness of it. Lack of consciousness does not mean false consciousness. It is simply that individuals who have constructed their lives around particular discourses cannot conceive of alternative ways of framing their situations even when their day-to-day experiences are dissonant with their worldviews. Such reframing can occur through the consciousness-raising endeavours propounded by Paolo Freire (1972) when the individual concerned develops a different narrative by participating in different types of experiences or someone engages that person in formulating other ways of understanding and acting upon his or her world.

Social work can be defined as an exercise in engaging with people to facilitate the telling of their story around a particular problem relating to their well-being, that is, to articulate what has happened to them and why. Its interactive base makes social work a *relational profession*. In this, practitioners and clients become co-participants in elaborating other narratives in which new possibilities for action open up (Hall, 1997; Cedersund, 1999). Their 'new' narratives are formed through interactions between the worker(s) and client(s) and the worldviews to which they individually subscribe, as these shape the realm of the possible for them.

Social work is the practice of intervening in the lives of individuals who need assistance in the acts of everyday living. Even at the best of times, it is a deeply problematic practice, mediating as it does the relationship between an individual in need and others in society who may or may not be in need. That those privileged enough to have the welfare resources they require have to be convinced of the value of helping others acquire theirs is a problem for social workers. They have to address queries about entitlement to services and assume responsibility for their provision in tricky and contested circumstances. The neo-liberals' severing of the direct connection between service provision and the state's responsibility to pay for meeting acknowledged need further complicates the relationship between practitioners, as representatives of the state, and their clients. It does so by raising barriers against the fulfilment of unmet needs. Responding to the needs of vulnerable people requires equality amongst citizens as expressed through entitlement to services; the human rights that underpin citizenship; solidarity as articulated through reciprocity between providers and users; and access to resources and services. Practitioners' difficulties also arise because they have to act as if there were certainties of practice when few are present.

The philanthropic gaze: Privileging residual welfare provisions

The personal social services can be provided by a plurality of providers – the state, the voluntary, commercial or household sectors. Professional social work occurs within particular social contexts and is guided by specific legislation, social policies, cultural practices in a given locality and accumulated professional knowledges termed 'practice wisdoms'. Each of these elements is constantly argued over and changing, and those whose knowledge or narrative counts assume a critical position in setting practice agendas. Although social work can be practised amongst people at all stages of the life cycle, involve people from all classes, genders, ethnicities and abilities, contemporary provisions accessed through the welfare state have become reserved largely for poor people (Jones, 1998) and those who are otherwise disadvantaged and under-resourced. Practitioners often struggle against a backdrop of the low status accorded to clients and working for members of the public who are in need.

Social work practice is complicated by its traditional association with residual provisions that target socially excluded needy individuals, families, groups and communities. Accessing publicly funded personal social services has been cast in charitable, almsgiving terms and adjudicated by knowledgeable experts who reinforce a sense of disentitlement or residuality. I term this the 'philanthropic gaze'. Under it, recipients of assistance are defined as a homogeneous group that can be segregated into 'deserving' and 'undeserving' members. The former may have some of their needs met under stringent conditions; the latter are left to rely on their own resourcefulness, or the expenditure of energy in activities which may or may not be lawful. The grouping and regrouping of clients into deserving and undeserving categories for the purposes of resource allocation forms part of the processes of regulation that Foucault (1991) called the 'technologies of governmentality', which are rooted in regimes of control.

Professional regimes of control are an important 'technology of governmentality' and are used regularly in social work. These are constantly being (re)formulated as different stakeholders attempt to shape welfare agendas. The state's responsibility to care for the casualties of a particular way of organizing social relations is offloaded onto the individual concerned through its employees, the practitioners who use knowledge and expertise to implement socially sanctioned regulatory regimes. Contemporary regimes of control in social work are embedded in neo-liberal discourses about welfare.

The philanthropic gaze is not restricted to those securing help from the welfare state. It is also practised by other providers whose beneficiaries are divided into deserving and undeserving clients (Whitton, 1931). Encapsulated by charitable giving, the philanthropic gaze undermines citizenship. Organizationally sanctioned rules and regulations guide interventions in the voluntary sector too. These are no less controlling than those exercised by welfare state professionals. Under the philanthropic gaze, asking for help is an admission of failure. Negative responses to these requests affirm clients' perceptions that recourse to the residual provisions on offer proves malfunction on their part. Their definition as failure has also been confirmed in Culpitt's (1992) analysis of neo-liberal welfare provisions.

Social workers are associated not with universally accessible benefits placed at the disposal of citizens, but with residual ones handed out as charity to deserving supplicants. Working within the philanthropic gaze embroils practitioners as key architects of regulatory practices that impact negatively upon excluded peoples. Residuality constitutes clients as passive beings dependent on others for their welfare and reinforces the negation of both active citizenship and the affirmation of individual and collective human rights and agency. Consequently, services are not designed within a rights framework by those needing them, but are determined by others and offered on a 'take it or leave it' basis (Dominelli and Khan, 2000).

In compromising the citizenship status of recipients, residuality reinforces a charitable rather than a rights-based notion of entitlement to services. Practitioners are assumed to know what is best. Clients are cast as deficient individuals who display little initiative for planning their own lives and are expected to behave according to professional diktat. Social work practitioners have also been constrained by a lack of professional autonomy, practising as they do within a contingent reality that has been shaped by a dependency on the state and the goodwill of its citizenry to operate.

The location of public provisions targeting poor people within a multilayered context of pluralistic providers has meant that wealthy people who require personal social services can purchase unstigmatized professional assistance through the market and avoid being compromised through residuality or being subjected to the philanthropic gaze. Through market-based provisions, they can exercise voice by using their purchasing power and exit strategies to favour those arrangements that they find empowering, in a way that those reliant upon public sector professionals cannot.

Practitioners can transfer from one provider sector to the other through a revolving door of employment opportunities, often created by state policies that promote the marketization of social services (Dominelli and Hoogvelt, 1996b). The kind of relationship established between workers and clients is determined not only by the capacities of individual professionals, but also by the contexts within which they deploy their skills to configure particular possibilities in practice. In the public sector, practitioners and clients work to establish emancipatory frameworks for practice within tightly constrained and constraining parameters, particularly with regards to resources at their disposal and the range of structural inequalities that they can directly address. Where chronic underfunding has made a difficult job more so, the capacity of both practitioners and clients to exercise agency is more contingent. But as they are involved in constituting their reality as well as being constituted by it, they may challenge their position through these interactions. Operating within a wide variety of controls and contexts, social work practice has become the art of the possible.

In this book, I examine social work as both the art of the possible and the science of creating a better future by drawing on empirical research, experiential knowledges and practice wisdoms to consider how social work can respond more appropriately and urgently to the social problems that beset our world at local, national and international levels. In a postmodernist framework, attempting such a project would be diminished through the accusation of being 'modernist' and out of touch with current realities. To this charge,

I reply that one only needs to look at the myriad manifestations of injustice in both British society and other countries to appreciate that in the current historical juncture, the privilege of taking for granted the benefits of modernity is reserved for the few. I would rather place what energies and talents I have at the disposal of those who are not so privileged to help them realize their goal of improving their situations. Conceptualizing social work according to liberationist precepts places it within moral discourses concerned with the realization of social justice in the local, national and international domains.

Continuities and discontinuities in practice

British social work since the Second World War has been located largely within the state sector and has engaged primarily with socially excluded people who are poor and vulnerable. Its location within the welfare state reflects a change from its nineteenth-century origins as a primarily voluntary activity with indirect links to the nation-state (Walton, 1975). The balance between social work and the state has been a constantly shifting one. During the latter part of the twentieth century and the beginning of the twenty-first, it has changed again to encompass a different mix of statutory, commercial, voluntary and domestic provisions. The processes of change are likely to continue initiating further innovations in practice as the twenty-first century evolves.

In countries like the United States, social work has been consistently less embedded within the statutory sector. Those accessing services through public provisions are stigmatized because these are aimed at socially excluded individuals and families with no other resources. Public services have been set aside as inferior and available only under strictly controlled conditions (Alinsky, 1968; Teeple, 1995), an arrangement that currently exacerbates public perceptions of clients as unworthy and incapable individuals (Zucchino, 1997). This stratification also enables wealthier people to purchase high-quality personal social services from the commercial sector without loss of face.

The situation differs again in low-income countries. In southern Africa, social work professionals have been more concerned with developing people's capacities within their communities, usually geographically defined, to promote social and community development (Kaseke, 2001) and redress the imbalances of a social work profession that was initially established to meet the needs of white settlers (Kaseke, 1994; Simpson, 2002). In these countries, social work concerns are more in keeping with an agenda based on addressing structural inequalities than with individual improvements, although these are also evident. In Zimbabwe, social work professionals have played key roles in initiating structural responses to social problems (Kaseke, 1994), whereas in post-apartheid South Africa, the black majority government has taken a direct role in promoting the social development approach through its Reconstruction and Development Programme (RDP) (Simpson, 2002). Consequently, social work discourses that favoured casework primarily for the white population during the colonialist apartheid era have given way since 1994 to those endorsing social development and community action (Simpkin, 2001; Simpson, 2002).

The emphasis on structural inequalities and community mobilization in Britain has parallels in the preoccupations of the Settlement Movement at the end of the nineteenth century (Walton, 1975) and the Community Development Projects supported by the British government from the late 1960s to the mid-1970s (Loney, 1983; Dominelli, 1990).[2] The shifting popularity between individualizing and structural discourses in the profession has marked continuities and discontinuities in social work practice as different actors have gained control of its agenda and sought to (re)make it in their image. This has included benefactors, practitioners, educators, policymakers and sometimes clients, organizing to ensure that certain discourses hold sway over others in particular localities at different times (Kendall, 2000, 2002).

Social workers have consistently been charged with the duty of upholding the human rights of vulnerable groups (Ife, 2001), although what constitutes these rights has been hotly contested and what has been encompassed within them has shifted throughout the profession's history. A human rights orientation is an extension of the expectation that practitioners facilitate the expression of citizenship for those who have been denied the opportunities to exercise it in the course of their daily lives. Affirming the human rights of socially excluded people renders social work a politicized profession, an aspect of practice which may place its practitioners on a collision course with employers, politicians, policymakers and the general public.

Intervening to advantage those who have transgressed hegemonic social norms even though they may be disadvantaged or oppressed persons can be unpopular. As a result, not everything practitioners do is applauded, even if it proves to be in the best interests of the client in the short term, and society in the long term. Examples of

British social work interventions that have not carried much public confidence include social workers' attempts to prevent young deprived offenders from perpetrating crime by taking them on trips abroad to instil in them a sense of responsibility for their behaviour (Burchard, Burchard and Farrington, 1989; Barry and McIvor, 2000; Russell and Phillips-Miller, 2002), and using social work practice to alleviate the damaging impact upon clients of oppression in society-at-large (Mishna and Mushat, 2001), to develop self-respect and respect for others, and to acquire interpersonal skills, including collaboration to achieve goals (see Phillips, 1993, 1994).

Supporting people who are experiencing human rights violations can aggravate social workers' relationships with their ruling authorities. In some situations, practitioners have paid for supporting the underdog with imprisonment and/or their lives (Fariman Fariman, 1996; Ife, 2001). In promoting human rights, social workers tread a tightrope over a chasm that requires considerable knowledge and skill to cross safely. Taking action to support human rights is risky and the outcome of their negotiations cannot be guaranteed. They are constantly negotiating risks, sometimes with respect to clients, at other times in relation to themselves.

Unity and fragmentation in social work

Social work covers a wide range of client groups, activities and settings. Its remit extends from work done with isolated individuals with few social networks to work encompassing complex social systems involving the many sub-systems associated with them. Social work is constantly being defined and redefined as it evolves in response to shifting contexts and demands. Its base is constantly changing by fragmenting and regrouping, although it retains unity around its core values and overall purpose. Social work's broad reach and interdisciplinary nature have challenged practitioners and educators who have tried to put boundaries around its remit, if only for strategic purposes like establishing discrete training programmes and professional credentials. Social workers also have to negotiate complex and contradictory sets of demands and expectations.

The desire to be inclusive of diversity in practice at the local level within what has become a globally recognized profession has prompted the International Association of Schools of Social Work (IASSW) and the International Federation of Social Workers (IFSW) to agree a definition of what constitutes social work:[3]

The social work profession promotes social change, problem solving in human relationships and the empowerment and liberation of people to enhance well-being. Utilising theories of human behaviour and social systems, social work[ers] intervene[s] at the points where people interact with their environments. Principles of human rights and social justice are fundamental to social work. (IASSW and IFSW, 2001)

This definition is an inclusive one and indicates the variety of roles and functions that social workers occupy across the world. Ranging as they do from one-to-one interventions to groupwork and community action, these reveal that social workers can act as counsellors, therapists, clinical practitioners, probation officers, social care workers, youth workers, planners and community workers. Its scope makes it difficult to draw exact boundaries around the profession and can get social workers involved in demarcation disputes with other professionals in allied fields, particularly those in health/social care work done in community settings, therapeutic psychology and rehabilitative psychiatry. It also involves social workers in a number of different tasks which include securing changes in individual behaviour, providing direct services, co-ordinating the provision of services by others, advocating for change in social structures, reforming government legislation and reformulating social policies.

This diversity in practice is also reflected in the wide range of educational training arrangements that exists worldwide (Garber, 2000) as social work educators have to prepare practitioners to work in a broad spread of settings, with different legislative remits, cultural traditions and client groups, and using diverse practice methodologies. The IASSW and the IFSW are endeavouring to increase the international profile of the profession and create unity within its vast diversity. They are also seeking to address the implications of these complexities by developing global qualifying standards for the profession (see Sewpaul, 2002) through another joint effort.[4]

While certain interests promote a degree of unity in the profession across national borders, there are counter-pressures leading to the deprofessionalization and fragmentation of the profession. Deprofessionalization has occurred as a result of managerialist imperatives that further Fordist relations of production in service provision and delivery, as exemplified in specific countries including New Zealand, Australia and Britain. The exigencies of Fordist production, sometimes referred to as Taylorism, have been codified under the rubric of competence-based social work (Dominelli and Hoogvelt, 1996a).

Competence-based social work is bringing Fordist methods of mass production developed in the manufacturing sector into the service one. This can be construed as the proletarianization of professional labour because a key aim of Fordist regimes is to simplify complex tasks as routine activities that can be undertaken by anyone. Fordism is being fostered by management anxious to exercise greater control over the activities of practitioners and gain more labour flexibility (Dominelli and Hoogvelt, 1996a; Clarke and Newman, 1997). The attempt to mimic industrial production processes in human services has not received universal acclaim (Black Assessors, 1994; Dominelli, 1996). The practices and attendant pressures generated by this approach are more in keeping with the demands of bureaucratic accountability and the rise of a corporatist culture intent on securing profits from the delivery of welfare services at the expense of a caring profession that is a moral activity practised for the benefit of others.

Competencies have been endorsed for drawing a broad segment of the social care workforce into training. This is a much needed improvement given that many of these workers are not qualified. I am concerned about this training being set at a low level in Britain, primarily National Vocational Qualification (NVQ) level 2, and its failure to address the absence of a career ladder or low pay for front-line staff. Poor wages and the lack of career opportunities exacerbate and reinforce the low professional status ascribed to social work as 'women's work' (Wilson, 1977; Toynbee, 2003). These shortcomings contribute to my scepticism about the capacity of competence-based approaches to raise the status of social work (Dominelli, 1996, 1997).

Competence-based approaches rely on functional analyses and the processes of risk assessment and risk management to draw boundaries around unacceptable behaviour and curtail 'dangerousness' vis-à-vis others or limit self-harm. Risk assessments attempt to predict the likelihood of a particular individual engaging in dangerous behaviour and thereby inculcate a sense of certainty in uncertain situations (Quinsey, 1995). Convicted sex offenders and families with children in abusive situations are often subjected to risk assessment and management processes by practitioners to reduce the potential for harm. Risk assessments as currently practised have become mechanisms of (self-)regulation, a technology of governmentality (Foucault, 1991) whereby professionals engage with those concerned to enable the latter to themselves control the risks that they may either produce or encounter and limit the potential of identified risk factors to disrupt their lives. Sadly, risk assessments have unreliable outcomes despite their alleged scientific basis (Quinsey, 1995). In emphasizing individual control, risk assessments enable the state's representatives, practitioners, to evade their responsibility for ensuring the existence of a general life-enhancing environment for all. Producing such a climate is a trust the state holds on behalf of all its citizens. Its violation is of direct concern to social workers, who are charged with promoting people's well-being.

Self-regulation occurs primarily through individual input. The category of deserving and undeserving clients is relevant because regulation is fostered through the deployment of scarce state resources to deserving cases. Clients who benefit from limited family support services in deserving cases of child abuse or from special programmes for sex offenders illustrate this trend. Despite their precarious condition, those excluded from such programmes are expected to fend for themselves. For them, risk can continue or even increase rather than reduce. Notwithstanding the fact that risk assessments give the impression of imposing order in difficult circumstances rather than curtailing actual risk (Quinsey, 1995), the capacity to identify or calculate potential risk is still an advance over a total indifference to it.

The 'new managerialism' (Clarke and Newman, 1997), competence-based approaches and risk assessment and management have wrought significant changes in an arena of work that has traditionally been dominated by relational concerns and professional autonomy practised as discretionary interventions in the lives of individuals with few resources and opportunities for subverting professional power relations. Like other forms of bureaucratic developments imposed on practitioners, these have yielded mixed results. On the positive side, the new managerialism has curtailed the privileging of professional autonomy; demanded greater accountability for practitioners' use of scarce resources; sought to increase service users' choice as consumers of services provided by social services agencies; and attempted to raise the standards of both practice and qualifications amongst the many workers who previously practised social care as personal care without appropriate training.

On the negative side, the new managerialism has not resulted in the anticipated additional resources and services necessary for hard-pressed individuals, families, groups or communities. Nor has it led to the empowerment of either clients or workers; contributed to a reduction in the heavy workloads that obstruct the creation of innovative forms of practice; promoted the evolution of client-centred methodologies; encouraged stability in practice; or furthered the development of the dedicated professionals who work hard to meet the needs of clients in impossible situations (Dominelli and Kahn, 2000; Dominelli, 2001).

These pressures keep social work in a creative, if stressful, tension which may become counter-productive as practitioners respond by leaving the profession in droves. Staff turnover in Britain is particularly high in urban areas like London. Vacancies remain unfilled for substantial periods of time and have prompted overseas recruitment.[5] Depending on the borough, London vacancy rates vary from 12 to 56 per cent. How can social work meet today's challenges when so many forces are undermining its capacity to assert its rightful place in the panoply of professions that have the express purpose of serving people?

I answer this question in this book by arguing that social work is a profession that continues to be worth having. It has a unique remit as the profession charged with mediating the 'social', that is, working in the contentious spaces between the social conventions that guide individuals' behaviour and determination to conduct their lives according to their own agendas, whether these are socially acceptable or not, and the problems that structural inequalities engender in their lives. Social workers have the task of helping clients assume responsibility for their individual behaviour alongside addressing the inadequacies of the social configurations in which they are located. These features have characterized the profession for some time and constitute what has been termed the 'individual-in-their-social-situation' (Younghusband, 1978; Kendall, 1991; Dominelli, 1997).

Social work is a locality-driven profession struggling to respond to conflicting agendas set by clients' needs, professional imperatives and the demands of employers and policymakers. The mediating role of social workers is further complicated by forces emanating from outside the profession and the boundaries of the nation-state, particularly global forces that (re)structure and (re)shape economic and political directives nationally. Practitioners are expected to address macro-, meso- and micro- levels of intervention, even when working with individual clients (Dominelli, 2002a). Social workers seek to create a unity within the diversities that separate them from clients and struggle to find new balances for meeting the challenges that arise from a combination of local, national and international factors. To address these challenges, social workers need both generalist and specialist knowledge and skills.

I focus on the former in this book to argue that there is a role for social work in the third millennium. To secure their place within a society that demands greater responsiveness, efficiency and accountability from professionals, social workers need to redefine the profession, retheorize it and develop new paradigms of practice so that they straddle the demands of public officialdom for promoting social inclusion and the aspirations of individuals to play a greater part in making decisions about their lives. Handling uncertainties, contradictions and conflicting demands in highly charged atmospheres are routine features of contemporary social work practice. Social workers also have to work in partnership with a range of people who have an interest in creating the new practice theories and methods of the future. These include clients, employers, professional peers and policymakers.

To forge the necessary innovations, social workers can draw on an existing strong theoretical and practice base. This can be supplemented by research of both qualitative and quantitative kinds, as insights drawn from research will become indispensable in developing new theoretical frameworks and models for practice. Research will have to focus on many different ways of looking at reality, of accepting that both empirical and experiential knowledges influence how people see the world and act within it (Belenky et al., 1997). Meeting these objectives will require social work educators and practitioners to begin making their own claims for recognition of the contributions that they have already made and will continue to make to research; ensuring that the distinctive knowledges that arise from social work research and practice are acknowledged; and securing funding for social work research on a par with that obtained for other disciplines. In Britain, social work educators will have to give greater priority to research than has been the case in the past. In countries such as the United States, greater space should be accorded to qualitative and critical theoretical research. Amongst low-income nations and oppressed populations, the emphasis could be on research that produces locality-inspired and relevant theories and guidelines for practice.

Structure of the book

My desire to contribute to forms of practice that enable practitioners to meet the challenges of the future is the driving force behind this book. Any discussion about how this can be achieved has to take place within specific historical, socio-economic and political contexts. It is impossible to encompass the whole of these either in practice or in the leaves between the covers of this book. Therefore, I have been selective in what I can cover. My choices have been guided by producing materials that will equip practitioners to engage in a critical reflexive practice that encourages the exploration of transferable skills that can be adapted to various situations, with different client groups in diverse settings.

I have based my choices on the realities of practice, informed largely by a British context that has an international reach. So, I consider the local, national and international contexts within which social work occurs and the implications of this for practice with individuals and communities. In exploring these, I focus largely on the two key client groups that social workers address, namely children and adults. I consider the social divisions that differentiate experiences for individuals and groups as they arise. Contexts impact upon individuals, groups and communities with both holistic and specific dimensions, but there are dynamics that they hold in common. For this reason, I do not cover all social divisions and forms of oppression in separate chapters. For a detailed elaboration of this argument, I refer readers to *Anti-Oppressive Social Work Theory and Practice* (Dominelli, 2002a).

I also engage with the political context of social work to explain variations within and across countries. This is strongly illustrated in work with offenders, which is increasingly being defined in England, Wales and the USA as a corrections and not social work service. I challenge this view by arguing that offenders are part of the communities in which they live and that rehabilitation must become a major element in the work done with them if they are to be returned to community life. This stands against the warehousing principle that Bauman (2001) asserts is the raison d'être of imprisonment, replacing the disciplining of workers highlighted by Foucault (1977). And, since communities form the locales in which practice occurs, I have included a chapter that deconstructs and reconstructs these for practice.

Social workers have to oppose existing structural inequalities and oppression, including those which they perpetrate, if they are to become more inclusive. New orientations in theories and modes of social work intervention have to address the complexities of practice in a more holistic and fluid manner than has been the case hitherto. In these, social workers will engage with the uncertain and fraught worlds clients inhabit, alongside meeting the demands of those who provide the resources necessary for pursuing the objective of social justice in the daily lives of socially excluded people without themselves becoming sources of further exclusion and oppression. This brings us to an active citizenship basis for practice within a human rights and social justice framework.

I examine the contexts within which practice occurs in this regard in chapter 2. Here, I analyse the changing contexts of practice to consider their impact upon practitioners as they respond to globalization, neo-liberal shifts in national policies and the new managerialism. Though usually neglected, these macro- and meso-level contexts are integral parts of micro-level practice. In the subsequent chapter, I reflect upon the continuities and discontinuities in social work's values and ethical orientation. I also explore connections between social work values, identity and social inclusion.

In chapter 4, I focus on practice with a specific client group – children. In this, I consider contradictory relations within families and social workers' involvement in their (re)production. This includes examining the balance between child protection-led interventions and preventative services that promote child welfare within the context of seeing children as human beings with rights of their own. I consider social work with adults, particularly the care of older people, in chapter 5. Adults currently comprise the bulk of social work clients. Here, I scrutinize the changing nature of social work practice as it becomes subjected to market discipline and explore the implications of this for practitioners' and clients' capacities to create effective working relationships. I highlight the increasingly contractual nature of social work practice and the opportunities and limitations for practice that this development presents.

I go on, in chapter 6, to explore why working with offenders is part of social work practice and should be retained as such. In it, I suggest that it is unhelpful to pit the rights of offenders to rehabilitation against those of victims and citizens to live in safe communities and reside in crime-free areas. Each of these groups is part of the same broader community and reconciling their interests to make communities worth living in requires dialogue across the criminal–non-criminal divide to address the causes of crime; assist offenders in making worthwhile contributions to their communities; and ensure that they refrain from treating communities and residents as objects for their self-gratification. To achieve these goals, practitioners will have to find a balance between the rights and responsibilities of all concerned.

In chapter 7, I consider the potential of community work to deal with problems caused by structural inequalities within the context of a globalizing world. I consider the basis for developing new directions in practice in the following chapter, in which I argue that the concepts of agency, power-sharing, interdependence, reciprocity, citizenship and social justice can underpin the development of new forms of practice. Together, these concepts place human rights at the centre of social workers' agendas. Realizing human rights in everyday practice facilitates social workers' becoming more proactive and adventurous in pursuing social justice goals. To incorporate this vision in their work, practitioners have to reconceptualize human rights as relevant in both individual and collective contexts.

In chapter 9, I conclude that social work professionals have to promote the rights of people to receive services according to their needs whilst maintaining their rights and duties as citizens. Claiming rights as citizens, individually and/or collectively, carries the responsibility of being mindful of the rights of others and the need to enhance others' well-being alongside their own. The state as the guarantor of people's rights has to accept responsibility for ensuring that the structures and resources necessary for their implementation are in place. Taking these abstract rights on board requires governments to underpin the activities of all stakeholders, including the public, commercial and voluntary providers of the services.

In leaving matters to the laissez-faire ideology of the market, the state abrogates its responsibility for upholding the rights of its weakest citizens. The regulatory state has to rein in the excesses of the market and respond to people's demands for a rights-enabled existence. In short, if more than band-aid solutions to social problems are to be found, the state, through its practitioners and policy-makers, in dialogue with all its citizens, has to be fully committed to transforming inegalitarian social relations. Doing nothing is not an option, because in doing nothing, politicians use the state's powers to confirm existing social exclusions and inequalities.

For social workers, human rights-led practice is based on respecting the dignity of people who are accepted as full citizens wherever they may live and eliminating structural inequalities. Following through on this approach requires social workers to make the case that access to the personal social services and involvement in their formation and delivery is the right of every individual regardless of status, attributes or place of residence. In short, people are entitled to services that have been freed from residuality. Such provisions have to address the different starting points and needs of those asking for assistance. One type of service provision will not meet the needs of all. Paraphrasing Seebohm, it means that the one-stop shop will have to have many departments and boutiques. Responding to individuals in their diversity and engaging in direct dialogue with policymakers who can release resources and unblock structural impediments to progress will challenge social work educators and practitioners to end the separation of theory, policy and research from practice.

SOCIAL WORK
A Profession in Changing Contexts

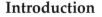

Introduction

Social work practitioners have consistently worked within changing contexts and played major roles in creating the contours of
the profession. These encompass the micro-level of interpersonal
relations, the meso-level of local institutions, legislation and policies, and the macro-level of a globalizing world. However, social
workers have been able to impact upon some contexts more easily
than others. Though difficult, those which have been under their
specific remit, particularly those at the micro-level of individuals
or families, have been easier to shape according to professional
precepts. Those embedded in the meso- or macro-levels have been
less amenable to their interventions. In the current historical conjuncture, policymakers have been resistant to social work pressures for movement in less oppressive directions.

In Britain, this is ironic given New Labour's concern with issues
that are distinctively social work in their orientation. Few ministers
dare utter the term, preferring the less contentious 'social care'
phraseology and all it implies. Nonetheless, the modernizing agenda,
with its goals of eliminating social exclusion, getting rid of poverty,
especially for British children and poor people overseas, and promoting social cohesion, picks up themes that lie at the heart of
social work practice.

The modernizing agenda is currently a major context shaping
social work policies, education and practice. It is a constantly shifting one and central in impacting on the sites in which British social
work occurs and how it is conducted. Modernization is only one of

the myriad policy contexts that affect the social work profession, however. Others include legislation not associated with modernization, international forces such as globalization, privatization of the welfare state and European harmonization. For poor people, modernization as practised in programmes like Blair's 'New Deal' and regeneration of communities initiatives is aimed at providing security in a context of insecurity.

Whatever differences there may be within its ranks, the New Labour government's modernization agenda is embedded within a narrow view of social exclusion that is linked primarily to exclusion from the labour market (Jordan, 2000). Policies for social inclusion embodied in 'New Deal' programmes seek to integrate people into waged work. The emphasis on getting poor people into paid employment has a long history in British social policy. The requirement to look for work has been a continuous thread in accessing benefits and was a central feature of the post-war consensus (Kaim-Caudle, 1973; Kincaid, 1973; Dominelli, 1991b). A key difference now is the more upfront role the state has in enforcing this ideology. Another is the media's interest in reinforcing discourses of those on benefit as 'workshy'.

Under modernization, paid work rather than citizenship entitlement is the main avenue for securing welfare. This approach ignores those who are unable to work for a range of reasons (Levitas, 1986), and fails to appreciate that poor people have developed a wealth of strategies for dealing with insecurity and are not reliant on one – the state providing for them. Clients seek state help as a last resort (Morris, 1995; Zucchino, 1997). To quote a young mother whom colleagues and I interviewed:

> I didn't choose to go on welfare. If I could have had a great career fallen on my lap, I would have taken that over welfare any day. But a lot of financial aid workers, and sometimes social workers too, think we choose this lifestyle. I chose nothing, I mean there may be people out there that do. But it's so stereotyped. . . . They think a single parent on welfare is this typical welfare case. That all we're going to do is sit on welfare and pop out more kids. Well, not everybody is like that. I'm trying to get off welfare. (Dominelli et al., forthcoming)

Political devolution, with its aim of facilitating decision-making at the local level, is an integral part of the modernizing agenda. Yet the contract culture at the level of service delivery goes in the opposite direction. Carried out in the name of deregulation, 'contract government' has resulted in the increasing interference of central government in the activities of local government and the everyday private lives of citizens. Neither the public sector nor the private lives of citizens have been free of the various regulatory codes enacted by central government (Dominelli and Hoogvelt, 1996a). Meanwhile, *financial* deregulation has ensured that private entrepreneurs have been able to organize their businesses in ways that best suit them. While reinforcing these 'regulatory codes', the nation-state has simultaneously divested itself of responsibility for providing services and direct involvement in the activities of organizations that have assumed the tasks previously performed by the state. These dynamics lie at the heart of contracting out services to the voluntary and commercial sectors and form an essential part of the purchaser–provider split.

This regulatory process relies on procedural and bureaucratic means, the contract, to assert control over the types of services delivered and their quality. In these, trust becomes a technocratic instrument rather than a relational one – part of the technologies of control, which cannot ultimately guarantee quality. These developments demonstrate how the architects of the technologies of control have lost sight of trust as being built on a relationship that links ends and means. Bureaucratizing trust can ensure that managers are not held accountable when things go wrong as responsibility can be passed from one part of the system to another without finding a culprit. Moreover, this process gives rise to cynicism as people lose faith in the system being able to deliver on its promises. Rail privatization in Britain provides a classic example of this process. Similar dangers are evident in social work assessments that do not yield anticipated outcomes.

Insecurity has been a persistent feature of poor peoples' lives, and they have become resourceful in finding strategies for surviving its ravages in a daily struggle to make ends meet. What they need are policies and resources that enable them to transcend this basic level of existence – a position that seems beyond their reach under social arrangements that propose that they personally deal with whatever comes their way. Rising above poverty requires a certain amount of social capital, which is lacking for them. A member of the steering committee for a single regeneration budget (SRB) community project I have been researching commented upon this by saying:

> They [poor residents] need resources that will enable them to go outside the endless projects that provide a bit of work and get something sustainable in the long run.

The short-termism of the limited employment opportunities provided under the modernization programmes are unable to take people out of poverty in the long term. This is a key failing of the 'New Deal' welfare model and needs urgent attention. In privileging paid employment, the modernization agenda has been unable to address the range of cross-cutting structural exclusions that operate through interpersonal relations and to deal with scarcity, which lies at the heart of insecurity, particularly the lack of well-paid jobs, housing, health opportunities, education and personal social services (see Pattison, 2002; Dominelli, 2002c). The complexities of contextualized insecurities provide major challenges to good practice in a changing profession.

Insecurity today is no longer a problem only for poor people. Middle-class people fear its incursion into their lives as professional jobs no longer guarantee their livelihood through the adult years and into retirement. The future looks bleak as job insecurity increases, pension plans fail to deliver planned incomes and endowment mortgages cannot guarantee repayments on home loans. Many middle-class people have become paralysed by fear stemming from these insecurities. Like poor people, they have looked for scapegoats and other individuals to blame for their plight. This reaction has not only hindered their capacity to transcend the limitations of existing strategies for containing insecurities, but has also added to these sources of unease. As a result of these material conditions, forms of oppression, particularly those rooted in the 'isms' such as racism, are undergoing a resurgence in everyday social interactions, while opposition to them mounts ideologically.

In this chapter, I examine the many contexts within which social work is situated, and argue that although these are constantly in flux, their parameters shape the range of the possible in practice. The constraints and opportunities that these contexts create may or may not accord with social work's value base, the judgements made by practitioners or the aspirations of clients. Social workers face a key problem in having to act with certainty in situations saturated with uncertainty, ambiguity and contradictory expectations. They are exercised in doing the best they can under extremely difficult circumstances, rather than being able to implement an ideal type of practice. These complicated demands make social work a contested political activity that does not have the luxury of simply saying 'this is what professionals should do'.

Macro-level contexts

The impact of globalizing forces on welfare provisions

Globalization is a crucial contemporary context of practice. Beginning at the macro-level, its many tentacles reach all aspects of public and private life and draw social workers into managerially driven technologies of governance that often affirm their policing role at the expense of their caring capacities. The forces of globalization embed local practices in the international arena through neo-liberal forms of welfare and internationalization of social problems. These developments make globalization an important dimension of policy and practice at micro-, meso- and macro-levels.

Elsewhere, I have defined globalization in social work as

> the organization of social relations in ways that promote the penetration of capitalist forces of production and reproduction into arenas of life hitherto deemed sacrosanct from market-driven imperatives. Globalization involves the global spread of capitalist social relations and their integration into every aspect of life – the social, political, cultural, economic and personal, and the consequent reordering of social relations in all these spheres (Dominelli and Hoogvelt [1996a]). This includes opening up public services to private providers, providing 'value for money', re-asserting managerial control over the workforce staffing 'the caring professions', and altering the relationship between the individual and the state. (Dominelli, 2001, p. 261)

Globalization has been created as a force for change by capitalist entrepreneurs who have allied with governments to find new arenas for profitable exploitation. They have little regard for its impact on the lives of those it touches and are heedless of the merit of keeping some areas of life outside its ambit. The changes they promote include: regulating the conduct of private life through consumerism and commodification of interpersonal relations; opening up public services to private providers; emphasizing 'value for money'; re-asserting managerial control over the workforce staffing the caring professions; and introducing new forms of governance. These have altered personal relations, working relations and the relationship between citizens and the state in profound ways from those practised traditionally. And they have also blurred the public–private divide, reduced state responsibility for the welfare of individual citizens and perpetrated the Americanization of cultural forms worldwide (Reitzer, 2000).

New Labour's worthy goal of eliminating poverty within Britain and abroad is stymied by the dynamics of globalization. Although not a force for evil in and of itself, globalization is organized as a set of capitalist relations that penetrate every aspect of life to produce winners and losers. Globalization involves five interactive features:

- a global market principle that shapes national decision-making and domestic economic behaviour and integrates the nation-state into global economic relations;
- altered national and international divisions of labour;
- deregulated and liberalized financial markets;
- conditions suitable for 'flexible accumulation'; and
- an increasingly regulated personal sphere (Dominelli and Hoogvelt, 1996a; Dominelli, 2001, 2002a, 2002b).

Their interactive dynamics have contradictory outcomes. Enhancing as they do the centralization of power and decision-making alongside deregulated markets in which corporate elites are free to construct realities that produce highly profitable conditions for investment purposes, they limit the space within which the private individual without resources can exercise choice when his or her expectations for doing so are at their height.

Globalization has changed the nature of social relations and had a direct impact on the local state. The process has been accompanied by the internationalization of the state (Cox, 1981), whereby the nation-state becomes a vehicle for promoting the adjustment of the domestic economy to the imperatives of the global market (Dominelli and Hoogvelt, 1996a), and by the emergence of 'contract government' (Greer, 1994). Corporate elites have achieved these changes by drawing the state into global capitalist networks on the basis of making the domestic economy more competitive and its workforce more flexible in order to turn production capacity into a commodity and produce goods at the lowest global price (Jaikumar and Upton, 1993). Social services provisions have been drawn into this ambit (Dominelli and Hoogvelt, 1996b) both as a site for the accumulation of profit and as a market in their own right.

Contract government in Britain has proceeded on the basis of several successive planned stages which involve the management of change through economic processes: the Financial Management Initiative (FMI) of 1982; the Next Steps Initiative (NSI), launched in 1988; and the Private Finance Initiative (PFI), begun in the dying days of John Major's Conservative government, but subsequently endorsed and implemented by Blair's New Labour governments.

Interestingly, the link between the vagaries of the market and the regulatory regime of the state is one that has been consistently missed in Foucauldian analyses of the disciplinary state (see Foucault, 1977; Chambon, Irving and Epstein 1999). These *assume* the context of capitalist social relations. As this link has enormous implications for the (re)formulation of cultures of control at both individual and institutional levels and for the social lives of individuals, these implications have to be made explicit.

The cultural paradigm for contract government includes: the definition of overall strategic goals and identification of sequential performance objectives within these; operationalization of performance targets; clear and detailed specification of input and output measures and the costing of these, including a critical scrutiny of 'value for money'; concrete specification of the relevant contributions and responsibilities of all the actors involved; and, among other things, the formulation of reporting and monitoring tools (Dominelli and Hoogvelt, 1996a). Contract government intensifies the commodification of relationships within the public sector and hastens the development of a corporatist managerialist culture to accompany the contract culture. This too has penetrated the social services arena.

During the FMI stage, the provider units were located largely within public sector departments. Under the NSI, the state created semi-independent executive agencies which operated at a distance from government and which contracted specific tasks to other private sector agencies and enterprises. Compulsory competitive tendering (CCT) legislation was introduced in 1988 as part of the NSI initiative and applied to social services departments alongside the others in the public sector. CCT has now been replaced by Best Value and Quality Protects initiatives. The PFI now aims to create partnerships between public agencies and those in the private sector, primarily as a way of encouraging private financing of public sector activities. PFI has also enabled the government to divest itself of the responsibility of providing finances for public sector health and educational services. Through PFI arrangements, the purchaser has become even further removed from the provider equation. As a result, social work users cannot hold purchasers directly accountable for services received; they have to go through the political process. These developments have been highly contested, particularly when they have involved basic utilities, educational facilities and transport, including rail and air traffic control.

These initiatives have imposed a new economic logic of turning former public resource providers into purchasers of services from commercial and voluntary provider units, whose actions are controlled by being defined and held accountable through contractual means. Known as the purchaser–provider split, these developments have involved the state in the regulation and governance of economic relations. In these, the state commissions particular goods and services under tightly stipulated conditions that control outputs. These contracts have shaped social relations amongst those who purchase, provide and receive services. These are in turn shaped by both existing and newly emerging social relations.

Quality assurance Systems of quality management and advance process certification are crucial to at-arm's-length patterns of regulation promoted under contract government and have been incorporated into the new managerialism. These are now found in both private sector business and public sector services, despite the latter having been traditionally defined as outside the commodity relationship. In social work, regulatory frameworks are embodied in Total Quality Management systems (see Adams, 1998) as BS 5750 or ISO 9000 and ISO 9001 on the international level. These procedures have reinforced bureaucratic regimes of control over face-to-face contact in worker–client relationships.

Quality assurance has become a bureaucratized form of control where the mechanisms and processes of quality assurance are expected to ensure that work undertaken meets required specifications. The monitoring of workers has become an indispensable managerial tool for controlling workers, including those in the professions. Technological developments that allow for easy monitoring of the quantifiable aspects of performance have intensified managerial control and facilitated its spread throughout the service sectors. It is debatable, however, whether this produces the kinds of practice that best serve clients. High levels of contract non-compliance, litigious suits and complaints from service users reveal that reliance on bureaucratic means may not ensure high quality standards.

For example, the failure of risk assessment regimes to protect children from abuse exemplifies how the bureaucratization of professional practice does not necessarily safeguard their right to a violence-free home environment. As Parton (1998) notes, the first question asked following the death of a child in the care of the local authority (now euphemistically called a 'looked-after child') is 'Were the procedures followed?', not 'What went wrong?' The emphasis on procedures draws the worker into the equation of culpability and allows structural contributory factors to escape notice.

The successful avoidance of discussions about systemic inequalities and resource shortages that set social workers and clients impossible tasks prevents the identification of the *social* changes necessary to reformulate child welfare as a responsibility of society as a whole. It also by-passes consideration of how publicly funded resources such as child care facilities, decent homes and jobs that pay a living rather than a minimum wage can alleviate stress on parents. Yet their ramifications are central to social work with children and families. Moreover, the focus on procedures masks the responsibility of those who actually killed the child(ren), and with it the link between personal and structural factors.

Despite being a crucial feature of the modernizing agenda, the emphasis on economy, effectiveness and efficiency has not led to the improved public services promised by government. Instead, the new managerialism has fostered budget-led not user-led services by tightening eligibility criteria, limiting choice and reducing user input into decision-making processes about service design, provision and delivery. It has yielded a top-down approach that has left practitioners disillusioned with the state of social work under managerialist regulatory regimes. In a study I conducted with Parves Khan (Dominelli and Khan, 2000),[1] a social worker who voiced the views of most respondents expressed it as follows:

> I feel that managerialism and market forces within a supposedly mixed economy of welfare are destroying social work practice. Increasingly the organization is driven towards creating an expensive, callous bureaucracy which prides itself on delivering resource-led policies as prime measures of its effectiveness and efficiency. Not content with deskilling a professional workforce, the organization appears to have effectively distanced itself from accountability/ responsibility towards social workers. . . . This has invariably caused untold stress and perpetuates a culture of fear in the workplace.

The Dominelli and Khan (2000) study revealed that social workers have more negative views of the changes wrought by the new managerialism than do managers. One social work manager expressed his more positive outlook as:

> When people say, 'I don't do social work anymore', I say, 'That's not true. You always did assessments, you should always have done care planning. It's just that now it's more explicit. It's been managerialized. That's the eighties coming through.'

This statement ignores the loss of professional autonomy which social workers experience in a bureaucratized process. Professional autonomy has been curtailed through bureaucratized managerialism involving the surveillance of workers, proceduralized professional activities and decentralized budget management. For example, social workers who work with older people have their own limited budgets for purchasing services. Practitioners' capacity for action is affected by the amounts available for purchasing resources. Clients requiring costly facilities will have less access to the services they need when funding is low. Financial accountability requires more and not less form-filling. The wise use of professional discretion and autonomy is compatible with holding workers accountable and can be undertaken in more client-empowering ways through more equal partnerships than those possible in bureaucratic regimes.

Under contract government, workers transfer from the public to the private sector, largely through the processes of privatization and sale of publicly owned provisions. Social work departments have not been exempted from these developments, although in the early days, the sections that sold quickly were tangible assets that could be easily disposed of – old people's homes and residential facilities for children. Their sale caused public provisions in this sector to decline considerably. Rising costs coupled with reduced state contributions to the care of individual elders have left a £1 billion funding gap and caused unprecedented numbers of private providers to close their doors. These have caused older people to lose their homes. One person thus evicted, 102-year-old Rose Cottle, took her protest to Downing Street. Her local authority, East Sussex, closed forty homes in 2001 (Steele, 2002).

The shift to contract government has set up a 'revolving door' through which individuals pass, being employed by the public sector one moment, and the private sector the next, usually at lower rates of pay and with less security than previously (Dominelli and Hoogvelt, 1996a). This facilitates employers' capacity to move people and resources according to the demands of flexible production and the processes of accumulation. The need for flexibility has become apparent in both discourses and practice. Indicative of this trend is the emphasis on generic practice with transferable skills as central in the new qualifying training for social workers.

Bureaucratic surveillance features are spread more speedily and thoroughly through the new, often computer-based, technologies, to impact upon and become integrated into everyday practices. The effect of these processes on social work has been to recast the relationship between:

- the state and its citizens;
- the state and providers of welfare services;
- the state and social work professionals;
- the state and social work clients;
- the providers of services and social work professionals; and
- local and global relationships through the internationalization of social problems (Dominelli, 1998a; Kahn and Dominelli, 2000).

The ideology of the free market and the responsibility of citizens to take care of their own welfare needs have supplanted the ideology of solidarity and the pooling of welfare risks to provide the common threads of self-sufficiency that now underpin relationships between workers and clients, clients and the state, workers and the state. Their loss has undermined publicly funded welfare services, with far-reaching consequences (Zucchino, 1997).

With regards to the welfare relationship between the state and its citizens, people are now compelled individually to meet the gap between public welfare provisions and private welfare consumption as the state has withdrawn from being a provider of services that were once, at least in theory, accessible by all who needed them. The catch is most critical for those needing state support, who, by virtue of claiming public assistance, are now defined as inadequate (Culpitt, 1992). This shift has changed the nature of the relationship between the state and its citizens from being one of the sympathetic rights-based state caring about and catering for the needs of its citizens to that of the indifferent state that distances itself from its citizens and leaves individuals to care and provide for themselves. At the same time as public welfare services diminish through a thousand cuts and those that are provided become less accessible to the populace through the introduction of user fees, state expenditure continues to rise. Expenditure increases because a considerable amount of state revenue is directed towards private companies in the form of grants and subsidies, tax exemptions and infrastructural support (*Canadian Business*, 1997; Barlett and Steele, 1998).

These tendencies have been exacerbated by the commodification of the services delivered to clients. Commodification of services has followed the recasting of clients as potential customers who can exercise the power to choose amongst the various services on offer. This definition of the relationship between the service user and the facilities available does not acknowledge that clients can seldom exercise their preferred choice if they lack the money to buy what *they* want. Their choices as consumers are often restricted to picking from options that others present to them. They may have had little, if any, direct input into designing or running these services. They may think them completely inappropriate and undesirable, but find that their real choice is these or nothing. To quote a social worker from my study with Parves Khan:

> Much lip service is paid to consulting users and listening. Often they are told that a service can only be offered in a certain way. Choice is theoretically offered and then taken away. (Dominelli and Khan, 2000)

Clients are not able to enter or exit the marketplace on terms that they set in the way predicated by public choice theory. The notion of the autonomous and powerful consumer who can set his or her mark on the options available is absent for social work clients. Services on offer can reinforce and deepen the sense of exclusion felt amongst those without such possibilities.

Additionally, the commodification of services involves a degree of fragmentation in the kind of services that are presented to a client as multiple providers compete for his or her attention. This competition is often 'fixed' by contractual conditions that are set by the purchaser and tight financial constraints that providing agencies have to abide by. Their restrictions on innovative practice and limits to effective interventions have been documented by a number of authors, including Barnes and Maple (1992).

The commodification of service provisions and the bureaucratization of professional practice have played major roles in reducing professional autonomy and the scope of decision-making powers held by professionals. This trend has replaced the bureau-professional (Parry, Rustin and Satymurti, 1979) with what I call the bureau-technocrat. An avalanche of new circulars and guidance providing procedural formulation of practitioners' tasks have now replaced the Orange Book,[2] severely curtailing the autonomy of those involved in heavy-end social work such as child protection to practise as they deem best, or in accordance with the specific needs of the individual with whom they are working. Similar difficulties are evident in work with violent offenders. National standards dictate how they must carry out their work. Though clear procedures and processes are important, over-bureaucratized practice makes it difficult to think beyond set tramlines and is a danger encountered by practitioners working as bureau-technocrats.

Managerial controls over professional judgement have intensified as a result of the growth in what is called the 'risk society'

(Beck, 1992) and the imposition of 'risk assessments' in complex areas of practice including child protection and work with offenders. In the 'risk society', individuals are expected to manage their own risks rather than rely on the welfare state to do so. If they unsuccessfully manage risk, they are also expected to take the consequences of their failures. Risk management becomes a technology for passively managing the self today and tomorrow by enabling individuals to assess the future consequences of present decisions (Rose, 1996). This makes risk assessment and management an important technology of governance affirmed through professional practice. Social workers assist in the management of personal risk through bureaucracy-led forms of practice rather than forming relationships which treat clients as subjects with the capacity to change or eliminate structural inequalities.

The internationalization of social problems

Globalization has facilitated the internationalization of social problems. These include features such as: the spread of poverty both between countries and within countries (Wichterich, 2000); the importation of social problems from one part of the globe to another, as in the sex trade in children; and the impact of migratory trends, including cross-country adoptions, asylum seekers and refugees. These developments have challenged the locality-based nature of social work and encouraged practitioners to think about the international dimensions of the work they do in a more systematic and organized manner. In the study I undertook with Parves Khan (Dominelli and Khan, 2000), social workers demanded training that would enable them to meet these conditions.

The internationalization of social problems involves the globalization of the local and the localization of the global. Internationalization has ruptured the tight national boundaries that previously featured in the profession. In bringing these to local attention, globalizing trends have enabled social workers to appreciate the interdependent nature of the world and problems that mark its social landscape. Tackling these social problems requires solutions that cross borders and bring social workers into the political arena in the national and international domains.

The changing contexts of social work indicate a realigning of power relations. Under neo-liberal social regimes, the interests of the employers and state through its managers are emphasized over those of professionals and clients. Individual or group responses to these changes can be those of acceptance, accommodation or resistance (Dominelli, 2002a). The boundaries between these options are often blurred as one can shift to another depending on a specific constellation of factors, events and personnel in any action. Those who accept a particular situation are likely to accede to the status quo rather than question existing arrangements of their own accord. Those who seek to adjust or accommodate to difficult circumstances have a more flexible and reflective approach that may result in a resistance response under certain conditions.

Those embedded in resistance responses are keen to demand changes in the positions in which they are located. They are also more likely to develop alternative provisions and look to other ways of defining their situation than those proffered by supporters of the status quo. Current resistance to globalization has been rooted in locality-based humanistic responses that contrast with the impersonal and bureaucratic measures favoured by corporate elites (Gilbert and Russell, 2002). Complex dynamics in these responses indicate that resistance is not an inherent part of power, as is signalled by Foucauldian analyses (Foucault, 1980). It has to be worked for, or brought into being.

Meso-level contexts

National policy frameworks: Social inclusion and exclusion

As part of the nation-state, social work is embedded in policy frameworks that shape the contexts of practice. These are constantly shifting, affected as they are by electoral politics, political allegiances, legislative remits and social policies. A key framework within the modernization agenda revolves around issues of social integration and the inclusion of excluded groups into mainstream society. The social inclusion agenda is part of the national policy context in which practice is embedded. This is shaped by international globalizing forces, and its implementation locally carries implications for government responses to globalization.

Social exclusion is a difficult concept to capture as it encompasses all aspects of life, whether in the public or private domain, the personal or the structural. The European Foundation for the Improvement of Living and Working Conditions (1995, p. 4) makes this evident in its definition of social exclusion as the 'process through which individuals or groups are wholly or partially excluded from full participation in the society in which one lives'. Others, such as Duffy (1995, p. 1) claim that it is 'the inability to participate effectively in economic, social, political and cultural life, and in some characterizations, alienation and distance from mainstream society'. De Haan and Maxwell (1998, p. 2) have a more narrow focus in their approach, suggesting that social exclusion is the 'failure or inability to participate in social and political activities'.

Peter Mandelson (1997), representing New Labour thinking on this issue, suggests a broader dimension to social exclusion by asserting that it prevents participation in 'everyday life', but without linking it directly to wider economic forces. Instead, he links it to the New Right notion of the 'underclass' (Murray, 1990, 1994), which is already contested as a flawed exclusionary concept. Not only does the underclass terminology pathologize poor people, and blame them for their poverty, it also situates them within the context of being *unwilling* to work (Morris, 1995) when jobs are plentiful. These discourses reconfigure poverty as a personal issue and call for personal responses to structural problems. Consequently, the policy injunction in both Britain and the United States is to get the 'underclass' back to work, with limited regard to their capacities or the fact that the jobs that they can obtain are low paid and cannot lift them out of poverty (Morris, 1995; Wichterich, 2000).

The applicability of an imported American concept to Britain is debatable. The 'underclass' concept is a racialized one and its relevance to Britain, which has a different demographic composition amongst welfare claimants from that evident in the American situation, is questionable. Significant numbers of black people in Britain are not on welfare. According to the 2001 Census, their age profile locates them mainly amongst the active workforce. They make few demands on the welfare system, despite their overrepresentation in low-paid jobs. These complexities indicate the multiple processes through which social exclusion occurs. These inadequacies also highlight the poor explanatory power of a concept which is incapable of addressing both the personal and the structural components of an individual's or group's failure to make it in a globalizing capitalist society.

Despite variations, these definitions of social exclusion have one element in common: highlighting the *personal* nature of social exclusion. In doing so, they underplay the significance of structural inequalities and power relations in producing exclusionary outcomes. I identified this problem for social workers in 1993 at a conference in Bellaria, Italy, when I linked social exclusion to globalization. Marketizing and commodifying personal social services has become structurally exclusionary because poor people, already excluded by low income, cannot participate fully in exercising choices about service acceptability. Nor are they engaged in designing these facilities and evaluating their performance. Their choice is limited to commenting upon an individual practitioner's work after services are given.

New Labour's policy and media endeavours have been crucial in formulating and promoting a new consensus about welfare in the wake of globalizing forces. It advocates the view that work combined with education is the only way out of poverty. This belief helps create what Peters (1997) calls the 'normative consensus' which legitimates the current (re)structuring of social relations and ignores structural inequalities despite a rhetoric that acknowledges them. Social policies such as the 'New Deal' attempt to reinforce the work ethic and labour discipline for those receiving welfare benefits (Craig, 2001), despite the unavailability of work that pays decent wages, that is, enough to lead an active citizenship-based life. Nor do these policies acknowledge people whose work is devalued or considered marginal to the overall economy. The new consensus also ignores the 'sponging off the state' perpetrated by rich people who benefit from unquestioned, formally legitimated schemes that reduce tax liability, including tax avoidance mechanisms and state grants for businesses (Barlett and Steele, 1998).

The rise in poverty amongst the working poor reflects the paucity of workfare- or 'welfare-to-work'-type policies (Craig, 2001), and one that has been ignored by New Right politicians, who continue to blame individuals for structural problems and accuse them of being over-reliant on handouts from the state. They have configured claimants as being on the make, or abusing a system that is there to help only those most in need (Murray, 1990, 1994).

I use the term *punitive welfarism* to characterize the patchwork of policy initiatives based on the *presumption* that benefit claimants abuse publicly funded benefit systems to obtain public funds through deception. It is an essential element of contemporary residualism and further marginalizes poor people's involvement in citizenship-based social lives. Research has consistently demonstrated that very few claimants are reluctant to work (Morris, 1995; Roberts, 2002) because they prefer the dignity of work to the stigma of being on residual welfare. Most rely on welfare for intermittent periods rather than one unbroken long-term dependency (Morris, 1995) as suggested by Murray (1984, 1990, 1994). Yet, as a category, they continue to be treated as undeserving abusers of other people's generosity (Roberts, 2002).

The threat to withdraw benefit from British welfare recipients who refuse to take up low-paid work adds a further twist to punitive welfarism. In 2000–1, benefits were withdrawn from 19,344 people, causing 'real hardship' (Roberts, 2002). Britain's Step-Up initiative aims to ensure that the number of 'scroungers' is further reduced. The emphasis on withdrawing child benefits from parents who fail to control their children is also part of punitive welfarism. This violates the children's right to an income that enables them to grow to full human beings, a provision endorsed by the UN Convention on the Rights of the Child, which the British government has signed. It also blames parents, who are reconfigured as bad or inadequate when the causes of children's behaviour may have little to do with their parenting: for example, the sheer boredom of a school system that does not capture students' interests or respond to their needs. That some students can cope with the structural inadequacies of the educational system does not deal with the problem of those who cannot. Nor does it affirm the matter as a personal one. If the structural inadequacies highlighted by the few were addressed, it is highly likely that the performance of the less bored students would be substantially enhanced. But in pathologizing individuals and following through with action formulated on such analyses, practitioners (re)inscribe the technologies of (self-)regulation upon both parents and child.

For women, this new approach has further downgraded unpaid work done in the home caring for children and dependent relatives (Levitas, 1986). Under the auspices of neo-liberal market ideologies, professional practice has fostered the realization of employment-led agendas. The ensuing changes in the worker–client relationship have exacerbated the difficulties that professionals have in providing the best services available to those requiring assistance. In addition, they enable the state to disclaim responsibility for meeting people's welfare needs.

These developments have resulted in public services that are starved of resources and private provisions that are inaccessible to those with insufficient funds. Despite claims to the contrary, private investors are reliant on state subsidies to supplement their own financial investments (Barlett and Steele, 1998; Hencke, 2001). Packaging together sufficient financial resources to launch a business creates an uncertain situation for entrepreneurs and clients. Resources may be inadequate for the purposes envisaged. The pressures of the tendering process favour those who offer the cheapest alternative in giving 'value for money' and retain profitability by constantly reducing expenditures even when costs are rising. As staffing is a key consumer of finances in the service sector, the tendency to reduce wage levels, workers' job security and social insurance benefits, particularly those financing health care and pensions, becomes an integral part of this process. The added political priority of cutting state expenditure on publicly funded welfare provisions and state industries intensifies the instability of the purchaser–provider split.

The fragility of the system has been evidenced by the closure of older people's and children's homes when the state has been unable to subsidize places to the levels required by the private entrepreneur (Brindle, 2001). These dynamics promote social exclusion by pushing people out of homes to which they have become accustomed, either leaving them as a homeless problem for someone else to solve or shunting them from one residence to another in a succession of closures – one that amounted to 18,700 places in 2000. Older people are moved through a series of musical chairs and left standing in empty space when someone else stops the music. In the process, they lose their unique individuality, rights to a stable environment, a home and the power to control their lives.

Social workers get sucked into reproducing exclusionary discourses through policy directives that they integrate into their practice. They can counter the assumptions upon which hegemonic discourses and policies are based by accumulating evidence from clients' everyday lives and showing that their daily routines continue to be embedded in processes of exclusion, of which dire poverty is only one manifestation. In validating the legitimacy of client knowledges, practitioners play a key role in having their views of situations accepted by others. Social workers engage clients in exchanging knowledge about their life experiences so that their voices can be heard and their stories can expose the inadequacy of official constructions of their lives. By supporting the creation of counter-discourses, social workers assist those outside their circles to understand the world from client perspectives.

Having played an influential role in establishing alternative discourses rooted in data about clients' lived-in everyday realities, social workers can use the media to popularize them. These discourses can challenge the normalcy of seeing clients as members of the 'underclass', a less than human species that gets involved in anti-social behaviours of various kinds, but particularly in law-breaking activities such as violent behaviour, drug abuse and burglary. Creating new discourses can ensure that clients are seen as real people having agency and a stake in society and what happens within it. Without condoning inappropriate behaviours, social workers can make links between those who are considered normal and those deemed deviant. Though implicated in them, social workers are not condemned to supporting hegemonic discourses. They can challenge how myths about poor people are created and deployed. Take substance misuse, for example. Wealthy people abuse these too, but the media furore about them is different, as is illustrated by the publicity around Prince Harry's misuse of drugs and alcohol. This paints him as a victim of his life circumstances rather than a demon for breaking the law.

Imagine the reaction of people if the headlines for poor people displayed similar understanding. The reader might be more likely to sympathize with Joe and Jane Bloggs if their storyline in the papers shouted 'Poverty and Poor Housing Drive Jane and Joe into Drugs' or 'Anna and Mark Take to the Bottle for Relief from Isolation and a Crime-Ridden Estate'. These challenge the use of mainstream social work interventions to 'write off' vulnerable people as worthless (Jones, 1996). Alternative approaches attempt to include poor people as an integral part of society and avoid their exclusion from discourses about it. This point is identified by Ruth Levitas (1997, p. 19) when she argues that the ' "real" society . . . is that made up of the whole 100 per cent in which poverty is endemic'.

Micro-level contexts

Power and authority

Micro-level practice focuses on the worker–client relationship. Power relations are central to understanding it. Power relations and the sources of legitimacy and authority are integral aspects of the contexts within which social work interventions occur. In these, power has traditionally been conceptualized as a negative force appropriated by one party in the relationship while the other does without, and so the practitioner is all-powerful; the client powerless. This formulation posits power dynamics in zero-sum terms that require one person or group to impose their will upon another whether at an individual or a collective level (Parsons, 1957), and has been found inadequate (Dominelli, 1986; Dominelli and Gollins, 1997).

Intentionality is a major element of zero-sum notions of power (Weber, 1978) and legitimates the authority of particular power-holders. Weber (1978) characterizes the basis of authority as legal precept, tradition and charismatic appeal. Following his understandings through into social work, authority can be seen as derived from legislation (legal precept), the state bureaucracy (institutionalized tradition) and the individual professional (charisma). Useful as this is in comprehending some complexities of power, it remains conceptually a quantitative instrument to be exercised as 'power over' others.

In this schema, power relations become coercive measures for exploiting individuals and groups even if they accept their legitimacy over them. Power relations are perceived as static except when people compete with each other to grab what is defined as a finite resource – power. Those who do not have power become subjugated and marginalized. Those who accept this definition of their lives are unable to conceive of alternatives to their situations. Unable to visualize a possibility in which altering their condition is achievable, they are unlikely to be interested in the potential to change it. Those who reject their subjugated position but who accept zero-sum definitions of power have only one option: to resist their oppressors, gain power for themselves and replace the current power-holders. This approach creates another incessantly repeated dance of musical chairs where the goal of those participating is not to be standing when the music stops.

Foucault (1979b) cautions against conceptualizing power as a repressive force and suggests that a more fruitful approach is to consider it a productive network that permeates society through various institutions and cultural practices. As such, power promotes and nurtures subjectivity rather than suppressing it (Miller, 1987). By being nurtured and endlessly re-created, the subject acquires a stake in the status quo. Its very permissiveness becomes a regulator of individual behaviour and contributes to its stability. This is because internally imposed regulation is more reliable than externally enforced controls.

Post-structuralist analyses focus on the creation and re-creation of power through 'discursive practices' using language to describe and convey meanings. Power works through language to construct discursively what is possible and what is not (Clegg, 1989), thereby opening up new possibilities for the exercise of power (Foucault, 1979b) or even closing them. Foucault (1977) conceives of power as occurring in relational interactions that are negotiated by people through discourses that frame what counts as legitimate power and what does not. For Lukes (1974), power is split between the power of structure and the power of agency. Generally, post-structuralists emphasize the link between structure, as simultaneously constraining and facilitating agency, and agency, which produces and reproduces structures (Giddens, 1993). Some post-structuralists see power as resting in temporarily fixed sets of meanings about agents and their practices (Laclau and Mouffe,

1985). There is some limited agreement between these theorists, although their emphases are different.

Regardless of their particular emphasis, these theorists continue to conceptualize power in terms of 'winners' and 'losers'. They focus largely upon *power over* relations (Dominelli and Gollins, 1997) that constitute people in relations of domination and subjugation. In contrast to zero-sum visions of power, feminist (French, 1985) and postmodern thinkers link power to the fluidity of meanings and the absence of pre-determined forms. Consequently, power is a complex phenomenon or force that is constantly created through negotiations and renegotiations between and amongst social actors (Clegg, 1989; Giddens, 1990).

Power as an interactional negotiated force is not simply a matter of control over others, as is suggested in zero-sum conceptualizations that produce winners and losers (Parsons, 1957). It can be a force that creates positive environments for communication and action which can result in 'win-win' situations (Brandwein, 1986). Creating and re-creating power through social interaction means that no one individual can be either totally powerful or completely powerless (Dominelli, 1986). As a negotiated phenomenon, power is formed in and through the similarities and differences that exist between people when they interact with one another. Their similarities and differences are (re)constituted through the dynamics of their negotiated interactions. Taking the idea of negotiated power into the practice arena as empowering practice, practitioners become engaged in creating spaces in which clients can exercise a greater sense of agency through their interaction with others regardless of their formal status (Dominelli and Gollins, 1997). This way of discussing and refocusing practitioner–client interactions can facilitate the potential for positive changes in clients' lives.

A technology of governmentality: 'The social' divides clients into deserving and undeserving groups and rations resources

Social workers both constitute and contextualize their practice in the web of relationships that weave the individual within a number of other social systems and networks, ranging from the person's family and local community to the broader society with its links to the national and international levels. Social workers navigate the interstices of 'the social' or the sites in which individuals conduct the routines of their daily lives. But as the practitioner is negotiating these spaces, so is the client. Both are exercising agency in their interactions with each other as they simultaneously constitute and are constituted by the other. These dynamics evolve between them regardless of the method of intervention being used or the setting within which the intervention occurs. Negotiated agency is central to relational practice and forms a key dynamic in social work interventions. The negotiation of understandings and experienced realities provides the bases for *the work* that practitioners and clients do together and constitutes *the social* that shapes and is shaped by their interaction. *The social* is a contextualized negotiated space within which practice occurs, providing a panorama that can change or remain the same.

This preoccupation with 'the social' is a distinctive feature of professional social work and provides the crucial contextualizing environment within which practitioners operate. Because this context involves caring as a fundamental service of life, anyone caring, whether a paid professional or not, feels able to participate in the discourses that configure this field. As anyone can have a say in how this sphere is shaped and subsequently regulated, it is created as a fluid, multidimensional, contradictory, ambiguous and uncertain domain. Rooted in its locality and experienced as immediate, this context contains continuities and discontinuities between the past, present and future. Over time, 'the social' is shaped by forces outwith the professional arena as well as within it.

'The social' involves the layering of many contexts and their intersection across and within one another. Whilst the shifts in the specific contexts within which professional social work is undertaken have varied across time and space in any one locality, there have been key defining moments which provide continuity within these variations. Some of these have been deliberately transferred to localities other than those in which they have originated. The history of social work in Britain and countries such as the United States is full of examples of policymakers, practitioners and academics learning and borrowing from each other (Kendall, 2000), although not always with beneficial effects (see Armitage, 1996). Practitioners and social work educators involved in such exchanges try to make sense of these contexts through their mutual interactions and learn from one another as they share knowledge about their situations and utilize the insights gleaned in their own locale (Dominelli and Thomas Bernard, 2003). The interplay between theory and practice is used to develop a range of innovations and possibilities other than those which appear important to educators and practitioners at first sight.

'The social' simultaneously creates helping relations and controlling ones as part of the technologies of governmentality. By forging these relations, 'the social' mediates the space between the respectable working class and its more dangerous elements. In doing so, it forges divisions between individuals who are able to exercise political voice and excluded people who cannot (Philp, 1979, 1985). At the same time it creates and shapes the contours within which they exist. It is inadequate to conceptualize 'the social' as sitting between mainstream society and those who have been alienated from its remit. Those who are excluded from the mainstream are also part of it because the mainstream can only exist insofar as there is an outside group with which it can compare itself.

Social workers display this inclusivity in their practice when they argue, often against the opinions of other professionals, that every person has some good that needs to be coaxed out for him or her to flourish as a member of society. Social workers' philosophy is both a conservative one that reinforces what has been defined as 'normal' and a radical one that challenges those encompassed by 'the normal' to include those who are outside it. By engaging in such practices, practitioners reproduce the 'dividing practices' that categorize people as opposites – 'normal' or 'deviant' (Foucault, 1977) – while simultaneously going beyond these to (re)constitute the 'deviant' as part of the 'normal' (Philp, 1979, 1985). The 'normal' becomes part of the 'deserving' group who can be helped; the 'deviant' becomes the 'undeserving' group that cannot be aided.

Foucault (1977) argues that power involves representation. Naming involves exercising the power of representation and inclusion (or exclusion). Those phenomena that are not named remain invisible and marginal. Categorizing people as 'deserving' or 'undeserving' exemplifies the power of naming. The awesome power of naming erases the needs of those left out through the simple act of labelling them 'undeserving'. Through naming, social workers normalize certain behaviours and marginalize others.

To constitute clients as subjects, social workers obtain their stories by getting them to talk about their lives, tell them what they have done (confess) and think about how they might act differently in future. Practitioners engage clients in their own naming, representation and (self-)regulation. Foucault (1991) suggests that clients become subjects of the technologies of governmentality thereby controlling themselves individually, as fragmented and atomized beings isolated from others.

Through differentiated inclusion, social workers become involved in (re)constituting 'deserving' people who have been objectified as subjects. They ensure that people acting as agents establish themselves as subjects through discourses about empowerment and self-determination (Rose, 2000). In promoting subjectivity by investing in individuals and enabling them to develop personal projects that are contiguous with the social order (Miller and Rose, 1988), social workers have facilitated a constrained type of citizenship amongst the 'deserving' poor. Yet their inclusion occurs at the expense of those labelled 'undeserving'.

Determining entitlement on the basis of which individual is more needy and deserving than another has been incorporated into practice. Differentiating between clients has become an integral part of social work's mandate that continues to the present. Dividing claimants between the deserving and undeserving poor has become useful in scientifically rationing resources. Though helpful in stretching resources, ideologies of governmentality that differentiate amongst clients create a gulf between them and social workers. Thus, clients see practitioners not as sources of assistance in time of need, but as hurdles that they have to overcome to reach the services they require (O'Connell, 1983).

Regardless of its aspirations, changing the individual behaviour of some clients is beyond the capacity of the discipline. Difficulty in securing individual change has prompted social workers to see some clients as incapable of acting according to the accepted social norms of the day. They have attributed their failings to the individual pathologies of clients without exploring the links to structural inequalities and the limitations of particular ways of organizing social relations in capitalist societies.

The development of theory from practice and of practice from theory has been an important dynamic in the change processes of the academic discipline of social work and professional practice. The constant interplay between them provides the basis not only for conceptualizing social work practice as an act of both thinking and doing that is encapsulated in the notion of reflexive practice (Schon, 1983), but also for seeing the research of practice, and research in practice, as important components in furthering understanding of what happens in social work interventions. The review and evaluation of practice is undertaken throughout an intervention from its conception to its termination and beyond (Compton and Galaway, 1975).

Practitioners seek to determine what would constitute their preferred or best intervention in any given instance, even though the contexts within which they operate might mitigate its realization. Social workers are responsible for both thinking and doing in their practice, despite identifying with the doing, or the practical. Reflexive practice is about the constant interplay between these two elements in the processes of practical interventions. Additionally, reflexive practice focuses on processes, particularly those that acknowledge the importance of client agency and seeing clients as full partners in practice, that is, people capable of contributing or giving to the relationship not just taking from it. Making headway in reflexive practice involves practitioners in power-sharing endeavours and a search for equality even though they may be unable to achieve it (Panet-Raymond, 1991). That social workers and clients should both act as subjects within an interaction rather than social workers treating clients as objects of their ministrations is central to this approach (Dominelli, 2002a).

Multi-disciplinary and inter-professional working makes demands of social workers' expertise that are not addressed in current training (Dominelli and Khan, 2000). Being reflexively critical requires a wide range of practical and theoretical knowledges alongside the skills to apply these in practice. It also involves social workers in thinking, feeling and doing their work – an integration of the practical, intellectual and emotional elements of any intervention. Teaching students to do this is a major challenge for social work educators.

Defining moments in professional social work: Shifting contexts for practice

Social work as a micro-level activity has been carried out formally by paid practitioners, sometimes professionally qualified, and informally by family, friends and neighbours. As the latter, it is unpaid work carried out on a voluntary philanthropic basis. Social work has been conducted in a variety of settings – the family as the key private domestic institution, commercial operations, religious agencies, various voluntary bodies in the community and public institutions. These provide contexts for practice. Social work has been sponsored by philanthropic benefactors, voluntary, state or private sector employers. Its spread across a breadth of locations within a rich tapestry of networks has meant that social workers have always engaged in a mixed economy of care, although the balance between the state, voluntary, commercial and domestic contributions has varied at different points in time and in diverse localities. The reign of the state as both purchaser and provider of the personal social services in Britain has been brief.

The early concerns of British social workers covered delinquency, family breakdown, sanitation and health problems, the economic fragility of people's existence and the disruption of traditional value systems (Mendelsohn, 1980). This list sounds similar to one that could be compiled now. Its practitioners, mainly white women, were originally drawn from the ranks of the middle and upper classes to work with those of the lower or poor classes and provide them with '*concrete* services' (Mendelsohn, 1980). The picture of a white middle-class woman-led profession is familiar to social work clients today. Working-class 'agents' subsequently joined the wealthy volunteers, but held poorly paid positions as low-status technicians. These agents provided the model for today's social workers (Lappin, 1965).

Professional social work education and practice has existed in the Western world for over a hundred years, having started with programmes of professional training in Britain, the Netherlands and the United States between the end of the nineteenth and beginning of the twentieth centuries (Kendall, 2000). Its development has coalesced around four key defining moments. These moments periodize the development of social work in terms of major concerns that are conveyed in discourses about its activities at particular points in its history without any one of them having achieved satisfactory resolution. These are not linear moments that follow each other sequentially in chronological time. Rather, they are a series of multi-lapping transitions on the path of professional evolution and recognition. At any specific juncture, the shifting contexts of practice enable particular discourses to dominate others. I identify these moments as:

- the early beginnings of the profession;
- a period of professional consolidation;
- a fragile consensus around the post-war welfare state; and
- the (re)fragmentation and (re)regimentation of social work under the auspices of globalization.

I examine below the significance of these moments for their impact on work undertaken with clients. I call these movements 'moments' to escape the linearity implied in stages and because the trends initiated in and through one moment carry over into the others. This conceptualization problematizes the development of social work and moves it away from neat chronological spaces.

A new profession makes its claims: The early beginnings of social work Social work is the product of its time. It has its own social, political, economic and cultural histories and actors engaged in creating, writing, reading and interpreting its story or stories. Professional social work developed as the handmaiden of the nineteenth-century nation-state with the objective of turning deviant individuals into acceptable citizens (Lorenz, 1994). In Britain, this task was engineered under the auspices of the Charity Organization Society (COS), whose members were instrumental in shaping the profession (Walton, 1975) as an essential element in the state's project of modernity.

The person-focused casework methods developed by the COS superseded the more structurally oriented analyses of poverty and its impact on human behaviour advocated by those practising community-based interventions and favoured, amongst others, by the Settlement Movement. In eschewing the links between structural conditions and individual behaviour, the casework approach set the scene for concentrating practitioners' minds on the personal attributes of clients and facilitated their being held responsible for their predicament. From here, it was a short step to pathologizing them for their failure to 'get on' in society. The tendency to hold poor people responsible for their plight threads through to the present.

Men headed the COS management structure.[3] Only one woman was on its original council (Dale and Foster, 1986), thus instituting a managerial pattern that is evident today (Grimwood and Popplestone, 1993). The COS brought together a number of voluntary agencies whose activities had proliferated over the years, although only those claimants worthy of help received charitable assistance. The workhouse catered for the others. Many of these 'unworthy' others were women who bore children out of wedlock. The Settlement Movement, by contrast, focused on poverty and poor housing as key issues for the workers to address.

The triumph of the COS over the more community-oriented Settlement Movement in establishing social work as a profession (Lappin, 1965) submerged for a time the contentious nature of social work. The victory of the COS and its espousal of the individualized casework method of intervention resulted in social work receiving legitimacy and financial support from the state to carry out its remit, thereby turning social work into a state-dependent profession (Walton, 1975) that lacked autonomous structures of governance – a feature which remains. A similar tension between individually focused casework and structurally oriented interventions like community work developed in the United States when Jane Addams imported British ideas for practice into that country (Lappin, 1965; Kendall, 2000). A significant element in this moment is the erasure of client voices and knowledges and the usurpation of the space so created by professional ones.

Social work differed from the other professions gathering strength in Britain at the same time in being led predominantly by unwaged and disenfranchised white middle-class women for whom social work offered employment outlets, albeit largely in a voluntary capacity (Walton, 1975). Working within a paradigm of residuality, although its clients were the most disadvantaged people in society, they could not demand remuneration for their services, even on a differential basis of charging rich people more to defray costs accrued in providing services to poor people. Moreover, they encountered more needy people than they had resources with which to respond. These characteristics made social workers dependent on the state and wealthy benefactors to fund their activities (Walton, 1975). This created a financially dependent profession which was constantly underfunded and unable to fulfil its mission of meeting the needs of all vulnerable people. Social workers have had to find methods of rationing the scarce resources that they have had at their disposal (Dominelli, 1997). This concern dogs contemporary practice and reinforces practitioners' incapacity to be effective and efficient gatekeepers of services as needs and resources become mismatched.

That people must look after themselves when public provisions are unavailable has been reinforced at the highest level in recent judiciary hearings. British court judgments have reaffirmed that purchasers' resource allocations can determine what services are provided for specific clients (Carvel, 2001). In backing the limitations imposed on social work practice by inadequate resources, they have confirmed that local authorities do not have to provide services they cannot afford, even when the person concerned has an established need vindicated by their employees' assessments. These decisions have (re)affirmed resource-led practice and restricted what social workers can do for elders and disabled people (King's Fund, 2001).

Of the multiplicity of contexts within which social workers have been embedded, a key one has been rooted in professional preoccupations and revolved around practitioners' struggles to establish professional credentials. Their early aspirations were dealt a severe blow by the Flexner Report of 1915, which rejected their claims to professional status on the grounds that social work lacked its own body of knowledge and failed to maintain its professional boundaries through restrictive training practices (Flexner, 1915). Further complicating their ambitions was the ideological unacceptability of women making claims to paid professional work. Social workers' inability to establish the credibility of a profession that defined itself through discourses that differed from prevailing professional ones also jeopardized its cause (Dominelli, 1997).

Social work's distinct professional base, training programme and paid employment pattern have been realized to some extent subsequently, but the status of the profession remains ambiguous. Its paradigms for practice, theoretical base and training requirements do not quite fit the 'normal' pattern evident in the more established professions of medicine and law. Moreover, social workers' attempts to pursue their claims have been hampered by society's tenuous commitment to them and their clientele. In Britain, the state's unwillingness to make the personal social services a universal provision as recommended in the Beveridge Report after the Second World War further undermined their aspirations. And so the struggle to establish social works professional status continues to bedevil it.

Britain's heritage as a colonial power has impacted upon social work's professional standing, not always in positive directions, by expanding beyond its national borders to solve 'home' problems and fulfil a proselytizing mission overseas. In the process, British models of social work, education, policy and practice spread to other lands. Caught up in the ideologies and practices of the day, social work became implicated in the spread of imperialist worldviews and projects that at times endangered the lives of people at the receiving end of practice. Cast as integrating and assimilationist moves in their time, current evaluations of their impact have revealed that by engaging in power over exchanges that endorsed the rule of white middle-class elites, social work practice reaffirmed gendered, classist, homophobic, disablist and racist orientations that continue to bedevil practice in developing countries today (Simpson, 2002; Sewpaul, 2003).

Social workers in the UK became drawn into dealing with the problems of modernity, particularly those associated with ensuring social stability within the nation-state, and promoting its imperialist interest overseas. Practitioners' complicity in exporting Britain's problems elsewhere lent credence to the view that its residents could enjoy a good life in other countries, especially in the new Commonwealth. This good fortune was posited for the 'home' children – the 'orphaned' working-class British children sent overseas, in many cases compulsorily. These initiatives drew poor families into regimes of surveillance and control in which the caring dimension was in short supply. Their experiences depict a series of inappropriate social work responses to poor people's need for assistance (Bagnell, 2001).

Professional consolidation   Social workers' preoccupation with establishing their professional credentials has been evident since the beginning of the twentieth century. To consolidate their pursuit of professionalization within a supportive social mandate, social workers focused their attention on finding a scientific basis to their activities. Freudian analysis provided the opportunity to develop a professional base grounded in scientific theory (Walton, 1975). This favoured certain parts of their enterprise, namely psychiatric and clinical social work. These endeavours re-emphasized working with individuals as Freudian insights enabled practitioners to help people deal with past personal traumas and link these to current behaviour. Psychodynamic casework became the prime method marking this point in the evolution of professional social work. Little, if any, attempt was made to address the impact of structural deficiencies upon individual biographies. Making connections between the two would have constituted unprofessional conduct, an irony that would have intrigued Freud, for a crucial innovation in his analysis of human behaviour was to situate personal development within at least one aspect of the social system – family relationships.

The construct of family favoured by Freudian analysis is the ahistorical, decontextualized nuclear family. Freud's ideal family takes no cognizance of: the structured inequalities that exist within families (Pahl, 1980); cultural diversity; the variety of family forms; or the differential valuing of families in society-at-large (Ahmad, 1990). These failings create difficulties in meeting the needs of diverse family forms that do not fit the stereotypical model of two white middle-class heterosexual parents with children (Callahan et al., 2000). Positing the 'normal' family of a father, mother and children as a universal form without conflicts and messiness, practitioners have labelled as deviant and dysfunctional those who do not fit this image.

Strengthening of the profession's status was patchy and uneven. Its progress as part of the project of modernity positioned social workers as significant participants in the formation of the British welfare state immediately after the Second World War. A social work professional, Clement Attlee (1920), even became prime minister. This trend received a major impetus from the Seebohm reorganization of 1970, which brought about the ascendancy of generic social work at the expense of specialist practice, on which professional credibility depended (Jaques, 1975, 1977). Working within a local authority base, social workers became one small professional grouping within vast social services bureaucracies aimed primarily at providing social care services from cradle to grave in one location. Their numbers and voice were dwarfed by those of other local government employees. By the late 1970s, practitioners assumed the form of junior partners operating in the bureaucratic structures of local government (Parry, Rustin and Satymurti, 1979) and became enmeshed in the bureaucratic rationality of the nation-state. Social workers became street-level bureaucrats or bureau-professionals (Parry, Rustin and Satymurti, 1979) whose influence on the profession's development waned.

The small number of qualified social workers working in large local authority bureaucracies is problematic. Their voice and concerns have limited space in competition against the demands of other state employees. The situation was particularly difficult for those in the National Association of Local Government Officers (NALGO), whose remit encompassed social workers. Their numbers were a tiny proportion of its constituency, and its record on taking up social workers' issues during the 1970s was poor. Social workers sought to enhance their impact by forming Local Action Groups within NALGO to take up specific issues associated with 'race' and gender. NALGO subsequently amalgamated with other public sector unions to become UNISON, now one of the largest service sector unions in the country. It has a much better record on taking up issues of concern to women workers and defending high-quality services. Social workers have participated in strike action aimed at improving their own working conditions and the services made available to clients on several occasions during the intervening years (Carvel, 2001).

Within this bureau-rational context, social workers' focus on individuals unable to function adequately within their social environment was both a help and a hindrance. It was useful in underpinning the profession's universalistic ideology and code of ethics. These provided the framework that nested the worker–client relationship within a general consensus about welfare and promoted its expansion as a caring profession. Social work's dependent status, however, became an obstacle to its autonomous development as a profession because practitioners could not challenge structural inequalities within existing social relations without getting into trouble with policymakers who employed them and funded and provided the bulk of services that clients could access.

Conflicting loyalties in contentious cases placed British practitioners on a collision course with their employer, the local state. When it came to choosing between retaining their jobs or supporting clients, social workers often became paralysed into doing nothing. Those that do take actions that their employers or local politicians condemn become labelled troublesome practitioners and, if they are not actually dismissed, they may find it hard to obtain employment in other authorities (Dominelli, 1990). Sue Richardson, the social worker at the heart of the Cleveland Affair of the mid-1980s (Butler-Schloss, 1988), found its impact detrimental when she supported paediatrician Marietta Higgs' diagnoses of child sexual abuse. It took a further ten years for her position to be vindicated (Campbell, 1998a, 1998b). In the meantime, she had lost a job that she loved. Her experience suggests that being technically competent does not automatically protect workers from the vicissitudes and politics of practice.

Raising the status of the profession has also floundered against public attitudes. The public's negative views have pathologized the clients that practitioners encounter in their work and accorded them low priority for publicly allocated expenditures. The ensuing discourses have demonized poor people (Jones, 1998) and are often at variance with those espoused by practitioners, who tend to be more liberal and tolerant than the general population (Bagley and Young, 1982). These differences in the perceptions of clients and their worth have become sources of conflict for social workers, who seek to empower clients and satisfy the requirements imposed upon their work by those who pay for their labour. The demise of the British Community Development Projects (CDPs) provides a classic example of dissonant discourses between practitioners and the state (see chapter 7, pp. 204–5). In these, practitioners emphasized the structural nature of the destruction of local communities whilst politicians endorsed models of individual pathology. CDPs were closed down when official discourses were undermined and workers' demands for local development became too troublesome (Loney, 1986; Dominelli, 1990). Similar parallels can be made about initiatives fostered under the American War on Poverty. Despite the initial optimistic notes sounded about consumer participation, pessimistic conclusions about the experiences of welfare claimants at the end of this Programme abound (Piven and Cloward, 1977, 1982).

A brief period of consensus around the welfare state   The establishment of the British welfare state after the Second World War gave

rise to an interventionist state form of welfare in which the governance of social life through bureaucratic and fiscal means was
central. It was known as 'welfarism', which Rose and Miller (1992,
p. 192) define as the securing of 'social and economic objectives
by linking up a plethora of networks with aspirations to know,
programme and transform the social field'. Social work was crucial
to this project. According to Donzelot (1980), the bureaucratic
rationality engendered by welfarism aimed to promote national
well-being through the idea of social responsibility tempered by
the mutuality of social risk and underpinned by social solidarity
and the optimistic belief that social problems could be solved and
difficult individuals and families could be treated or rehabilitated
back into society.

To realize these objectives, welfarism drew upon the economic
philosophy of John Maynard Keynes and social policies formulated by William Beveridge. These encouraged the state to manage
economic demand through the manipulation of public expenditures
within a market economy and to insure against the risks posed
by this economic arrangement through full employment and social
insurance. Social insurance was actuarially based and people
had to contribute to benefit. By following actuarial prescriptions,
Beveridge anticipated that the five Giants of 'want, disease, idle-
ness, ignorance and squalor' would be conquered at the same time
as individuals became bound together in a system of solidarity and
mutual interdependence. As the system was wage-based, this
formula left unwaged people, primarily women undertaking
domestic responsibilities, out of the beneficiary loop unless dependent on men as wives or daughters (Pascall, 1986; Dominelli, 1991b).
Without direct access to benefits, women were in a structurally
induced dependency that excluded their needs and concerns from
the state's purview.

For a period, this vision was shared across the political spectrum
and the practitioner–politician divide. It was a benevolent view
aimed at producing a harmonious and stable society. Under its
arrangements, the interests of the state, the social worker and the
client were expected to converge. Professionals would work through
the state apparatus to deliver social services. In meeting social
needs and furthering social justice, politicians expected to achieve
social progress. However, closer scrutiny of its impact revealed a
high degree of exclusion and differentiation. Its 'citizen' became
exposed as a passive recipient who was primarily a white male
in waged work (Pascall, 1986; Williams, 1989; Dominelli, 1991b;
Lister, 1997).

The consensus unravels   The contradictions and ambiguities in bureau-professional social work became increasingly evident as it failed to meet the aspirations of clients, who complained of feeling disempowered and abused by the professionals charged with helping them become 'self-determining' individuals. Interventions that fostered the professionalization of social work such as psychodynamic casework (Towle, 1965) were attacked from within and without for not meeting clients' needs and perpetuating social exclusion. Criticisms of inadequate interventions intensified when those in the 'new' social movements of the 1960s and 1970s had their intentions frustrated by the absence of services responding to their needs as they defined them. In Britain, the first of these drew upon the claimants' movement and castigated social workers for failing to respond to class stratification as a major issue (Corrigan and Leonard, 1978; Simpkin, 1979). Others followed with additional social divisions: 'race' (Dominelli, 1988; Ahmad, 1990), gender (Hanmer and Statham, 1988; Dominelli and McLeod, 1989), sexual orientation (Hanscombe and Forster, 1982; Arnup, 1995) and disability (Oliver, 1990; Morris, 1991; Begum, 1992; Begum, Hill and Stevens, 1993).

Those in the 'new' social movements critiqued the oppressive nature of social work practice and its inability to encourage agency amongst its clientele. They also succeeded in giving collective voice to what had previously been expressed as individual concerns and refused to accept the legitimacy of ascribing to social work professionals the sole expertise on their life stories. Another key objective of those in the 'new' social movements has been to challenge the dynamics of residuality. They have used their collective voices to call for non-stigmatizing citizenship-based services that meet people's needs and are under their control (Dominelli, 2002b). They have also sought to make alliances with people who have not been clients to assist them in pursuing their demands. Social workers' responses to their claims of the 'new' social movements, however, have been patchy and fragmented.

The demands emanating from the 'new' social movements have formed part of the broader challenges to the current social order and have strongly influenced the development of social work theory and practice. The women's movement, black activist movement and disability movement have had a particularly powerful impact. Seeking to realize social justice, their critiques have highlighted the power of social workers to oppress marginalized and disempowered groups by providing inappropriate services and shutting out their voices. The social actors associated with these movements insist that social workers respond to their needs as they define them. More recently, their political passions have focused on improving the position of poor working-class peoples, dealing with the by-products of industrialization and environmental degradation and meeting the needs of those involved in migratory movements on a global scale (Wichterich, 2000).

These critiques have contributed to unravelling the post-war consensus on welfare, but they have also inspired the growth of alternative models of social work: feminist social work (Dominelli and McLeod, 1989; Dominelli, 2002b); anti-racist and black perspectives in social work (Dominelli, 1988; Ahmad, 1990); and the social model of disability (Oliver, 1990). Despite the extensive literature developed to help practitioners integrate their insights into practice, mainstream providers have not fully incorporated these into their work. So, alternatives that respond to critiques of traditional practice with innovative initiatives that have improved services according to client-led agendas remain marginalized.

At the same time, academics and practitioners who had defined themselves as on the Left began to expose the exploitative foundation on which social work as a state activity rested (Corrigan and Leonard, 1978). Others followed and they retheorized the basis on which practitioners could improve their practice to promote interventions that were more responsive to the expressed wishes and needs of clients, particularly those espoused by the 'new' social movements. Meanwhile, New Right politicians conveyed their exasperation at social workers' lack of success in keeping children safe, reducing offending behaviour amongst young people and supporting traditional family groupings. Their concerns peaked during the 1980s and 1990s in an attack that further undermined the post-war consensus on welfare.

A new consensus forms around the precepts of neo-liberal market ideologies Under Thatcherism, the Left's critique of bureaucratic welfarism was partly appropriated by proponents of the New Right. Rightwing ideologues used legitimate concerns about failing services to mount an ideologically driven attack against universal welfare provisions and impose financial market-based controls to regulate reluctant professionals (see Gilder, 1982; Murray, 1984, 1990, 1994). Linking their views to monetarism, they intensified their own brand of critical rhetoric and turned it against both practitioners and clients to advocate a free market ideology with policies attached to it. Redefining client empowerment as choice was central to this project.

The New Right's hostility towards the gains of the 'new' social movements (Gilder, 1981), the power of professionals and intellectual elites who opposed their dogma ensured that once rightwing politicians ensconced themselves within the state, they utilized their powers to implement a social revolution in favour of the market and deal wounding blows to its 'enemies', the professional 'do-gooders' (Brooks, 1996). The New Right implemented the social changes it desired by usurping much of the Left's libertarian ideology concerned with client-centred practices; restructuring the sites of professional power through legislative fiat and financial inducements; imposing new managerialist imperatives on welfare provisions; and institutionalizing quasi-markets in welfare regimes. In Britain, their objectives were achieved by using economics as ideology rather than an outright ideological attack decrying public welfare (Dominelli and Hoogvelt, 1996a).

Meeting market imperatives meant introducing a new set of conditions within the welfare state and subjecting it to a series of reviews and policy changes aimed at increasing British competitiveness in international arenas; decreasing the powers of professionals ensconced within welfare state structures; and encouraging the development of a mixed economy of welfare in which the state acquired a new role as purchaser of services whilst the independent sector made up of private (commercial) and voluntary providers became more deeply involved in delivering them (Griffiths, 1988). The largely invisible domestic sector became harnessed to this project through its capacity to fill the gaps between the services that were needed by individuals and what could be publicly provided or privately purchased. Community care policies encapsulate this vision. Key tools for managing its success include audits and the documents *Quality Protects* and *Best Value*.

Legislative developments in social work layered further complications into market-driven practice. These were later incorporated in New Labour's modernizing programme, but they started out as initiatives for facilitating the creation of quasi-markets that turned clients into consumers with rights that could be attributed to them individually. The key pieces of legislation were the 1989 Children Act, the 1990 National Health Service and Community Care Act (CCA) and the 1991 Criminal Justice Act (CJA). The first two of these shifted the balance of power away from professionals and onto clients. The three Acts brought the new managerialism into social work and inculcated new managerialist cultures of control into social work organizations. These developments integrated the profession into corporate management systems that promoted capitalist social relations in an arena that had traditionally been considered outside their reach. Combined with internationalization of the state, these responses have drawn social work into the global system and have begun to impact considerably upon day-to-day practice (Dominelli and Khan, 2000).

The new managerialism was significant in changing the policies, practice and culture of the workplace. From the beginning, managerialist imperatives were directed not solely at social work practitioners, but at all local authority and state employees within the civil service, health and education. In social work, the attacks against bureau-professionalism ultimately encompassed both practitioners and educators. A manager in the study I conducted with Parves Khan articulated the objectives of the new managerialism as

> a shift from social workers doing things for people towards much more user-empowerment, valuing people, listening to people. (Dominelli and Khan, 2000)

This shift in climate has been facilitated by the major 'moral panics' that developed around the deaths of a succession of children who had been subjected to local authority scrutiny. Beginning with Maria Colwell in 1973 (Berridge and Brodie, 1996), these have run through the intervening decades to include Victoria Climbié (Laming, 2003). The consequent inquiries have led to specific measures directed at improving social work practice (Parton, 1985). The ensuing changes have entrenched bureaucratic forms of regulation and surveillance on practitioners, who had previously enjoyed a considerable degree of autonomy.

Surveillance is conducted not only through managerial imperatives and controls, but also through mechanisms of peer review. Social workers are experiencing a growth in quality assurance mechanisms that rely on the quality of their services being assessed by 'clients' and peers. The complaints procedures which have been introduced to ensure compliance with bureaucratic regimes are peer-administered. Surveillance regimes run by the inspection services draw on the mechanisms of peer review. The Social Care Institute for Excellence (SCIE) constitutes a further component of the peer review process in which best practice is identified and propagated. Those who do not comply with its proposals can expect their shortcomings to be noticed.

The market ideology is most evident in the 1990 CCA. It was crucial in setting up the quasi-markets which have now become endemic in social work. These provide a major context in which practitioners from various backgrounds operate as case managers assuming tasks once performed solely by social workers. Begun in relation to the care of older people, its methodology has now encompassed other client groups, including children. The 1989 Children Act established parents as consumers with rights by reducing social workers' powers in child welfare cases, curtailing their arbitrary powers and empowering parents when in conflict with them. The Act endorses the idea that children have rights to their own culture, although these entitlements are not always observed.

The 1991 Criminal Justice Act (CJA) intensified managerial control and surveillance over probation officers' work with offenders through performance indicators and national standards. Additionally, the CJA required the monitoring of inequalities based on gender and 'race' as enacted through probation practice, and it provided magistrates with a wider range of sentencing options whilst retaining a belief that offending behaviour can be changed. Magistrates were encouraged to use prison as a sentence of last resort and for the most obdurate offenders. The government also authorized the privatization of some prison services and the greater involvement of voluntary and commercial providers during this period.

Globalization reframes the social work agenda   Globalization has penetrated daily life and reformulated people's experiences by normalizing global capitalist relations in everyday routines. Social work is being reshaped by actors involved at the meso- and micro-levels of practice, while macro-level forces emanating from the dynamics of globalization are reorienting the practice agenda. In the interplay between these, the interventions of New Right theorists and politicians have supplanted discourses about the social contract by endorsing individual self-sufficiency, market rationality, contract government and bureaucratic controls to govern the design, provision, delivery and quality of services (Dominelli and Hoogvelt, 1996a). Under their aegis, social life becomes guided by choices individuals make in the marketplace rather than the tenets of welfarism. The importance of globalization and its attendant neo-liberal ideology for social workers is that they have become redefined as part of the problem of modern life for failing to deal with issues of poverty, disintegrating family structures, increased juvenile delinquency, a declining respect for authority and the loss of individual responsibility in providing for one's welfare needs (see Gilder, 1981; Murray, 1984, 1990, 1994).

A crucial part of global capitalist ideology is that globalization works for the good of all, through its 'trickle-down effects'. Rising

levels of poverty, crime and alienation are symptomatic of the failure of the 'trickle-down' society to deliver the goods in a way that
is inclusive of all human beings in the nation-state and globally.
In the UK, there are increasing signs of immiseration and social
exclusion (Craig, 2001), despite attempts by New Labour to place
social inclusion high on its wish-list for changes in the body politic
(Giddens, 1998b; Jordan, 2000). Evidence compiled by the United
Nations and others highlighting increasing levels of poverty and
social exclusion both within and between countries counters the
New Right assertion that globalization improves living conditions
for all through 'trickle-down' effects (UNDP, 2000; Wichterich, 2000).
Poverty and other forms of exclusion provide important contexts
of practice that have been created by policymakers, capitalist entrepreneurs and international intergovernmental organizations such
as the International Monetary Fund (IMF) and World Bank through
structural adjustment programmes (Wichterich, 2000).

Globalization has altered the labour process in professional
practice by bringing the methods of industrial production into
professional labour. The proletarianization of professional work
has been referred to as Taylorization or Fordism and describes how
complex qualitative *relational* tasks involving several processes of
interaction and multiple levels of judgement have been simplified
into neat, discrete, separable elements that can be quantified or
measured and monitored. In social work, this is epitomized in
competence-based social work with its routinized checklists and
risk assessment schedules – tools invented to provide security in
complex professional judgements where certainty of outcome cannot
be guaranteed. Professionals are not omniscient as they do not
control all aspects of an intervention process, nor do they know all
factors that go into producing a particular outcome.

The Taylorization of professional work has intensified trends
towards technicist approaches to social work and undermined the
relational aspects of its interventions in favour of codified professional knowledges and rule-based behaviour (Currey, Wequin and
Associates, 1993; Barnett, 1994). Through it, bureau-professionals
have been replaced by bureau-technocrats. Competence-based social
work has provided the means whereby management has been able
to impose its requirements upon the labour process, and reinforce
the regulatory regime known as the new mangerialism.

In this, the relationship between social workers and clients and
between the state as employer and social workers as professional
employees features managerial control and surveillance rather
than trust and empowerment. The new managerialism assumes

absolute control. Yet contingent control is the sole possibility because clients expose only fragments of their realities to practitioners, who then select amongst these and those that they can uncover through their own investigations for intervention. An assumption of absolute control features heavily in the 'what works' school of thought. Rooting professional practice in the idea of absolute control, however, is done at the peril of both client and practitioner.

The fragmentation of the labour processes under globalization has encouraged the professionalization of practice at the lower levels and its deprofessionalization at the higher levels. It does so by feeding moves to improve qualifications amongst social care workers, primarily untrained women who have provided personal and physical care in the social care arena for many years. These women are now receiving minimum training in the form of recognized qualifications at the National Vocational Qualification (NVQ) level. Although now performing duties previously done by social workers, NVQ holders are not guaranteed access to jobs requiring higher qualifications. So, they may become locked into a fragmented, low-status, low-paid gendered ghetto. At the same time, a three-year basic qualification at degree level has been set for social workers. A significant improvement over the previous two-year limit, this qualification has yet to establish the professional credentials of social work and its practitioners still spend substantially less time in training than do key professionals they work with, whether doctors, psychologists or lawyers. Additionally, as the qualification is driven by competence-based approaches to social work, there are limited chances of this driving the professionalization of practitioners to higher levels. Unless subverted by reflexive practice, it is more likely to turn them into competent technocrats.

Conclusions

Practitioners do not have the luxury of ignoring the micro-, meso- or macro-contexts of practice with their attendant power relations as these are constantly negotiated and renegotiated through and during their interventions. Social workers operate in and have to be sensitive to a multiplicity of contexts, each of which is complex. Addressing these is difficult and complicates their work in ways that require the considerable expenditure of energy and resources. Since they cannot intervene at all the levels that are relevant, social workers make choices about which ones they will prioritize and give attention to. Thus, being aware of the choices they make and the reasons for them is an important dimension of practice.

Globalization, particularly its tendency towards the internationalization of the state and the exploitation of public welfare resources for the purposes of flexible production and profit accumulation, has added its own demands on social workers. These require practitioners to work collaboratively across national borders as well as within them, often with a range of clients and other professional groupings, and to respond to managerial imperatives. These include: the duty to realize the three 'Es' of economy, efficiency and effectiveness in service delivery; requirements that are monitored through performance indicators; and outcome-oriented assessments of their work. These subject practitioners to forms of surveillance and regulation similar to those experienced by the clients with whom they work.

ES, ETHICS
EMPOWERMENT

Introduction

Values have been a cornerstone of social work practice, standing alongside knowledge and skills (CCETSW, 1976). In Britain, values, particularly a commitment to anti-oppressive values, have been seen as a protective cloak that has been expected to deal with problematic individual behaviours and provide a cover against the ravages of increasing structural inequalities and other deleterious changes that have recently damaged the quality of life for social work clients (CCETSW, 1989). These have included: structural forces linked to the global economy that have resulted in the loss of skilled jobs, particularly for working-class men; a deterioration in the physical fabric of run-down communities with rising rates of crime; and unsympathetic social policies that, since the advent of Thatcherism, have promoted punitive welfarism.

Whilst useful in creating a basis for uniting a fragmented profession, values cannot of themselves bring about changes necessary for eradicating structural inequalities. Their elimination is a contentious issue requiring political commitment and action at the highest levels. Holding appropriate values helps in this process by enabling people to appreciate the wastage of human potential caused by social problems; promoting egalitarian discourses; and endorsing activities that target the elimination of inequalities. Inegalitarian power relations perpetuated by decision-makers and resource-holders have to be changed at the same time as egalitarian values are enacted. Social workers have an important role to play in promoting these issues.

In this chapter I examine the traditional values of social work and the extent to which these have changed in recent times. I also consider the limitations of values as agents for change at the macro-, meso- and micro- levels of practice, and their potential for mobilizing people individually and collectively in pursuit of an egalitarian social order that encourages people to behave as active citizens with responsibility for both their own well-being and that of others in an interdependent world in which the (dis)welfare of one impinges upon everyone else. Rising levels of poverty, crime and alienation are symptomatic of the failure of the 'trickle-down' society to deliver welfare goods to encompass all human beings individually and globally. Social workers are asked to deal with the casualties of this form of social organization.

Empowering clients has been seen as a way of moving towards a more egalitarian social order (Gutierrez and Lewis, 1999). I argue that, useful as empowering practice is, it is unable to do more than deal with issues at the micro-level of practice in the practitioner–client relationship, and has little impact on structural inequalities, which also need to be ended. To ensure that such changes occur, social workers need alliances with others across a broad spectrum of agencies and actors directly concerned with matters of social justice and the transformation of inegalitarian social relations. They also have to become involved in reconfiguring the knowledge base that structures people's understanding of their realities. Realizing these changes requires practitioners to rethink the epistemological base on which their practice is founded and take action at local, national and international levels.

Practising social work values: Reconfiguring continuities and discontinuities

Values are the principles that have been elaborated to guide professional behaviour by highlighting what is accepted as meaningful in establishing the priorities that guide particular interventions. Values aim to create a professional culture that improves practice through their practice. They are encapsulated in a code of ethics that attempts to draw boundaries around what is acceptable conduct and what is not. Embodied in the code of ethics, values become incorporated into the technologies of control through which professionals become self-regulating individuals who exercise control over others.

Codified as ethics, values control professional behaviour and ensure that social workers, as those caring for vulnerable people, do not abuse their power (BASW, 1996). These codes of ethics are highly individualized (for both practitioner and client) and people-focused. Sarah Banks (2001) argues that this is because social work values are ultimately predicated on the Kantian one of 'respect for the person', a value that is firmly embedded in the Enlightenment and reflects professional social work's modernist origins in Western Europe.

This claim is somewhat problematic. Although undoubtedly true in the European and Christian context of social work, my excursions into other countries and faiths suggest that these also have 'respect for the person' at their core. In these, the person is embedded within broader social networks more often than is the case for the atomized, possessive individuals of the West. Additionally, other cultures have had their own forms of social work, and many of these have had their own periods of 'enlightenment'; they were simply different from those of the West. I add these words of caution because it is too easy to fall into the trap of claiming all 'good' values as European, and assigning the 'bad' ones onto the category of the 'others'.

Social work's traditional values were propounded by Father Biesteck (1961) in the profession's happier days. These he identified as: individualization; the purposeful expression of feelings; controlled emotional involvement; acceptance; a non-judgemental attitude; client self-determination; and confidentiality. Biesteck's values are rooted in an ethic of care that has encouraged social workers to help others in difficult circumstances and represent society's general commitment to assisting in an unobtrusive manner those who are vulnerable to life's exigencies. Traditional values assume that people need help because they have fallen on hard times and not because the conditions in which they live are harsh. The implementation of traditional values in practice requires social workers to show empathy (Egan, 1998), the capacity to step into another's shoes and thereby move beyond the realm of their own experience or transcend the limitations of what they know and accept as valid forms of behaviour.

Traditional values have been framed as if they occur in a vacuum. They are decontextualized from the social environments in which they are formulated, developed and practised, and void of any epistemological underpinnings which add a further layer of context. An important part of the latter is seeing the world as ordered around binary dyads wherein each part is in opposition to the other and ranged in a hierarchical ordering which defines one part superior and the other inferior. Ignoring the social context within which practice occurs can restrict social workers' capacity to understand the meso- and macro-level opportunities and constraints that shape the range of possibilities that can be explored in a relationship at the micro-level.

When presented as decontextualized entities, values are abstract and have a considerable degree of universal appeal. They may occupy professional discourses in ways that imply that they are fixed entities that survive changing trends and fashions (see Biesteck, 1961). But, in being practised, values have proved to be both more robust and fluid and more contradictory and controversial than anticipated in these theories. As the social and knowledge contexts within which values are embedded impact upon their use, practising values exposes the deficiencies of being cast as universally valid and fixed.

Stability and change in traditional values

The values propounded by Biesteck (1961) over four decades ago have endured despite the 'contract culture' and its ensuing deprofessionalization of practice. The terminology referring to values has been updated somewhat and highlights both the continuities and discontinuities evident within them (Dominelli, 2002c). Their abstract formulation partly explains their continued presence. Another reason for their persistence is that they have been adapted and modified in practice to take account of different contexts and critiques of their inapplicability in many circumstances. In practising values, social workers draw on a fluidity that stems from their being redefined through social interactions. The values expounded by Biesteck (1961) display continuities and discontinuities over time (history) and space (locality) as a result of being practised in context-specific situations.

Working with individuals is an important aspect of individualization. The individualization element in Biesteck's formulation has persisted to the present. Social workers continue to emphasize that they work with *individuals* whom they seek to bring to social health (Younghusband, 1978). They have traditionally articulated the causes of individual difficulties in the dichotomous categories of individual pathologies or structural inequalities and concentrated on one category or the other, but not both. Practitioners understand that in focusing only on the individual, they ignore the social or collective context in which a person is embedded. In failing to address the structural issues that impact upon individual behaviour, they collude with ideologies that blame victims for their plight (Mullaly, 1993). More recently, social work has been theorized as dealing with both individual behaviours and the structural contexts within which they are embedded (Dominelli, 2002a).

Biesteck's phrase 'the purposeful expression of feelings' is one that contemporary social workers might find strange. But they do subscribe to the value of either detachment or distancing as a professional stance. Viewing their relationship with clients as neutral is challenged by social workers who claim that becoming involved in what they are doing, and being passionate about eliminating social injustices, is unavoidable (Mullaly, 1993). However, even this group of professionals insist that they should not impose their values upon clients, or reveal too many of their own values and political preferences (Dominelli, 2002b). Their passion is expressed in their analyses and the search for allies and resources, not in treating their clients as pawns in political power games. This sounds like Biesteck's 'controlled expression of feelings or emotional involvement', an attribute that is central to maintaining the dignity and worth of the individuals with whom practitioners work.

Social workers continue to favour acceptance of their clients as people and the portrayal of non-judgemental attitudes towards them. The value of non-judgementality is more problematic than its terminology suggests, particularly in those areas where elements of identity, or who people are, become important. Social workers subscribe to totalizing definitions of identity whereby in treating everyone the same, they fail to *value*, or ascribe worth to, difference and end up reproducing oppressive relationships along the lines of 'race', gender, class, age, disability, sexual orientation and other attributes. In other cases, maintaining non-judgementality requires social workers to draw a distinction between the person and his or her behaviour. They may demonstrate understanding for the individual whilst condemning his or her actions. Such distinctions are particularly apt in social work with offenders, where probation officers and youth justice workers constantly have to work with people whose actions defy the imperatives of respecting the dignity of others, for example, sex offenders.

Client self-determination continues to be an important value in social work. Practitioners are constantly trying to help clients make their own decisions and thereby assume greater control over their lives and outcomes. More recently, the terminology has changed to one of empowerment rather than self-determination. Although the intent is the same, empowerment discourses are more likely to focus on the processes whereby clients take control of their lives, while self-determination is more focused on the end result of particular interventions.

Social workers are now more circumspect about what they can achieve through empowerment processes, not only because people in the 'new' social movements have highlighted the controlling dimensions of practice (Oliver, 1990), but also because they have become aware of the co-option of empowerment rhetoric by those on the New Right whose commitment to social work clients is at best suspect. Moreover, they have seen its use as a bureaucratic instrument that has failed to change power relations as experienced by those with whom they work (Dominelli, 2000). Thus, empowerment has been used to create discourses that suggest that consumers have choices which it may then turn out they have only in theory. Or, as expressed by a social worker in the study I conducted with Parves Khan:

> User consultation and involvement has become a tokenistic exercise flawed by a lack of resource commitment and a misunderstanding of politicians as to the involvement of users. (Dominelli and Khan, 2000)

Confidentiality, another important value identified by Biesteck (1961), was considered an uncontentious issue which restricted information flows to those involved in the casework relationship. The commitment to confidentiality, however, can contradict or cut across other values, such as user self-determination. If it is defined in non-contextualized ways, it can embroil a practitioner in agreeing to conditions which become unacceptable when its implications for people who are in trouble or vulnerable are clarified. At other times, invoking confidentiality can be dangerous, as in instances when a social worker asks a client or colleagues to keep unethical practices quiet, or if practitioners do not declare conflicts of interests.

Practitioners now acknowledge that confidentiality exemplifies the difficulty in setting tight boundaries around practising values, and the ethical dilemmas that arise when values are conceptualized as absolutes. Confidentiality can be used as cover for horrible acts of oppression. Restrictions on 'blank-cheque' confidentiality have become increasingly necessary as social workers have become aware of the range of sexual and physical abuse of vulnerable children and adults perpetrated by carers and others who work with them (Pritchard, 2001a). In consequence, practitioners advocate a more conditional and contingent confidentiality.

Stories by abused children indicate that secrecy dominates the relationship between abusers and those they abuse. The recent exposure of the Catholic Church's failure to deal with reported sexual abuse of children by priests suggests that confidentiality has been misused to protect adult perpetrators at the expense of abused children. Adultist power relations[1] can be utilized to reinterpret confidentiality in favour of adult interests. In some countries, notably Canada and the United States, reporting the abuse of children is mandatory. Americans also have mandatory reporting of elder abuse to redress power imbalances between perpetrators and those they abuse. British practitioners are discussing the extension of mandatory coverage to the abuse of both children and older people. Currently, mandatory reporting is imposed only on social workers and probation officers, primarily when children are being abused.

Confidentiality is now recognized as culturally contingent. In some cultures, for example, Gujerati Muslim culture, the right to share information about particular cases is not limited to the individual and professionals concerned, but can include extended family or community elders who have an interest or role to play in a given situation. Similar traditions are evident in Maori peoples' cultures and have been embodied in the family case conference approach (see Ruwhiu, 1998). This fluidity can cause white social workers discomfort as they become anxious about being unable to control information flows to others.

Practitioners should not jump to the conclusion that all people who share a given culture will view a particular situation in the same way and inappropriately reveal details of a particular case to anyone from that community. They have to check out the specific understandings of confidentiality with each person they work with and arrive at a meaningful definition of the term – one that takes account of specific contexts. British social workers also need to be mindful of legal obligations under the Data Protection Act. This Act individualizes information and requires that consent is obtained in writing for a person's details to be shared with others for particular purposes. This requirement can have a significant impact on client–worker relationships and increase the bureaucratic dimensions of the job.

Biesteck's (1961) values are primarily about guiding relations at the micro-level of practice or in the practitioner–client relationship. These assume that whatever is needed to act in an ethical manner is bounded by and contained within this relationship and suggest that the practitioner is all-powerful within it. Biesteck fails to acknowledge the role of the client in creating that relationship. Power relations are nuanced and complex. Clients are not just passive recipients of social work interventions. They also shape the relationship and influence the range of options on offer through their belief systems, the way in which they behave, and how they construct the problem(s) that they wish to address.

Practitioners are not all-powerful. They are subject to pressures from both above and below and have to create and mediate power relations through their interactions with clients. Whilst they have situational powers conferred upon them through their role, know-ledge of resources to hand, and statutory and legislative remits, they do not control dimensions of power that are dialogical, national or international. Dialogical power is created in and through inter-action with others in response to what they do, and vice versa. I have conceptualized negotiated power relations as embodied in the power of the powerless and the powerlessness of the powerful (Dominelli, 1986).

Trust

Values are also expressed in concepts that practitioners use to describe their work and how they think about identity as it impacts upon them and their clients. An important one of these is trust, which is crucial to the relationship between a professional and a client. The *Collins English Dictionary* defines 'trust' as 'the placing of confidence in or relying upon a person or thing'. The presence or absence of trust is a vital aspect of social relationships and affects how a social work relationship is perceived and experienced. Trust in a relationship can act as a catalyst for behavioural change, as occurs when someone emulates a trusted person as a role model. Trust tends to be seen as a good thing in and of itself, but it is abused in intimate or close relationships where sexual abuse or domestic violence takes place (see Dominelli, 1989; Mullender and Morley, 1994; Hester, Pearson and Harwin, 2000). People can endorse poor role models of people they trust when they are unaware of abusive behaviour because they assume trustworthi-ness prior to discovering the other side of a person's character.

Social workers have emphasized trust as an important element in client relationships when initiating change in individual beha-viour. The potential to use *relational trust* has been curtailed by the purchaser–provider model of practice, where social workers are restricted to commissioning services from others. But even here, trust remains important. The social worker has to rely upon trust expressed as contractual mechanisms and bureaucratic procedures for the delivery of appropriate services. I call this *legalized trust*. Legalized trust does not obviate the relational dimension of trust. Without this element, legalistic approaches can substantially reduce the power of social workers or clients to adapt as their relationship and assessment of a situation alter. In a relationship, perceptions are fluid and dynamic and constantly being (re)formulated as people (re)negotiate relationships through their interactions.

Trust provides stability or certainty in changing contexts and enables people to achieve more by pooling their resources to secure agreed goals. Relational trust enables practitioners and clients to use goodwill more effectively and stretch limited resources within a caring relationship further, without feeling exploited in the process. It provides the basis for 'extra-contractual care' (Dominelli, 1997). 'Trust' between carers and those cared for enables them to renegotiate their relationship outside the bounds of a contract to enable clients to receive more than their legal entitlement to care, to the mutual satisfaction of the parties involved.

A commitment to social justice: A contested value

Debates about values today have new elements that were not evident in Biesteck's (1961) day. Amongst these are: commitments to social justice; elimination of structural inequalities; and structural change. These were introduced following the critiques of social work as an oppressive profession mounted by women, black people, disabled people and others. Their criticisms have incorporated considerations of the impact of both macro- and meso-level forces upon micro-level interactions, particularly through analyses of the contexts in which practice is embedded. As practitioners and academics began to highlight structural inequalities, celebrate the values of social justice and social transformation, social workers' role in society became hotly contested in the media, government, academia and practice (see Phillips, 1993, 1994).

In the UK, the most overt manifestation of the dispute over values centred on social justice and erupted around the issue of anti-racist practice in the summer of 1993. In this, the regulatory framework for social work education and training, Paper 30, with its commitment to tackling all oppressions, particularly racism (CCETSW, 1989), was challenged in the media by a range of powerful opponents in opinion-forming positions – government

ministers, journalists and academics from the more traditional elements within social work, usually associated with the 'maintenance'
school of thought (see Appleyard, 1993; Phillips, 1993, 1994; Pinker,
1993). The ferocity of their attack, which caricatured the basic tenets
of anti-racist social work, and their control over both the media
and the profession ensured that theirs was the dominant voice.
Although the first student cohort under this regime had barely
graduated, the Central Council for Education and Training in Social
Work (CCETSW) was compelled to restructure and compromise its
stance by abolishing the Black Perspectives Committee and amending the offending line in Appendix 5 of Paper 30.

Despite these pressures, little has changed on the values front,
particularly in their written form, and social work's commitment
to social justice has continued to be expressed, albeit in different
ways. Nonetheless, the attack highlighted both the contentious
nature of values and the appropriateness of defining social work as
a profession that challenges structural oppression, whether perpetrated individually or socially through institutional structures and
cultural norms.

The ensuing debate, if it can be called that, because key proponents of anti-racist social work were not given equal space in the
media to express their views,[2] revealed a crucial flaw in the attack-
ers' construction of the case. Rooting it in a binary world of opposition and hierarchy, their epistemological worldview envisaged
professionals as all-powerful individuals who could impose themselves in the worker–client relationship in total disregard of clients'
agency, and without accountability for their behaviour. This construction of the situation is a travesty of the complex contextualized
relational basis of social work practice and the negotiated nature of
the interaction between practitioners and those with whom they
work. This controversy demonstrates the political nature of social
work education and difficulties that can be encountered when
social work educators champion social justice.

Reconfiguring the ethic of care

Crucial to understanding the trend in which budgets determine
services is an examination of the vocational aspects of social work.
These are rooted in an ethic of care (Sevenhuijsen, 1998), which sits
unhappily alongside the market discipline which has been imposed
on practice by government fiat. The market ethos ignores the relational basis of social work or the human relationships within which
social work practice based on an ethic of care is enacted. An ethic

of care draws on altruistic values held by a professional who is usually selected for training precisely because those traits are already evident in his or her personality.

Altruism is an essential ingredient in this ethic of care and is central in establishing an empathy that promotes an understanding of others. Empathy enables social workers to form relationships with individuals who differ from them on a range of dimensions (Egan, 1998) whilst drawing on self-knowledge, values and ethics to propel them into meaningful engagement with others. The capacity to be non-judgemental, caring and supportive is central in (re)configuring a professional's repertoire of skills. Making these connections with others provides the key to securing behavioural change in individuals seeking help. Research has consistently indicated that clients appreciate an empathetic element when interacting with practitioners.

A capacity for empathy alone is insufficient for responding to a person in need. From a client's perspective, a professional's inability to address structural issues that impede individual progress is a major failure in social work interventions. This is exemplified by practitioners' inability to tackle the poverty within which the majority of clients live (Jones, 1998). Sadly, the structural elements in clients' circumstances continue to be neglected under the purchaser–provider regime of competence-based social work. Competence-based approaches to social work can incorporate traditional values because these ignore the contexts within which social work is practised and, like casework, focus primarily on an individual's behaviour. Decontextualized values within a competence-based framework are compatible with the traditional emphasis on individual weaknesses rather than strengths.

The ethic of care can be exploited by managers concerned with balancing budgets and keeping within resource constraints. One way of doing this is to call primarily on women to make the personal sacrifices necessary to bridge the gap between what a client needs and the capacity of a service agency to provide. This action may save bureaucratic resources, but it ignores the price that women and other carers pay to look after dependent children, husbands and other relations. Some carers become freely involved in caring; a number give their services out of a sense of obligation or duty, feeling they must put aside their own interests to ensure that an incapacitated person receives the care they require. This *obligated care*, provided as a 'labour of love' (Graham, 1983), is different from altruism and empathy, which produce more *reciprocated relationships* than those conducted under a sense of compulsion.

Despite unmet need in the caring arena, social services along with health departments have not expended all financial resources allocated to them for this by government. This can be construed as unethical behaviour amongst management, but managers are not necessarily bound by the codes of ethics that apply at practitioner level. The likelihood that managers in social work offices do not adhere to the same code of ethics and values as the practitioners they manage is increasing as more and more of them are appointed from outside the profession without qualifications or experience in social work. This is a change from the days when social work practitioners became managers by rising through the ranks from frontline positions (Walton, 1975).

Rethinking the life-course within identity

For the sentient human being, life can be considered a series of non-ending transitions that starts with birth and ends with death. Social workers have to understand the transitions that people make between one part of their lifespan and another. Although the lifespan of an individual can be reconceptualized as a journey towards death, this is an inadequate summation of it because even in death, an individual's atoms change their energy state from being encapsulated in a body to becoming molecules embodied in a range of other things. However, people's experiences of living in and through their bodies are used to order their lives in particular ways.

On an individual level, the life-course is the period of existence between birth and death. It involves a number of transitional changes. Some of these follow a linear development and are straight-forward; others are more fragmented and circuitous. In traditional discourses, these transitions have been taken to follow each other chronologically and so the life-course has been variously described as covering a series of stages from infancy to adolescence to adulthood, with varying degrees of maturity to old age. Early versions of the life-course theorized these as discrete stages of development, each having a beginning and an end, and with specific attributes and characteristics identifying each phase and following one another sequentially. Erickson's (1959) work provides a classic illustration of this approach and has been influential in professional discourses.

These constructions have treated human and personal development as fixed, objective and knowable. Individuals who do not meet the prescribed attributes at a stipulated point in time are deemed to have a problematic development that could lead to a personality disorder that produces anti-social behaviour. Such rigid views of development have been challenged through critical theories. For example, black and white feminist psychological theories have confronted definitions of adult women as immature and dependent beings who need to have decisions made for them (hooks, 1984; Hollway, 1989). Instead, they have posited women as agents with the capacity to act on their own behalf individually and collectively. They have also questioned chronological approaches to women's development. Interrogating human growth has revealed the messy and uneven processes that produce variations within individual lifespans and amongst different individuals. Thus, human development is seen as a gendered, racialized and classed phenomenon that makes it difficult to speak of fixed patterns with any degree of certainty.

Sadly, this alternative knowledge has been slow to percolate practice, and many professionals continue to draw on outmoded understandings of human growth and development. Static formulations of people's development have been given a new lease of life through risk assessment schedules and the various indices used to establish different levels of psychological development. These have been especially influential in relating to children who have been abused by their carers, and in profiling and analysing the development of convicted adult sex offenders (see Wyre, 1986). By drawing on official discourses that promote rigid views of the development of human personalities, practitioners may deny both client agency and their own potential to engage in relationships that can change a person's behaviour.

Following the dictums of risk assessment procedures reduces capacity to begin where the client is at. Social workers should use risk assessment instruments with caution. These tools may be useful in determining whether or not something has gone wrong, but they are not substitutes for a thorough investigation and analysis of the situation and individuals that they are actually dealing with. Practitioners aware of the interactive creation of practice scenarios should be circumspect about the rote application of risk assessment instruments and focus their attention on how and why a particular feature comes to dominate an individual's development or behaviour at a specific point in time.

To facilitate people's ability to respond to loss and death, and to help them to come to terms with their own future demise and its implications, practitioners have to understand the process of grieving the loss of particular capacities during a person's lifespan, and the complex emotions and relationships that have to be handled by those who survive the death of loved ones. In this worldview, practice becomes movement through a series of transitions to achieve human well-being through interaction between interdependent individuals, groups and communities. The interdependency that exists between one person and another requires practitioners to engage with people's concerns about what happens when they have departed. The dependency of people on their physical environment also has to be taken into account in their activities for these carry implications for themselves and those with whom they share it now and in the future. Pillage of the environment, for example, can lead to a loss of livelihood.

Identity

Traditional views of identity have drawn on linear models of human development, as just described, which specify set stages of progress at different points in an individual's life cycle (see Erickson, 1959). These static views of identity have been challenged by postmodernists, who argue that identity is complex, multifaceted and fluid (Hall, 1992; Dominelli, 2002a). Its features change over time, according to context and through interaction with others, thereby making identity a negotiated social entity. Under this scenario, people present different aspects of their personalities and emphasize some roles more than the others to fit in with the expectations of those around them in specific situations. 'Fitting in' does not necessarily mean losing one's own particular sense of identity, even if individuals become involved in relationships that make precisely such demands of them because they can resist these characterizations without demonstrating it until more propitious circumstances prevail. In other words, they are not who or what they seem.

Patricia Hill Collins (1991) makes this point when she refers to a black woman domestic servant who retains her own sense of dignity and self when her identity is disparaged by her white woman employer. While keeping her own counsel in her employer's presence, she expresses her belief in herself and in her dignity and self-worth elsewhere when it is safe to do so. Giving up one's sense of self or affirming it when appropriate can be strategically important in surviving oppressive relationships or achieving a specific goal.

'Othering' processes

'Othering' processes are integral aspects of identity formation. The 'self' exists because there is an 'other' to whom one can compare oneself. The self–other dichotomy or binary dyad enables the self to externalize the 'other', and facilitates the act of viewing the 'other' in an antagonistic and hierarchical relationship to itself. This dyad involves comparisons that evaluate some people as superior to others, thereby creating inegalitarian relations in identity formation and hierarchies of valuing human beings. These dualisms become the basis of oppressive relationships which reinforce negative evaluations of others and reproduce relations of domination in and through interactions with other people.

'Othering' processes create divisions for policing populations labelled 'other' – those set outside the 'normal' population. They do so by configuring people as 'desirable' (the normal), or those who can be included within social relations, and 'undesirable' (the deviant), or those who can be excluded or considered outsiders. The legitimation of certain claims and practices has been central to the regulation and disciplining of groups that have been 'othered'. This goal is constituted as an integral feature of discourses and is achieved by stipulating which actions comprise 'normal' behaviour (Foucault, 1977) and which do not.

Like other professionals, social workers are implicated in 'othering' processes. These are particularly evident when they construct the 'other' as being deviant or outside prevailing social norms. In externalizing the 'other' as out there, beyond mainstream society, clients become constituted as not part of society. They thereby become socially excluded individuals to whom or for whom things can be done. 'Othering' becomes a barrier that keeps excluded people away from those who are included – a process of separation that distinguishes the 'deserving' from the 'undeserving'.

'Othering' is crucial to the process of defining the 'deserving' client as different from the 'undeserving' one. The concepts of deviancy and normality confirm a particular way of constituting people and are useful in dividing 'normal' individuals from 'deviant' ones. Although othered and treated as separate and distinct, the 'deviant' person, like the 'normal' one, is part of society. The most positive aspect of this process is that what is constituted can be deconstituted or altered. Consequently, social workers should not feel defeated when they begin to acknowledge their participation in the dynamics of oppression for they can use their new understandings to change their practice in more life-enhancing directions.

Valuing people's identity and appreciating the significance of identity relations are important, if unacknowledged, parts of the values framework in social work. People's sense of who they are, whether as policymakers, employers, practitioners or clients, has a dialogical relationship with the values to which they subscribe. Consequently, identity has a substantive impact on interpersonal interactions regardless of whether these are undertaken with members of one's own group or other groups. Identity formation is dialogical because it occurs in and through social interactions with other people. In these interactions, people draw upon available discourses to constitute the kind of identity that they want or feel they have to subscribe to. So, identity is multifaceted and fluid, and individuals choose which aspects of their identity they wish to emphasize in any particular context. Elements of identity that professionals share with friends will not be the same as those revealed to clients, other professionals or peers. The same holds for clients' use of their identity attributes.

Identity in social work relies on practitioners knowing *who* they are and understanding *who* their clients are, or how clients constitute themselves and are constituted by others for specific purposes. Identity relations in social work have been individualized and tend to be expressed in fixed and immutable terms, leading practitioners to think about identity as something that an individual acquires at birth and sticks with until death. Individuals belonging to the same category are deemed to have the same characteristics. This limited conceptualization of identity is applied to themselves as much as to clients. They deem identities as fixed and discrete rather than interactive, although they may concede that some 'discrete' characteristics overlap with others across a number of social divisions.

Social workers believe that once they learn the specifics of a given culture, they will become culturally sensitive enough to work with those who are different from them. This approach has ultimately provided the paradigm for 'culturally competent social work' (Lum, 2000). Like its earlier antecedents, colour-blind multicultural responses to racism and cultural difference, however, culturally competent approaches fail to treat identity as a fluid, multifaceted phenomenon formed through dialogical processes that are constantly being created and re-created through social interactions.

Social workers may recognize a person as 'black' but deem those subsumed within that category as all the same (see Lum, 2000). Although practitioners have moved beyond the normative 'colour-blind' approach of treating all clients as if they were white middle-class people to acknowledge socially constructed racial differences, they have replaced one stereotype with another. In relying on stereotypical definitions of 'black people', practitioners lose the uniqueness of the individual and draw unjustified conclusions about the commonalities among that grouping. Not valuing the complexities of diversity is a failing of both social work practitioners and educators. Casting a specific cultural group as homogeneous is evident in culturally competent approaches to social work (see Lum, 2000).

Unitary conceptualizations of identity are extremely powerful and deeply embedded in social work. All women, black people, older people, are treated as if they were like all the others in their particular category; individualism means being one of a homogeneous whole. Even when drawing distinctions within categories, social workers deal with each discrete element as fixed and lacking heterogeneity. And, as social workers discovered cultural difference, they began to ask for courses on each culture so that they could better understand the differences between their culture and that belonging to the 'other'.

Rigid views of identity make it easy for social workers to adhere to stereotypes about what features and attributes constitute a particular type of person. This formulation of identity can cause social workers endless difficulties in establishing dialogical relationships with clients because they are conceptualized as passive recipients of practitioner benevolence and expertise. Much of this dynamic has underpinned oppressive social work practice with marginalized peoples or those human beings whom social workers 'other', whether as individuals, groups or communities.

Social workers' reliance on unitary and fixed notions of identity reinforces dynamics that devalue people by labelling as 'manipulative' those clients who do not behave according to their expectations, or as 'having played the game' if they have gone along with them. In their research on young mothers, Callahan et al. (2000) refer to these dynamics as 'looking promising'. One practitioner explained it thus:

> . . . if in fact you [the young mother] are an active parent, a co-operative parent, a good parent, then I would suggest that you come to me and I'll go to my manager and I would support that [young mother's request] and that'll happen. (Dominelli et al., forthcoming)

These dynamics implicate practitioners in creating the client whose needs will be (un)met. They also draw the client into constituting him- or herself as professionally defined. Acting as a member of a specific client group may seem absolutely necessary when social workers treat social divisions as significant in establishing deserving client status. For example, a social worker responding to an older person as one of a dependent or vulnerable group in need of assistance in the community may find that he or she plays along to receive resources that allow him or her to remain at home. Mothers who argue that their children are 'at risk' so that they can access scarce family support services are also displaying this kind of behaviour. Their interactions constitute the persona being related to, thereby providing a 'truth' about negotiated realities that practitioners have to address.

Practitioners create their professionalism along with their clients while clients create themselves and their social workers. Traditional social work texts have acknowledged a danger in this dynamic: *dependency* as an avoidable hazard of professional practice. Practitioners create this state when they make clients dependent on their skills or force them to meet their needs. Subordinating clients' capacities to their needs encapsulates poor or unethical practice that practitioners should eschew (Butrym, 1976).

Understanding identity as a constituted phenomenon that is negotiated through social interaction is important to relational social work practice because it frees both practitioner and client to acknowledge each other as having the power to influence what happens in their relationships and exchanges with one another. Additionally, it enables practitioners to appreciate the boundaries around their capacity to change either individual behaviour or structural conditions by helping them to recognize the limitations of their own power.

In casework relationships, recognizing the agency of a client enables a practitioner to transcend the restricted vision embodied in seeing him or her as a passive consumer. The potential for change is also blocked in competence-based approaches which relate to clients primarily in their roles as consumers of the expert services provided by professionals. In drowning out the voices of clients, professional power is diminished as practitioners add another layer of oppressive practices to control clients and restrict their scope for self-directed action. Clients are 'othered' instead of being empowered in the process, and the vicious cycle of not getting the necessary services is repeated.

Fixed views of identity formation are evident not only in official social work discourses, but also in radical ones that attempt to create alternative ways of understanding the social world and acting within and upon it. Static and linear constructions of identity formation are evident in the portrayal of the development of black consciousness in the writings of black authors including Eldridge Cleaver (1971) of the Black Panthers; Malcolm X (Malcolm X, 1989; Lee, 1993) of the Nation of Islam; Robert Staples (1988) in discussions about black masculinity; and W.E. Cross (1978) and Lena Robinson (1995, 1998) on black psychology. These authors present identity as a fixed, chronologically determined phenomenon. Progress through specified stages of development is used to measure the extent to which black people are conscious of themselves as an oppressed group and can rise to the challenge of redefining themselves as a group capable of self-liberation. Cross's (1978) model of nigrescence and those derived from it, like Robinson's (1995, 1998), portray the use of fixed models of black people's identity formation for radicalizing purposes.

Unitary conceptualizations of identity formation have also been applied to white people (see Frankenburg, 1997). Some have focused on white women's social and psychological development. Amongst others, Jean Baker Miller (1978) ignores differentiation amongst women and treats all women as the same. Carol Gilligan (1982) does likewise when drawing distinctions between men and women's moral development. Although the writings described above have been useful in getting black people and white women to think positively about their capacity to change their oppressive situations by positing alternative ways of viewing society and their place within it, these models do not account for the less regimented ways that identity formation occurs and is experienced by oppressed peoples in everyday life.

Other thinkers have begun to theorize development differently and have looked for continuities and discontinuities in culture and identity that allow more flexible understandings of identity formation and radicalizing consciousness. These endorse oppressed people's capacity to resist being locked into a passive model of personal and group development that subordinates them as objects of other people's power to name their realities for them. In social work, John-Baptiste's (2001) model of Africentricity and Graham's (2002) Africentric analyses of identity and knowledge creation exemplify these alternative concepts.

By reframing continuities as sources of growth in diasporic conditions alongside the power to redefine reality to respond to exigencies in the daily life of people of African origins, John-Baptiste and Graham have validated the experiential knowledge of African-origined people as the basis for promoting their development as consciously aware individuals and groups. These authors show that people of African origins exercise agency rooted in the routines of everyday life to overcome oppressive structures. Although retaining a unitary dimension to identity formation, their approaches have the advantage of highlighting how daily life experiences and the transmission of knowledge across generations and geographical space become the basis of resistance, rather than presuming that it is simply there as a by-product of power relations in the Foucauldian manner (Foucault, 1983).

People's awareness of the realities of everyday life is more messy and partial than is presupposed in academic paradigms. People may be aware of their oppression in some areas of their lives and not in others. They may wish to exercise the prerogative of emphasizing a specific aspect of their identity in one situation, but de-emphasize the same trait in another, depending on what they wish to achieve in a specific interaction with another. Their capacity to take action in support of what they may or may not know is also contingent. Much will depend on the contexts within which people operate; the extent to which they think real alternatives exist for them; and their reading of the possibilities for acting in and upon these. Their experiences of life will be more instructional if they can realize opportunities to change their situation rather than count on purely abstract theoretical models that are not rooted in their specific realities. Practitioners can improve their practice by taking note of these dynamics and using everyday experiential knowledge as the basis for change. If our lives are socially constructed, they can be deconstructed and transformed.

Processes of intervention

Intervention provides the processes whereby change occurs. The processes of intervention are those elements of practice which focus on *how* social workers engage their clients. How practitioners work with clients is heavily reliant on the values they hold and use to guide their practice. Moreover, these values underpin social workers' activities throughout the processes of intervention. By engaging with clients, practitioners become aware of the conflicts and dilemmas evident in practising values and the steps needed to resolve them.

Predicating these processes on hierarchical values can preclude a practitioner seeing potential ways of acting other than those guided by a rigid vision based on expert authority. Hierarchical processes are reflected in forms of intervention that rely on the expert's voice and knowledge drowning out those of the clients and thereby contribute to devaluing their knowledge and skills. This can cause premature closure of other possible courses of action or the erasure of alternative ways of thinking about a problem and block the capacity to proceed differently. Practitioners adhering to hierarchical conceptualizations of the world expect clients to do as they are told and are more likely to subscribe to pathological views of clients' talents and abilities. Thus, valuable opportunities for change and movement can be lost.

Egalitarian processes are aimed at valuing client knowledges and establishing non-hierarchical relations between practitioners and clients. Practitioners focus more on client strengths and use these to initiate changes in a client's life circumstances. Practitioners who aspire to more egalitarian relationships with clients can still promote hierarchical forms of practice. This is particularly evident when they fall into the 'false equality trap' (Barker, 1986; Dominelli, 2002b). False equality traps spring when, despite their espoused values, practitioners work on the assumption that clients have access to the same level of resources and opportunities available to the 'normal' citizen – the ubiquitous decontextualized and individualized human being who is without class, 'race', gender, disability or other social division through which structural inequalities are expressed. The undifferentiated person is a function of an epistemology that draws upon and affirms the stereotypical white middle-class male image that underpins the current social order and the social relationships that are formed within it. This depiction of reality establishes the norms by which other persons are measured and found wanting (Pascall, 1986; Dominelli, 1991a).

The processes of intervention in social work practice involve a number of phases:

- referral;
- data gathering;
- assessment of the problem;
- planning and agreeing a plan of action;
- implementing the action plan;
- reviewing the action plan;
- evaluating the action process;
- evaluating the outcomes;
- evaluating client performance;
- evaluating practitioner performance; and
- reflection for/on future action.

Although it is useful to separate out these phases to understand them more fully, they should not be thought of as discrete and independent from each other. Each of these impacts upon the others, and each is revisited constantly during the course of an intervention. Practitioners tend to think about the first three elements in sequential order at a preliminary stage (Compton and Galaway, 1975). These are only a starting point when first responding to a referral. They do not necessarily follow one another in either a neat sequence or the order presented in practice. Many of these processes occur concurrently (see Clifford, 1998, for a more detailed discussion of assessment practice and Cheetham et al., 1992, on evaluating social work).

Empowering people or valuing client voices can and must occur in each and every one of these phases if egalitarian practice is to be enacted. If clients feel that the processes of intervention belong to them, they are more likely to participate in developing action plans. Playing a real role in formulating these from beginning to end promotes such ownership of process, which, in turn, facilitates change in individual and collective (group) behaviour by enabling people to take more effective control over the direction of their activities.

The dance of competing values within the major approaches to social work

As I describe below, mainstream social work practice draws on both traditional and new values.

Casework in action: Focusing on individuals

Traditional values à la Biesteck (1961) underpin casework relationships and help to define the parameters within which practitioner–client interactions occur. Traditional caseworkers prioritize expert knowledges and hierarchical order. They focus on individual behaviour and do not concern themselves with the broader social contexts in which such behaviour is embedded. Caseworkers' capacity to engage the person in a decontextualized manner reinforces the individualizing dimensions of practice and promotes the idea of the all-powerful practitioner and powerless client. This configuration of their relationship denies client agency and can perpetuate helplessness in clients' responses to offers of assistance.

Traditional casework can address family situations and dynamics and link aspects of individual behaviour at different points
during the life-course to family relationships. Traditional caseworkers assume that a family provides the ideal social setting for
an individual's development, although they accept that it can fail
some individuals. Because practitioners do not problematize
relationships that are formed within the family, they may overlook
tricky situations that underplay unequal power relations within it.
They also treat the family as an autonomous unit. Consequently,
they miss out its interaction with and dependence upon broader
systems and contexts, and so their understanding of its dynamics
in complex situations is inadequate.

More recently, some forms of casework, or one-to-one work with
individuals, particularly those associated with counselling, especially feminist counselling, have attempted to challenge both the
individualizing and pathologizing elements of traditional casework
(Chaplin, 1988). In conducting one-to-one interventions, these practitioners have to be careful not to abuse their power and must
establish clear boundaries around what they do in these relationships to ensure that they do not blur the distinction between being
a professional practitioner and a lay person or friend. By locating
the person-in-their-social-context, feminist practitioners help clients
draw links between their individual plight and structural position.
The values of supporting individual change have enabled feminist
social workers to embark on this path while retaining a commitment to empowering forms of ethical care (Dominelli, 2002b).

Groupwork: The acknowledgement of systems

Groupworkers have held an interesting position in social work,
occupying as they do a domain that lies between work with individuals, at one end of a continuum, and with communities, at the
other. Groups have been used to promote client self-determination
and confidence. They have been highly effective in bringing individuals together to identify common goals and take action to change
their situation (Ward, 1998). Systems have been targets of change
endeavours initiated through group action, although groups have
also been used to initiate changes in individuals when working
with offenders or helping individuals survive trauma, as in incest
survivor groups.

Groups have their own set of dynamics and issues that can produce value conflicts and difficulties amongst members. The structure

of a group can be hierarchical and authoritarian or egalitarian and democratic. Which it is will impact heavily on the conduct of relationships within the group. Tensions amongst group members can be heightened when there is dissonance between stated and actual behaviour. These can be particularly acute when group leaders fail to live up to expectations in guiding the group through its deliberations and courses of action. Understanding power relations within a group and their influence upon individuals within it is important in addressing differences between group members and handling the exclusionary practices that accompany the exercise of 'power over' dynamics by some participants.

Community work: A concern with structural inequalities

Community workers have sought to address the inadequacies of a casework orientation to practice and included structural change in their interventions (Loney, 1983; Dominelli, 1990). The desire to promote community empowerment by doing something about structural shortcomings, particularly in employment, housing, transportation, leisure facilities and environmental issues, has often provided the focus for mobilizing communities (Craig and Mayo, 1995). Community workers have generally eschewed interpersonal dynamics and individualized responses to hardship in their quest to target structural change through campaigns of action. Many of their varied activities have not resulted in structural changes of any significance. This weakness has been associated with the failure of community work to carry relevance beyond its locality, deal with conflicts emanating from different segments of the same community and sustain action over substantial periods of time.

Despite its commitment to collective endeavours, community work becomes competitive and isolationist through the action of defining the limits of community. By naming a community, whether based on geographic location, identity attributes or interests, those not encompassed by this definition are excluded. Drawing boundaries around communities raises important issues about exclusion and inclusion, including the question of whether exclusion is ethically acceptable. Similarly, difficulties can be identified over conflicts in the allocation of resources when community groups compete against each other for scarce material goods, particularly finances. Many small organizations lose out in the ensuing allocations unless steps are taken to prevent this. For example, in Duluth, Emerge organizes projects for men and has refused to compete for funding with women's groups working on domestic violence issues because men's community groups tend to get the lion's share of resources.

Competence-based social work: Fragmenting and technocratizing practice

Competence-based social work lends itself readily to the three 'Es', as the market-oriented values of economy, efficiency and effectiveness have been termed. Competence-based practice has become highly instrumental and individualized and given momentum to the processes of commodification unleashed by neo-liberalism. This has inhibited its capacity to support structural change. Relying on proceduralized interventions symbolized by checklists of varying lengths and administered with fluctuating degrees of confidence, competence-based social work lays claim to social work's traditional value base, alongside a commitment to social justice and anti-oppressive practice (see Lum, 2000). Its adherents argue that it combines traditional values with market-oriented ones. As it does not target social structures as objects of the practitioner's change endeavours, its claims to addressing social injustice and inequalities are somewhat suspect. Rather, it assumes that the social worker's intentions to work in specific ways with clients at the micro-level will produce the anti-oppressive practice that is being sought.

Valuing social justice and social change: A human rights context for practice

Social workers have focused on valuing social justice and social change in micro-level relationships and attempted to work with clients in ways that are ameliorative and respectful of difference. These concerns have provided the backdrop for the development of a human rights-based social work that promotes active citizenship amongst those requiring its services. Endorsing rights which have been enshrined in the Universal Declaration of Human Rights supported by all member countries of the United Nations can be a major challenge to social workers. Not only has this approach sparked debates about the meaning of social justice and social change, but even the concept of human rights has been questioned for being overly dominated by Western ideas and rooted in individualistic ways of seeing the world which do not meet the needs of more collectivist cultures elsewhere (Ife, 2001).

Human rights have provided important avenues for critiquing cultural practices that have oppressed and injured people on the margins of particular cultures, particularly those having deleterious consequences for women's well-being. This was aptly demonstrated in the 1995 Beijing Conference on Women, which argued that women's rights are human rights to undermine the inviolability of various 'cultural' practices such as female genital mutilation and men's violence that targets women. Crucial to this development was redefining such acts as assaults against women.

Redefining social problems, especially to turn private woes into social issues, is a well-known element of feminist social work (Dominelli and McLeod, 1989; Dominelli, 2002b) and is a technique that social workers can use in their daily work. Important in empowering and mobilizing women at the level of the group and community, redefining social problems for the purposes of changing life practices is also crucial to the process of deconstructing the technologies of control. Under control regimes, naming a problem in ways that suit those who hold power over others and not offering disempowered groups pathways out of their predicament are tools that reproduce relations of dominance that can easily undermine human rights and the pursuit of social justice. Focusing on human rights-based social work has been a response to client demands that practitioners engage in transformational social work. Practitioners' endeavours are unlikely to lead to transformative changes in existing social relations if they do not transcend the limitations of focusing only on individualized problems.

Private woes have to be redefined as social problems (see Mills, 1970) and affect change at the personal, institutional and cultural levels to realize citizenship-based human rights (Dominelli, 2002a). Without this, simply amending the label attached to an issue will do little to alter the overall balance of power and distribution of resources that negatively impact upon the practices articulated to deny individuals their human rights in a particular locality. Despite these caveats, the effect on an individual of renaming social problems should not be underestimated. It can disorient him or her by removing generally accepted certainties from daily routine activities. If badly handled, there will be little relief from the psychological pain that uncertainty can cause. Under these conditions, well-meaning interventions can play a significant role in making micro-practice or social workers' involvement in one-to-one situations more rather than less oppressive. Avoiding this outcome underlines the importance of paying attention to individual as well as structural dimensions in responding to individual, group or community needs.

Training is no longer the preserve of the academy

Like practice, social work training in the UK has become a political football flicked through the shifting regulatory fields of the new managerialism. From the late 1970s to the present day, social work education in British universities has come under an increasing barrage of more direct and visible forms of government intervention and regulation in its curriculum content and teaching practices. This has been driven by government and employer dissatisfaction with practitioners' skills and coalesced around their belief that teaching carried out through the Certificate of Qualification in Social Work (CQSW) and its successor, the Diploma in Social Work (DipSW), was irrelevant to practice. Employment-led critiques declared these qualifications too theoretically oriented and unable to meet the needs of the field. In the early 1980s, discourses around these anxieties resulted in a coalition combining political, policymaker and employer interests to actively 'take on' social work educators.

Employers' moves had begun earlier with the introductions of a practical, skills-based Certificate in Social Services (CSS) and ultimately culminated in the competence-based DipSW. Both developments were promoted under the auspices of a government quango, the Central Council for Education and Training in Social Work (CCETSW), which employer interests came to dominate. The CCESTW jettisoned a social sciences orientation to social work education in favour of workplace-based, competence-oriented training programmes offered under the aegis of employing agencies.

Academics were deeply divided over their own differing visions of the profession. They failed to dialogue with each other successfully and reach a negotiated agreement as to the way forward. Academics' inability to secure government approval for a three-year qualifying training programme in the mid-1980s resulted in the government imposing its own requirements for a more employer-friendly approach through the CCETSW in what proved to be a singularly contentious and unsatisfactory two-year DipSW, which is being phased out.

In broadening the struggle for the heart of the profession to encompass employers, practitioners, policymakers and academics, key players in the profession became divided from one another, and many of the controversies which had been debated 'in-house' became widely discussed public matters. By the mid-1980s, the weak and divided training arena became the site where the employers mounted a successful campaign to wrest control of social work's educational agenda.

Central to cementing together the alliance against social work education was the view of employers and leading New Right politicians in government that leftwing academics were too influential in shaping professional education and practice. As a result, they sought to regain control over social work training and education to ensure that it paid less attention to critiques of society and identifying structural inequalities highlighted through social science research and client experiences. The scepticism with which those under the radical social work banner evaluated social workers' performance as agents of social control and the stinging attacks which clients directed against practitioners' failure adequately to address racism, sexism and disablism perpetuated in and through practice, were redefined as fashionable trends that bore little relationship to the realities of daily living endured by disadvantaged people (see Phillips, 1993, 1994).

Instead of exploring the realities that critical analyses portrayed and drawing lessons from these for practice, New Right ideologues and employers disparaged the concerns raised as 'political correctness' and demanded that social work educators focus more on preparing social workers to sit at their desks the morning after receiving their qualifications and 'get on with the job' without making demands of their employing agencies or upsetting the status quo.

The coalition of interests involving employers, government and some academics unleashed an unending series of reviews and changes which culminated in 1993 with an ideological attack on anti-racist and anti-oppressive practice and what it stood for (see Pinker, 1993; Phillips, 1993, 1994). Ultimately, their endeavours have consolidated the power of employers over academics and exposed the suspicion with which government holds the professionals entrusted with the task of training those caring for vulnerable populations. Practitioners and academics charged with applying the technologies of governmentality were not complying with employer dictates, and so new strategies for reversing this breakdown in managerial control over professionals had to be devised.

In shifting social relations to accommodate new contexts, the Thatcher government initiated a profound series of changes in the social work profession. These have affected its role and purpose in society; its relationships with client groups; its methods of working; its workplace relations; and its training programmes. The localized educational struggle described above reflected the Thatcher government's response to changes in social relations emanating from the pressures of a market-oriented ideology, globalization and the state's fragmenting project of modernity. It augured a new phase in an employer-led orientation to the profession that privileges bureaucratic competence-based social work interventions and the requirements of the 'new managerialism'. The reign of the bureau-technocrat is replacing that of the bureau-professional and relational social work is taking a back seat.

Ironically, the DipSW was replaced in 2003 by a three-year qualification set at undergraduate degree level. But this development has failed to create a ladder of qualifications that go from pre-degree level to Ph.D., as is the norm in a number of Western countries and advocated by the Bologna Declaration for Europe. Thus, the struggle for the shape of social work education continues. On the one hand academic interests have begun to organize into a more coherent grouping through the Joint University Council's Social Work Education Committee (JUC-SWEC) and Assembly for Social Work. On the other, a strong, employer-led emphasis remains in the new award as it is linked to occupational standards set by the Training Organization for the Personal Social Services (TOPSS). Dominated by employers, TOPSS favours a highly bureaucratized form of competence-based social work. This arrangement allows some space for the articulation of academic concerns through the benchmarking statement devised by the educational quango, the Quality Assurance Agency (QAA), but the new award is contested space and its boundaries cannot be taken as fixed. CCETSW's successor, the General Social Care Council (GSCC), is likely to continue the preoccupation with occupational standards and bureaucratized competencies despite the inclusion of benchmarking statements within the new three-year award.

Meanwhile, probation training had its links to social work education terminated in 1998, under the New Labour government, thus completing initiatives begun by the Conservatives. The new regime for probation training, the Diploma in Probation Studies (DPS), is tightly controlled through the Home Office and the National Probation Directorate. Probation provides an excellent example of the logic of the market operating in education and training, as consortia of providers, which may include universities as partners, bid for the right to train probation officers for a fixed term. The DPS relies on occupational standards and competence-based training occurring largely in the workplace. This model also gives employers a strong hand in shaping the educational and training agenda, and is discussed further in chapter 6.

Changing agendas

The persistence of social work's core values, despite the range of attacks upon their practice, is both admirable and remarkable. It seems that altering social work's basic values and ethics requires second-order changes (Broadbent and Laughlin, 1990) which cannot be achieved through the instrumentality of either the new managerialism or its penchant for competence-based approaches to social work which use values as bureaucratic instruments for measuring and controlling practitioner behaviour and performance alongside client aspirations. From this perspective, the new managerialism can hardly be called a success story. It has not delivered the goods for either practitioners or clients.

Social workers deal with uncertainty in contexts demanding certainty. This expectation is contradictory as there are no fixed, agreed answers to the situations they encounter. The contentious nature of responses to social problems requires social workers to become involved in a dialogue around resolving social problems, or what I have called previously a 'dialogue around controversies' (Dominelli, 1998a). If such dialogues are to change clients' behaviour, social workers have to think differently about each situation. During this process, they have to challenge their own epistemological base. This requires them to eschew the either/or logic that is an integral part of traditional professionalism, which privileges practitioners' expertise over clients', and partake in both/and logic to allow for the joint creation of new spaces in which to address problems that clients encounter. Practitioners can act professionally when working with clients and be concerned about tackling the structural inequalities that erode their quality of life.

Values change as a result of competing discourses over a particular issue or forms of action. The success of a particular discourse in establishing a hegemonic position cannot be taken as forever fixing that value (or set of values) in time and space. Values will constantly be fought over and have to be (re)asserted and (re)affirmed if they are to provide continuity by surviving into the future and be applied in other situations. Through these struggles, discontinuities will occur, some previous values will shift position and new values will be formed while others are retained.

The persistence of social work's traditional core values has been revealed in recent research. Most of the social workers whom I interviewed with Parves Khan (Dominelli and Khan, 2000) affirmed their continued use of the profession's core values. These included:

helping people cope with their situation more effectively by working with the person-in-their-situation; meeting needs at an individual level; and enabling the self-determination of the user. These respondents also claimed that the promotion of social welfare throughout society in general and the creation of a just society constituted part of their value system. Respect for diversity and working in partnership with others were additional components of it. At the same time, a significant minority (18 per cent) felt that controlling people's behaviour was a key social work value.

However, social workers found it increasingly difficult to express their values in practice, with 16 per cent claiming that they could no longer underpin their practice with core social work values. The reasons they gave for the problems they experienced were: lack of resources; crisis management; management's antagonism to anti-oppressive practices; and prioritizing the cost-saving values underpinning care management. As one of these social workers put it:

> Resource-led assessments, not needs-led. I am compelled to adopt this 'value' rather than adopt it voluntarily. (Dominelli and Khan, 2000)

These findings highlight a worrying development. The current code of ethics promoted by the British Association of Social Workers (BASW) is consistent with Biesteck's values, but these cannot be easily implemented when resource-led values are in opposition to needs-oriented and people-led ones.

Conclusions

Values are important aspects of social work theory and practice. They are crucial in establishing the ethical basis on which social workers can and do work. Despite their longevity and seeming coherence, values are contentious and, at times, contradictory. They can also conflict with one another to produce ethical dilemmas that require skill, knowledge and sensitivity to address. Traditional values have focused primarily on the relational basis of social work and have been implemented primarily through a casework relationship that has privileged professional knowledge and expertise. This approach has been challenged by clients from the 'new' social movements, who have insisted that social workers support them in their struggles to realize their human rights, secure structural changes and social justice, and alter their practice accordingly. They have also gone beyond individualized identities to expose collectively shared dimensions of identity formation.

Responding to client-led agendas does not mean that there is no role for professional expertise. The knowledge, power and resources that practitioners hold can be critical in empowering clients at the micro-level, just as they can be used to disempower them. The key issue is the quality of the relationship that social workers establish with those requiring their services and the extent to which they are willing to share power to increase the degree of agency that clients can exercise in a relationship to determine the direction that it takes and exert some control over what happens within it. Crucial in shaping its quality are the values that social workers seek to implement in and through their practice (Dominelli and Gollins, 1997). Practitioners' values and understanding of the links between the different levels of intervention also impact upon their capacity and willingness to engage with change at the meso- and macro-levels.

The limitations of traditional casework-based approaches to social work interventions also present problems. By focusing exclusively on individuals, current practice prevents caseworkers from addressing structural inequalities, regardless of their impact on individual behaviour and life chances. Clients feel alienated from and disenchanted with existing social relations for failing to tackle existing inequalities that feature in their lives. Despite casework's avowed preoccupation with individual change, its weaknesses can be attributed to the epistemological base on which casework is founded, and the reluctance of practitioners to accept social change as a priority within this mode of working.

Within the repertoire of social work practice, human rights-based work or community development approaches offer some models of action that can involve social workers in empowering clients and nurturing their potential to initiate structural change. Social workers who engage in these forms of practice, however, are likely to become embroiled in political controversies that may detract their energies from the task at hand. To engage in actions that mobilize clients, social workers will have to cease becoming pen-pushers or, as their work becomes increasingly computerized, key-punchers in front of their workstations and leave their offices more. They must also engage in bureaucratized practice to a lesser extent than is currently the case. Bring back a well-resourced community social work! Progress along this road will be difficult (Simpson, 2002) and require the creation of new partnerships amongst clients, professionals, employers and representatives of the state at local and national levels. In some instances, even the international sphere, long ignored in professional practice, will become relevant. As clients realize self-empowerment, the need for professional social work intervention will decrease and ultimately cease altogether – a goal which all good practitioners should achieve for each client. Thus, client autonomy symbolizes a further measure for defining success which is itself highly valued.

SOCIAL WORK INTERVENTIONS WITH CHILDREN AND FAMILIES 4

Introduction

Children are central to society. They represent its continuation over time. They are our collective futures (Maracle, 1993). Yet the cross-generational links between children and adults in contemporary Western societies tend to be contradictory, poorly understood and, at times, tenuous. The varying social constructions of childhood are usually ignored in favour of one dominant template, which currently casts children as dependent upon adults, who become their benefactors (Ariès, 1962). This arrangement has given rise to adultist power relations in which adults exercise power over children in their care and can compel them to submit to various forms of abuse and exploitation (Dominelli, 1989).

Childhood is currently being appropriated by commercial interests for profit-making purposes, creating the 'tweenies' to cover 8- to 12-year-olds and encouraging the sexualization and commodification of young bodies in the media. In pursuing commodifying agendas, the media have individualized children, separated them from direct family and community control and turned them into consumers from whom enormous profits can be made.

Voices protesting this process, whether from children or adults, have little chance of being heard in the cacophony of cash registers and pleadings of children to participate in the consuming process because they want to be accepted by their peers and experience the thrill of empowerment that exercising power as consumers endows. These particular processes of commodification and consumption remain in adult control. Those in charge are the adults who own and control the means and processes of production and the media. In this context, childhood becomes a negotiated process between parents and children whilst being simultaneously mediated by both private entrepreneurs and advertising men and women who create demands for more glamorous items that mimic adult ones, especially in clothing. This produces a cycle of consumer manipulation that keeps the money rolling in.

The commodification of children and their consumerization provide an interesting example of the erosion of the public–private divide. Through these processes, the private lives of children have become public property or commodities that can be exchanged in the marketplace. Additionally, the processes that commodify children's bodies, needs and desires draw upon their sense as agents, that is, people with wills and purchasing power of their own. The Mary-Kate and Ashley range of products at Wal-Mart/ASDA, for example, portrays a sophisticated approach to pre-teens who have 'minds of their own', and can be viewed at its own special product website, *http://www.mary-kateandashley.com*. Analyses predicated upon the social construction of childhood cannot adequately critique such developments because they neglect children's participation in these processes as agents of their own futures. Ironically, values that oppose the exploitation of all human beings, whether of children or adults, provide a firmer basis for opposing the commodification of children. Challenging developments of this nature can be mounted from all sides of the political spectrum, but would not necessarily guarantee children's right not to be abused. Only anti-oppressive values promoting equality of outcomes and egalitarian processes can do that.

Under the anti-oppressive lens, the commodification of young children's lives and needs can be defined as systemic abuse. In the example of children's clothing, commodification provides a site in which the fight by supermarket giants to gain control of a niche market has sexualized children's bodies in a way that contravenes the interests of children advocated through a children's rights approach, or even child protection cases. Could British social workers take on a supermarket giant, or challenge parents willing to subject their children to such pressures by taking them to court for engaging in actions likely to cause 'significant harm' under the provisions of the 1989 Children Act? The answer is unlikely to be 'yes' unless the children concerned are already known to social services. If they are not, their activities are likely to be considered a 'success' story.

We know from research that poverty is a key predictor of coming to the notice of social services (Schorr, 1992). Poor children in Britain are more likely than middle-class children to be the objects of surveillance from middle-class practitioners (Parton, 1985). Aldgate and Tunstill (2000) have shown that family stress and social deprivation are the most common factors amongst children 'in need'. According to the Framework for Assessment (DoH, DfEE and Home Office, 2000), poor children in a one-parent family living on income support have a one in ten chance of being subjected to care proceedings. Children in a two-parent middle-class family, by contrast, have a one in seven thousand chance of coming to the attention of social workers (DoH, 2002). Similar disparities are evident in Sweden, where lone parents are less stigmatized (Hessle, 1998). This evidence suggests that the label of deviancy is more readily applied to those operating outside white middle-class norms.

Child welfare experts have become preoccupied with monitoring and policing certain kinds of families. As policing, risk assessments signify techniques of notation and are more likely to impact upon poor (white) working-class families than (white) middle-class ones (DHSS, 1995; Gibbons et al., 1995; Jack, 2000) and upon black families across the spectrum of family types (Dominelli, 1988; Barn, 1993). As managers of risk, social workers are more likely to expend energy and resources on poor families deemed to be more 'at risk' of harming their children than on wealthy ones. These include single parents, substance abusers, homeless people and vulnerable ethnic groupings.

By regulating the families of poor children, social workers police the social construction of families more generally, give credibility to the dominant white heterosexual nuclear family model above all others, and reinforce its continued status as the preferred one. Practitioners may have their own particular views about priorities for practice, but the constraints within which they operate suggest that certain choices make more sense than others in a particular context. They engage in actions through which practice becomes 'a technique of notation' (Miller and Rose, 1988) or a technology for reinscribing or modifying in predictable ways the behaviour of those who have been defined as objects of concern or social problems.

The family is a normalizing institution as well as a socializing one that teaches children how to be good little boys and girls who will become good citizens as men and women (Belotti, 1975).

Traditional ideas about childhood draw upon historical assumptions that deem children the chattels of their fathers, and if not them, their mothers, endorsing a view of childhood that remains strong (Ariès, 1962). Until recently, legally recognized family forms were familialist, that is, norms celebrating the heterosexual married couple with children in which the man was the economic provider and the woman the carer (Eichler, 1983). It assumes that relationships within the family are equal and that, as an institution, the family is capable of meeting the needs of each of its members when it functions normally (Parsons, 1957). This model continues to dominate policy discussions in Western countries (Kilkey, 2000).

As a hegemonic conceptualization of reality, the white heterosexual middle-class nuclear family formation normalizes a particular way of viewing the world that results in other constructions of the family – extended, single-parent or same-gender – being considered inadequate and pathological. Normalization occurs through discourses that legitimate certain knowledge claims (Foucault, 1977). It works by accepting certain possibilities as providing valid forms of knowledge and agency while rejecting others (Philp, 1985). The former are usually hegemonic or associated with the mainstream; the latter with marginalized people. As I have indicated in the previous chapter, the two can only exist in relation to each other. The dynamics of the binary dyad in which one part is in opposition to the other result in a family being defined as normal because alongside it there is one categorized as deviant.

In this chapter, I examine social work with children and families to question the idea that children should have fewer rights than adults. I argue against rooting our views of children within adultist power relations and suggest that children need to be thought of as autonomous beings living within collective contexts where their health and safety should be the concern of all members of society, not just their biological parents (Dominelli, 1999). I critique current developments in social work with children and families to show that defining children as private possessions has deleterious implications for children and adults, especially mothers solely responsible for their care. I contend that the development of social and community networks which can safeguard children's interests and rights are more likely to produce an environment conducive to promoting children's growth to maturity as full citizens and is an essential element of any child welfare service that focuses on child and parental well-being. I also consider child welfare systems in other countries to suggest how social workers can promote the creation of new more child-centred partnerships by learning from overseas experiences.

Familialist discourses: Understanding different conceptualizations of 'the family'

The term 'family', or even 'families', is an emotionally charged and contested one. 'Family' is not only a sociological entity, but also a politicized cultural one that means different things to different people, even those within the same 'family'. The meanings individuals attach to it often reflect their positionality within the family and its intersection with other social divisions such as age, 'race', gender, class, disability, sexual orientation.

Families are socially constructed and come in a variety of forms. The Copenhagen Summit on Social Development of 1995 agreed an open definition of 'family' that aimed to be inclusive of a variety of forms, but by 2000, at follow-up events to the Summit, attempts to revise it along more traditional lines were evident. In Britain, families range from those that are headed by a lone parent, usually the mother, to extended families that encompass several generations. As the 2001 UK Census indicates when compared to earlier ones, family shapes and sizes are constantly changing, reflecting demographic trends, migration patterns, social policies, immigration legislation and cultural norms.

Mainstream conceptualizations promote a nuclear family format defined as familialism (Segal, 1983). Its basic tenets are that every individual is equal to every other; each person's needs are the same; and resources are evenly distributed amongst members (Morgan, 1983). However, research indicates that family dynamics are internally differentiated by age and gender (Pahl, 1985). Others indicate that 'there is a tension between the idea that the family is a unit with shared aims and interests and the fact that individual members of a family often have conflicting needs and desires' (Leonard and Speakman, 1986, p. 86).

Whatever its composition, a family can be a source of both pain and strength. The actual position in any specific one has to be established rather than assumed. Families can provide joyful experiences and teach children the skills that they need to negotiate their way successfully through life, as occurs when black children are taught skills for surviving in racist societies (Comer and Poussaint, 1975). Inegalitarian familial relations are manifest in abusive situations. The abuse of children within the family can occur regardless of 'race', class or other social division (DoH, 1995). Abuse is a source of sorrow and damage, destroying as it does children's trust in those responsible for their care (Dominelli, 1989).

Inequalities based on 'race', gender, class, age, sexual orientation and disability add to the complexities of family dynamics and challenge many of the assumptions upon which hegemonic formulations of the family are based. Black feminists have identified 'the family' as a mainstay for black people's survival in (white) racist societies (Bryant, Dadzie and Scafe 1985; Collins, 1991) and rejected white feminist analyses advocated by Barrett and McIntosh (1981, 1985) that focus on its weaknesses (Bhavani, 1993). They have also highlighted women's strengths within black communities, including their substantial abilities to develop extensive networks of support to deal with the difficult circumstances in which they live (Stack, 1975). As part of this process, black women have also located responsibility for raising children within the broader community (Maracle, 1993) and questioned the dominant view that child care is the sole responsibility of biological mothers (hooks, 1990).

Social workers, particularly white ones, can use such knowledge to help black children and families receive the services they need and avoid the pitfalls of pathologizing family forms (Ahmed, Cheetham and Small, 1986; Dominelli, 1988; Ahmad, 1990). At the same time, white practitioners need to ensure that they do not endorse stereotypes of black families as being able to 'care for their own' (Patel, 1990), thereby colluding with denying them services when such support is impossible because family structures have been altered by social policies, immigration regulation and demographic changes. Similar care is needed in working with white families.

Roles associated with motherhood, fatherhood and childhood within the family are socially constructed and changing. *Motherwork*, the work that mothers do, is vital to family survival and provides physical and emotional care for children and men. Despite not being socially valued (Rosenberg, 1995), motherwork is simultaneously idealized and disparaged (Pugh and De'Ath, 1984). In a globalizing world which has decimated manufacturing jobs once employing men in the West and now emphasizes service sector jobs that women fill (Wichterich, 2000), many women have become main earners in the service sector to assure the bulk of a family's financial resources (Khan, 2001). This *structural* trend has undermined men's role as provider, advocated by hegemonic patriarchal constructions of the family, leaving a void in men's lives. Seldom addressed, responding to men's emotional and social needs in a changed and changing world is a task that social workers could undertake (Dominelli, 2002b).

Despite the image of the 'new' man, fatherhood in contemporary society remains conceptualized primarily in terms of meeting the economic provider or breadwinner role (Russell and Radojevic, 1992). Men continue to do little housework, so women undertake the bulk of the work around the home (Walby, 1997). Men who have challenged this depiction of their position in the family are in the minority and have encountered resistance to their endeavours by women, including their wives, other men and helping professionals (Russell and Radojevic, 1992). Men who have taken seriously their involvement in children's upbringing have been considered less manly for doing so by colleagues at work and often get teased. Here is how a professional man working for an international company concluded his story of challenging roles within the family when I interviewed him:

> Every time I asked for time off work to look after our sick child, I was asked, 'Who wears the pants in your family?' I could never get over feeling embattled by it all. And that was only a couple of years ago.

He now works in a smaller firm for less pay. Being ridiculed is more likely if men become involved in 'dirty work' such as changing nappies or cleaning toilets (Walby, 1997). Men's and women's experiences argue for a more balanced relationship between waged work and personal caring relationships, especially those associated with raising children – the 'work–family' balance. Without it, both fathers and mothers can experience strain arising from caring responsibilities. Redefining masculinity, fatherhood, motherhood and women's and men's roles in families and waged work becomes an urgent task that social workers can facilitate.

Adultist paradigms in child welfare

The family is different from the other institutions with which social workers interact. It is located primarily in the private rather than the public sphere, although it is subjected to the public gaze if things go wrong. The distinction between private and public institutions is crucial in that it creates difficulties for social work interventions because the private sphere has been created as outside the reach of the state and social workers are expected to respect these boundaries while breaching them if necessary. Work with families is contradictory because it is predicated on not shattering one of the most important illusions of modern life, the sanctity of the family, whilst simultaneously protecting weak and vulnerable individuals within it (Hirst, 1981).

The family plays a mediating role between individuals and society. This relation is expressed through the professionals with whom the family interacts, such as social workers, educators and health providers. These professionals may either reinforce nuclear family formulations, or be more open to family diversity. The family as a social institution is increasingly assuming a multiplicity of forms, each with strengths and weaknesses within specific contexts and situations. Yet social workers rely on normalizing and totalizing ways of defining identity in their interventions with both children and adults (Dominelli, 2002a). They have to negotiate with family members to shape the ensuing interventions around actual family formations. Having the skills to do this effectively is particularly necessary for social workers involved in case conferences which have the power to decide whether or not a child is placed on the 'at risk' register, with the profound implications that this may have for children's relationship with their parents or other carers, now or for the rest of their lives.

Familialist constructions of the family underpin social workers' work with children and families. Social workers have traditionally worked with children according to adultist paradigms. In these, children are deemed dependent upon their carers within the privacy of the family home. Contained within traditional models are further assumptions. These include the following:

- The family is powerful enough and sufficiently resourced to deal with whatever problems its members encounter.
- Only 'bad' or inadequate parents require professional intervention, usually because they lack parenting skills or abilities.
- Intervention is justified if it is in the 'best interests of the child', as stipulated in child welfare legislation.
- It is appropriate to separate children from their families when inadequate parenting is evident in the opinion of the relevant social work (or at times health) practitioners.

When working within this model, social workers presume that adult carers are benevolent beings who will look after children, nurture and provide for their welfare in unproblematic ways. Even when they are required to intervene because things have gone awry, social workers assume that adults can be trusted to care for children as long as they are 'theirs'. The treatment of children as if they belong to parents or carers reinforces their construction as possessions under adult control. In these interventions, practitioners combine the 'policing of families' (Donzelot, 1980) through their investigative mandate with offering support through their caring one.

Fox-Harding (1991) identifies four different perspectives used in this work: a laissez-faire patriarchy which endorses minimal intervention by the state; a child protection perspective that legitimates active state intervention in appropriate circumstances; a parent's right perspective which promotes birth parents' control over children; and a children's right perspective that sees the child as an independent person whose wishes need to be respected. These perspectives overlap with one another and emphasize rights over responsibilities. In highlighting rights, they diverge from the neo-liberal perspectives advocated in the New Right's emphasis on responsibilities that family members have for each other during periods of dependency like childhood or old age.

The perspectives identified by Fox-Harding are problematic. They individualize and decontextualize families. This makes it difficult for social workers to see the broader contexts within which families are embedded or even the structural inequalities that impact upon families and how these are shaped by members' interactions. Ignoring structural considerations in social work contributes to poor practice by leaving important issues unaddressed. Fox-Harding's models also neglect the collective and structural dimensions of family life. Although these may be more important for some family groupings than others, they cannot simply be ignored.

Britain's 1989 Children Act reinforces such individualizing and decontextualized conceptualizations of the family. Operating within a patriarchal framework, it claims that 'the best place for the child to be brought up is usually in his [sic] own family', and encourages social workers to work 'in partnership with the parents' in meeting children's needs (Children Act 1989, *Guidance and Regulations*, volume 2).

A difficulty with the Children Act is its assumption that the private family is the best place for children instead of making this a matter for discussion and deliberation. If practice is to respond to specific individuals and circumstances, practitioners have to determine the best course of action for a particular child through a careful consideration of his or her situation without prejudging it.

I suspect that a number of child protection cases have been mishandled precisely because social workers have operated according to presupposition and been unable to question whether a given child could be left in a given family. The tragic histories of Jasmine Beckford (Blom-Cooper, 1986) and Victoria Climbié (Laming, 2003) could be argued in this light: practitioners assumed that their carers *were* caring and truthful. The family as private space with hierarchically ordered relationships within it fails vulnerable children. Holding their carers publicly accountable could be enacted more readily if the family were to be created as public space.

Research sponsored by the then Department of Health and Social Security (DHSS, 1995) revealed that parents valued most those interventions in which social workers enabled them to 'retain their role as responsible, authority figures in relation to their children'. In the state versus parent antagonism, this position allows the rights of parents to supersede those of the state in determining what happens to children. Practice based on a parental rights stance affirms adultist relations over children. In supporting parental rights, the existing formulations of socially constructed entities and unequal power relations in families are reaffirmed.

Child welfare research exposes and perpetrates key dynamics within normalizing discourses that social workers enact in working with children and families. These include taking as irrelevant that not all parents have the same resources at their disposal to assist in parenting work; and assuming the immateriality of the unequal power relations and distribution of resources within families.

The DHSS research did not address the rights of children to shape their own lives. The views of children and their capacity to assert their own rights in difficult situations where their interests may be at variance with those of their parents were glossed over, although the 1989 Children Act allows for children's views to be taken into account. In arguing for equal partnerships between parents and the state, the DHSS ignored disparities of power between parents and the state; between parents (partners); and between parents (partners) and children. Research can easily become a technology of control, or a political instrument through which some messages become articulated and amplified above others.

Practitioners work primarily with women. Their adherence to dominant constructions of the family facilitate their being able simultaneously to take as given and neglect: women's role as the main caregivers for children; the limited involvement of men in caring work; and gendered power relations that disadvantage women. Hence, in working with children, practitioners ignore the actual power relations operating within a family.

The goal of retaining an unquestioned basis to family relationships is accomplished by passing normative judgements through bureaucratized means: dividing families into the 'good' or deserving ones and the 'bad' or undeserving ones. The 'good' families in this construction remain outside the interventionist paradigm and retain their entitlement to privacy. For the others, intervention is a must and they can be subjected to surveillance on behalf of society. As a result, becoming the object of the professional gaze becomes a stigmatizing event performed by bureau-technocrats who exercise 'hierarchical surveillance' over them (Foucault, 1991). That this action is a bureaucratic one is essential to maintaining control as a technocratic measure that keeps hidden the political nature of the act of naming or labelling families.

By configuring or labelling a family in negative ways, social workers legitimate their right to intervene within it whilst leaving to one side those families who are not so configured. The division of families into 'good' and 'bad' families, and parents, particularly mothers, into 'deserving' and 'undeserving' ones, has major implications for social work with children and families. When they intervene in families, social workers must do so in ways that do not challenge the basic distinction between 'good' families that can be left alone and 'bad' families that must not. Consequently, social workers cannot intercede in private affairs unless a family's failures have been disclosed in the public domain. Under the public gaze which is constructed by the professionals who become involved in a given situation, mothers who are deemed to have failed in their sacred duties as mothers – to 'protect their children' – become 'bad' or 'undeserving' mothers from whom it is permitted to remove children, in 'the best interests' of the latter. Such actions affirm hegemonic discourses about 'the family' and legitimate 'hierarchical surveillance'. The irony is that despite castigating people for being bad parents by taking their children away, the state itself is unable consistently to model good parenting to these children (Dominelli et al., forthcoming).

A number of public institutions have usurped many of the family's earlier functions, and in doing so, they have undermined the coherence provided by family organization around these activities. This may engender a sense of anomie about function and purpose at the level of the household (see Durkheim, 1957). Anomic relations may exacerbate conflicts and tensions within the family and cut across age and gender divides. The experiences of family members are stratified according to class and 'race': for example, white working-class and black families experience higher levels of surveillance than white middle-class ones, and in being scrutinized, their right to privacy is undermined. Private behaviour is put on public show for others to dissect in the name of protecting particular individuals in their midst.

Power, control and governmentality

The policing and regulation of families occurs through what Foucault (1979a, 1991) calls 'governmentality'. This refers to the 'ensemble formed by the institutions, procedures, analyses and reflections, the calculations and tactics that allow the exercise of this specific, albeit complex, form of power' (Foucault, 1979, p. 20). The regulation of poor families involves different sets of professionals of which social workers are one. Each group exercises power by negotiating and renegotiating its own interests and priorities to shift existing configurations of power and reconfigure these. Therefore, power relations enacted amongst them cannot be conceptualized as either monolithic or unitary.

Professionals use the 'techniques of notation, computation and calculation; procedures of examination and assessment' (Miller and Rose, 1988, p. 8) to create discursive fields that define problems and prioritize responses to them. Today, these techniques quantify the unquantifiable and render it amenable to measurement and surveillance. They also provide the basis for changing discourses from those focusing on relational social work to the commodification of practice consistent with Fordist principles and managerialist imperatives embodied in competence-based practice and the instrumentality of risk assessments. Competence-based practice and risk assessments (re)produce social work's status as a textually mediated profession whereby policy as text both informs and creates the discourses that authorize specific forms of practice.

Discourses are the structures of knowledge, claims and practices that people use to understand and explain phenomena and decide how to respond to them. Interpretation has to be included in understanding these systems. Different individuals can interpret the same knowledge system differently. Meaning is not separate from interpretation, but part and parcel of the same act. Philp (1985) suggests that discourses represent systems of knowledge that allow the expression of agency. Each discourse seeks to channel agency in particular directions. Alternative discourses arise by engaging with and countering existing ones. An example noted in the previous chapter is the critique of Eurocentric approaches to social work by Africentric theorists who have challenged their assumed universalism and relevance to people of African origins (John-Baptiste, 2001; Graham, 2002).

The family as an institution has been integrated into the mechanisms of both socialization, with its concerns for growth, and social regulation, with its preoccupation with control. Social workers have become an important part of the system used to regulate the family. Hirst (1981) argues that they have been essential to solving the state's problem of ensuring that the rights of its weak, dependent members are observed whilst retaining the family as the 'natural' arena for their care. By intervening only in pathological families or those that do not meet the criteria of normality, the myth of the private sphere is maintained.

In pursuing their tasks, social workers utilize the techniques of 'moralization' and 'normalization' (Donzelot, 1980). Material and financial rewards used to ensure that poor families rectify their moral failings are part of the moralization technique. Spreading accepted norms of living into households that request assistance constitutes part of the normalization process. Normalization is also embedded in policing processes in which social workers make judgements about people's behaviour and deploy their discretion in categorizing specific actions as acceptable or not. This establishes a binary polarity that privileges and rewards certain types of behaviour and punishes others (Foucault, 1977). Coercive intervention is authorized where moralization and normalization techniques fail to achieve the desired results.

'Normalizing' certain family forms facilitates the construction of those that lie outside these as pathological. Responsibility for defining what constitutes the 'normal' has become the remit of the 'psy complex' or social professions like medicine, psychiatry, psychology, criminology and social work (Ingleby, 1985; Rose, 1985). Foucault (1977) claims that practitioners working in these fields have colonized the terrain of 'the social'. They also work with each other on the same people, though often badly. Poor communication and professional rivalries abound (Laming, 2003) as each seeks to secure its status in the professional hierarchy.

In consolidating its position, each 'caring' profession vies with the others to establish its status as the superior one. This involves 'psy' practitioners in creating new objects of knowledge, accumulating new bodies of information and formulating new methodologies of intervention. These strengthen the 'technologies' of discipline which are used not only on the objects of the professional gaze, but also in establishing status hierarchies amongst and between those practising the different professions. 'Psy' professionals use three processes to discipline the *objects* of their intervention, or those defined as the people with whom they work: hierarchical surveillance, normalizing judgement and investigation (Foucault, 1977, pp. 169–77). These processes are particularly explicit in child protection work.

These hierarchies shape professionals' relationships with each other and legitimate the expertise of the older, more established and scientifically oriented professions over social work. Their more 'established' gaze reinforces the lesser position of social workers through the normal routines of everyday practice. In describing her work when she began her career, a hospital social worker I interviewed outlines the processes whereby hierarchical surveillance and normalizing judgements occur between professions. She is describing the voluntary admission of a mother whose child had been taken into care following an episode of violence in which the woman's partner had seriously assaulted both:

> We were doing ward rounds in [a psychiatric hospital]. I disagreed with the psychiatrist's diagnosis and questioned his opinion that the mother's pathology created the messy situation the family was in. He didn't even try to answer my question. Ignoring me, he turned to the next patient, spoke to him briefly and then we all carried on down the hospital corridors as if nothing had happened and I hadn't spoken. I was shocked. The cold-shouldering that followed my remark and my surprise at his reaction prevented me from pursuing it. I later asked my colleagues what they thought of it all. Although others agreed with my views [of the diagnosis], no one spoke out at the time. They said that the consultant's word was the law and as he brooked no criticisms, there was little point in making any. No one dared get on his bad side, and they said, if I had any sense neither should I. So I kept my mouth shut after that occasion.

In this situation, the social worker has been disciplined according to the medical regulatory regime which accords privileged status to 'expert' medical knowledge. The psychiatrist in charge rules through fear, which ensures that his formulation of a problem becomes the accepted one. The social worker's reaction also illustrates the lack of certainty in and contested nature of the terrain that 'psy complex' professions occupy. Fear becomes a means of quelling dissent and legitimating particular expert discourses, ensuring that these dominate and reproduce 'power over' relations.

Constructing childhood through practice

Social work with children and their families is a major area of practice. Child welfare work deals with complex and sensitive tasks. It is highly skilled work conducted under a specific national legal remit, although some international conventions also apply. Coping with the demands of diversity in family forms, cultural traditions, lifestyle choices and a range of other factors complicate the work, especially in child protection, to a degree that is hard for outsiders to understand. Health workers are key non-social work professionals who often find it difficult to grasp the complexities of child protection issues (Gillen, 2001a). Social workers involved in child protection have only one outcome that is acceptable – to get it right. Mistakes are not easily forgiven for the life of a vulnerable child may be at stake. Lauren Wright and Victoria Climbié are recent examples in a highly publicized list of poor outcomes. The complexity of the work and risks entailed in 'getting it wrong' provide the basis for rejecting the myth, often popularized by politicians and media, that any 'street-wise granny' can do social work.

Social work with children is highly contentious because practitioners struggle to balance a number of often competing interests. Key amongst these are expanding needs within a context of inadequate resourcing for those experiencing difficulties; and conflicting interests between child(ren), parents and the state, on whose behalf social workers intervene. British practitioners doing child welfare work operate under considerable pressures as caseloads mount and resources dwindle (Brandon et al., 1998). Despite the Audit Commission's (1994) call for family support services to be rooted in community organizations, a major piece of research conducted through the DHSS (1995) revealed that in Britain, child protection work detracts practitioners' energies from the development of preventative strategies which may do more to support child welfare in the longer term than crisis intervention work can ever aspire to do. The pressures of overload are not limited to social services (Cannan and Warren, 1997). Health workers who play a central role in supporting identification, investigation and intervention in child abuse cases are also overworked.

The problem of overload is illustrated by health visitor Veronica Egenamba, who was struck off the nursing register because 102 of the vulnerable clients she was responsible for had not been referred to the appropriate agencies. She was responsible for 300 families (Leason, 2001). Without commenting on the appropriateness or otherwise of this particular decision, it is worth pausing on the conditions in which this health visitor worked. Given the numbers on her caseload, even if she were to spend only ten minutes processing or reviewing each case each week, it would take fifty hours. As this is longer than her working week, it would leave her with no time for doing anything else, including writing up case notes for work undertaken. Health workers, like social workers, manage resourcing conflicts by prioritizing whom to see and not seeing people on each case every week. However, although prioritizing may help manage time, it cannot eliminate resourcing shortages.

The focus on crisis intervention constrains child protection work within a short-termism that is shaped more by the resources and skills that social workers have at their disposal than it is by professional judgements about appropriate forms of intervention in delicate situations. The New Labour government has recently identified the need for social workers to refocus on child welfare (DoH, DfEE and the Home Office, 2000; DfES, 2003) without losing child protection considerations. Whilst this is welcome, it is unclear how this can become a reality without substantial additional resources, if only to free up professional time in which to do preventative work.

However, I would argue that the entire system needs to be re-thought and refocused. This requires standing outside the child protection system to ask different questions. For me a crucial one is: how does society promote the growth and development of *all* children? Asking this question would move the debate from residualism and the highlighting of parental contributions and pathologies to turn the professional spotlight away from child protection, though without losing sight of this concern, because an abused or exploited child is not able to realize his or her full potential. In doing so, professionals would reorient the system towards a child's personal well-being within a social context that includes interactions with others from their communities alongside family members and tackling structural inequalities as these impact upon a specific child.

Dealing with structural inequalities is a neglected area of child protection considerations, even though New Labour has committed itself to eliminating one of them – child poverty, initially by halving it by 2015 (Colley and Hodkinson, 2001), now deferred to 2020 (Sure Start, 2002). Poverty is a key concern because, despite progress, one in three of Britain's children live in poverty

(Perlmutter, 1997; Miller and Ridge, 2001; Bonney, 2002). The figures are higher amongst single-parent families headed by women (Duncan and Edwards, 1996, 1997) and vary according to geographical location (Howarth et al., 1999). In parts of Inner London, poverty afflicts one child in two (Gaffney, 2002), a despairing picture also evident in the 'affluent' southeast (Dominelli, 2002d).

Social workers have little opportunity for tackling such issues unless they are community workers mobilizing people around low income. Few poverty campaigns have specifically targeted meeting the needs of poor children *in their own rights as children* within a non-stigmatizing framework. Though important, tackling family poverty will only provide limited help as doing so will not necessarily address income inequalities within families. Their impact is more uneven on women and children (Pahl, 1985). Nor do family campaigns address the issue of children as autonomous human beings with their own set of rights. To change the balance in intra-familial resource distribution, children have to be seen as having identical rights to resources to adults, as should women to men. Each individual within a family should have access to equal resources. Existing resource allocation in families, however, favours adult men.

As part of its strategy to help poor children, New Labour is providing support that targets needy children through early-years services. Sure Start for children under 4 years of age (Sure Start, 2002), Connexions for young people aged 13 to 19 years of age (DfEE, 2002), and parenting classes to increase parenting skills, especially amongst young mothers, aim to achieve this objective. The New Deal for Lone Mothers encourages women to join the paid workforce by offering limited training and child care support (Gingerbread, 2000). Social workers can and do play a significant role in these programmes. Each programme involves a 'personal adviser' who assists a particular person to meet specific objectives in turning his or her life around.

Personal advisers focus on a person's shortcomings and lack of skills development. Such advisers are explicitly charged with ensuring that people adopt certain paths above others, and so are involved in more overt forms of policing behaviour. They occupy crucial roles in implementing New Labour's technologies of control by passing 'normalizing' judgements. Personal advisers do work traditionally undertaken by social workers and provide a site for further training and professionalization. Although incorporated into networks of governmentality, personal advisers have not been given a remit to tackle structural inequalities, including the absence of children's voices from matters of extreme concern to them – enhancing their well-being. Consequently, systemic weaknesses are not considered part of the helping equation they engage in.

These initiatives may help some people, but they are problematic. They exclude in the name of inclusion by targeting failing families – parents whose children have dropped out of school or are in trouble with the law; lone mothers and children whose needs cannot be met because they live in poverty (Miller and Ridge, 2001). The flaw is that these programmes perpetuate residual services for needy children, reaffirm individualized blaming discourses and pathologize parents who personally may be unable to do anything about the structural inequalities in which they live.

Welfare-to-work-type programmes for single parents exemplify these difficulties. These are highlighted in the case of Tamarla Owens, the mother of a 6-year-old boy who shot a girl the same age in the classroom in Flint, Michigan, whilst his mother was working on these schemes. Leaving home early in the morning and arriving late at night, she hardly saw her children. Despite working seventy hours a week on two jobs, she was evicted for being unable to pay her rent just before the shooting. British social workers should take note of the impossible demands such programmes place on already stressed families and advocate for change in their structural conditions.

Residuality is enforced with regards to poor housing conditions, including high levels of homelessness, and poor health which accompanies poverty (Townsend, Davidson and Whitehead, 1992; Ward, 2002). Residual provisions are stigmatized, exacerbate the general difficulties faced by people in need, and reduce poor children's chances of improving their circumstances over their life cycle (Bradshaw, 2001). These problems were evident in the Owens case and cry out to be tackled with urgency.

Working in another context, Cannan (1992) addresses the issue of stigmatized services for children using family centres and concludes that these should be available to a wide range of users and provide a variety of services to enable families who need support to interact with those who do not. Thus, services would not be limited to cases in which child abuse has already occurred. Lack of social networks and isolation can contribute to poor mental health amongst parents and intensify the obstacles they face in improving their lives (Pitcairn and Waterhouse, 1996). Poor mental health contributes to poor parenting and increases the stigmatization of families. Mental ill health can be a critical issue for mothers because women, especially those who are married, are more likely to have mental health problems (Prior, 1999), particularly depression (Saraceno and Barbui, 1997).

Social workers are aware of structural inequalities, but they have an image of parenting that corresponds to that typified by the white middle-class mother, with the attendant resources that this implies. And they apply this image to situations where it is inappropriate to do so (Callahan et al., 2000). That white working-class mothers are expected to meet the standards of white middle-class mothers was noted long ago and has been reaffirmed by Holman (1988). Hills (1995) identified the 'cycle of poor parenting' experiences across generations of poor people living in rundown estates. His study demonstrates that personal inadequacies and lack of good role models in parental behaviour contribute to poor parenting in later generations. This research indicates that to be effective, intervention has to engage with both personal and structural problems.

Callahan et al.'s (2000) study reveals that problems experienced by young mothers are not caused by their ignorance of what constitutes good mothering; indeed, they subscribe to the same white middle-class model of good parenting as social workers. Instead, as these young mothers are well aware, their behaviour and aspirations are constrained by a lack of resources, but they cannot rely on social workers to provide these. Callahan et al.'s research suggests that to break the 'cycle of poor parenting', social workers need skills, resources and policies that address the personal and structural issues that undermine mothering capacities. Addressing these requires major changes in current policy and practice.

Securing the necessary changes cannot be the preoccupation solely of young mothers; their limited resources and low credibility, which is in part the product of negative media images and politicians' attacks, would detract from such endeavours. Media portrayals and public discourses have demonized and devalued young mothers and their skills, especially if they need public assistance and are unmarried. Demonizing and pathologizing unmarried mothers has been a theme articulated throughout the history of professional social work, beginning in the nineteenth century, when 'unmarried mothers' became construed as having moral rather than social problems (Strega et al., 2002). Defined as inadequate individuals, they were blamed and shamed into behaving as stipulated by prevailing social norms. Social workers colluded with these discourses and were employed to put them into effect. Moving forward now requires the media, politicians and practitioners to focus on the strengths that young mothers have, including the channelling of their desire to be *good* mothers, providing the resources necessary for doing mothering work and promoting life-affirming images of these women. These approaches to young mothers would enhance the potential of those who already hold this status to avoid becoming failing parents, and thus foster the well-being of their children. The issue of preventing or reducing the growth in the number of young women becoming mothers is a separate one and needs to be handled differently. Neither group is assisted by being stigmatized, but offering young women attractive options out of poverty and alienation would do much to delay motherhood to a more propitious (for them) time. Helping to bring this about is a legitimate social work endeavour.

In traditional scenarios, the technologies of control become technologies of inscription whereby the '(in)adequate mother' is (re)inscribed in ways that allow professionals to intervene in her private life. Through this process, the voice of the mother as either woman or mother is lost, as is that of the child, although the voice of the child has seldom been of direct concern in the process of (re)inscribing the mother. Pathology-based interventions in people's lives are not predetermined. They are the outcome of particular ways of defining and processing people. Changing the procedures whereby social work is undertaken and aiming for different objectives, especially those rooted in meeting people's needs as they define them, can produce change by initiating alternative discourses. And, as procedures form contexts, changing these alters how personal behaviour is structured. Professionals are constantly involved in change processes. These may be aimed at (re)integrating people into the structures and accepted norms of the status quo, as suggested by the maintenance school of social work (Davies, 1985), or transforming existing social relations, as advocated by the emancipatory school of social work (Dominelli, 1997).

Social workers can do more to support children, using the provisions of the 1989 Children Act and the United Nations Convention on the Rights of the Child, which the British government ratified in 1991. Unfortunately, progress in improving conditions for children has not been straightforward. When reviewed, the United Kingdom, like several other countries, including Canada, was berated for not meeting the targets set. Such verdicts can, however, be used to secure changes in national policies. British social workers could use the negative reports produced by the UN Committee on the Rights of the Child regarding their government's inadequate progress on the implementation of its provisions in 1995 (Franklin and Franklin, 1996) and 2002 (UNHCR, 2002) as leverage in demanding resources to enhance children's welfare.

The Convention stresses that the welfare of the child is paramount and covers broad areas like child survival, development, protection and participation, including children's right to be free from discrimination, inhumane treatment and all forms of violence, and receive health care, education and information (Lindsay, 1992). Social workers could gather data on children's lack of welfare opportunities through their work and utilize their advocacy skills to exert pressure on governments to release resources that would enable all children to have equal chances in life. If government were to act accordingly, it would accept that raising children is a social responsibility that involves the entire community (Clinton, 1996). Social workers could be involved in facilitating this goal by developing networks that link children and parents to the broader community so that family support in its widest sense becomes the basis from which other work proceeds. Promoting community responsibility for children could address structural inequalities currently hampering some children's development.

Devolution has begun to change the overall picture in the United Kingdom, although it is too soon to make predictions as to outcomes. It is unclear whether initiatives such as the appointment of a Children's Commissioner in Wales and a Minister for Children in England will tackle structural inequalities alongside parental deficiencies. The Children (Scotland) Act of 1995 and the Children (Northern Ireland) Order, 1995, have the 'children in need' focus evident in the 1989 Children Act. These two pieces of legislation target interventions on families' (i.e. mothers') ability to parent adequately. Children's Rights Officers exist in some local authorities in England and aim to offer an independent service to children in government care. I am sceptical about whether these institutions will address structural inequalities. And I question whether these structures are capable of providing unstigmatized services for all children, though they might succeed in getting some families to attend parenting classes and improve their situation a little.

Social work with children has become highly routinized and bureaucratized as it has increasingly moved away from professional and into managerial control. This development has yet to be subjected to full critique and debate. Inquiries into child abuse indicate that the child protection system is failing to protect children (Parton, 1996; Laming, 2003) and that harassed, inexperienced and under-resourced practitioners are unable to cope with the demands of the job. The problems of practice become highly visible in these cases and expose shortcomings in: resourcing levels; the training for social workers who undertake tough child protection work (although, in Britain, post-qualifying courses on child care aim to rectify some weaknesses in this area); the ability of managers to supervise and support practitioners appropriately; and the capacity of interagency personnel to work effectively with other professionals, parents or children. The long line of tragic child murders committed by carers constantly brings these failings to light (Berridge and Brodie, 1996).

One state response to the shortage of resources and personnel in child welfare has been to restructure the hierarchies of surveillance by focusing on calculating 'risk' in child protection cases so as to police populations and spread existing resources more effectively and widely. The management of risk becomes an important aspect of the 'risk society' (Beck, 1992) in which the calculation and mitigation of risk dominate policy formulation (Lupton, 1999). The assessment and management of risk change the role of practitioners from autonomous professionals who make independent decisions to technocrats who execute managerial imperatives which may have been formulated without specialist professional input (Castel, 1991).

Child welfare is an area where the development of child-centred services is largely driven and constrained by managerial concerns to protect the agency (Parton, 1998). In this, the voice of the child remains remarkably silent and those of parents only slightly less so. Adults can more readily protect their interests, and some have come together to create organizations to fight for them: for example, Parents Against Injustice (PAIN). PAIN was formed as a lobbying body during the 1980s to ensure that British parents had greater rights in challenging social workers' attempts to take their children into care (Brewer and Lait, 1980). Its success in asserting parental rights through the 1989 Children Act has downgraded those of the state and children.

Policing deviant families: Placing children on the 'at risk' register

The death of children at the hands of their parents and carers – approximately fifty per year in Britain – has prompted discursive practices rooted in notions of 'risk'. The criteria for establishing risk is that a child is 'likely to suffer or has suffered significant harm' (Children Act 1989, sec. 31(2)(a)). Establishing whether this is the case has skewed social workers' priorities towards an increasing number of child protection cases which have downgraded the value of spending time and resources on preventative work.

This hierarchy of surveillance also emphasizes the roles of forensic medicine and the legal profession in guiding deliberations in court.

Although there is no mandatory reporting in Britain, around 160,000 allegations of child abuse are investigated each year (Packman, 1994). Most of these are not substantiated, but they consume scarce social work resources that could be utilized elsewhere (DHSS, 1995). This dilemma exposes the contradictions that social workers have to face: protecting children from significant harm whilst simultaneously preventing unwarranted state intrusion into the private lives of children and their families. Family work tends to focus on women as social workers usually work with mothers and ignore men in the family. Social workers are also likely to be women policing other women, which assists the process of (re)affirming gendered relations and self-regulation in the caring arena (Dominelli, 2002b).

Risk assessment and management in child welfare work

Placing a child on the 'at risk' register is geared to ensuring that the child is protected from abuse. For parents, this act symbolizes the worst possible moment in their relationship with the intrusive state – losing the right to parent without surveillance from professionals. From the moment their children are placed on the 'at risk' register they become subjected to further regulation and discipline as professionals activate the 'technologies of control' to more closely police deviant parental behaviour.

Risk assessment involves the identification, evaluation and monitoring of risks (Kemshall and Pritchard, 1996) in the behaviour of individuals who are deemed to pose a danger to others. In child protection situations, risky behaviour is thought to carry the potential of harming children. The aim of risk assessments is to avert such behaviour by subjecting individuals suspected of committing acts of violence or abuse against others to various forms of regulation and control. In the process, the practitioner endeavours to distinguish the person who can self-manage from the one who has to be managed. Risk assessment and management as a technology for governing others is, however, an imprecise art, despite its pretence to scientific respectability. For as Quinsey (1995) claims, 'dangerousness' is hard to predict in given circumstances with specific individuals.

Risk management requires practitioners to make visible the decisions they take by documenting the information pertaining to clients in a prescribed form that managers can use to monitor their endeavours and pass judgements on the quality of their interventions. The systems and mechanisms for recording decisions provide the raw material or texts upon which the process of auditing takes place. Auditing of what has been or can be done (Power, 1994) affirms bureaucratic rationality and procedures and replaces the trust that relational practice utilizes to facilitate work undertaken with clients. It also reinforces control from the centre and enables managers to determine whether or not front-line workers have made decisions that they can publicly defend without their physically having to stand guard over them. In this context, whether the decision was the right one or even the best one that could be made from the point of view of the child or family involved becomes immaterial as agency preoccupations and priorities acquire precedence, despite the objective of protecting a child from harm. By controlling the processes of intervention, bureaucratic rationality embodies managerialist initiatives that aim to channel and manage the uncertainties of practice, and, in consequence, contributes to the transformation of the bureau-professional into the bureau-technocrat.

Risk management involves regulation not only of the client, but also of the worker. Practitioners become subjected to bureaucratic and managerialist forms of control and procedures that aim to reduce their scope for exercising discretion and making autonomous decisions. This should reduce the 'risk' of things going wrong, namely worker incompetence in missing important clues in the suspected individual's behaviour. Bureaucratic rationality shapes the field within which responses are negotiated between workers and clients, however, and often results in bureaucratic responses that leave the person who requires protection being left without it.

Children continue to be injured, abused and sometimes murdered. Not only do their own parents or close carers fail them, the system does too. These failures demonstrate that the system created to bring together information from a variety of professional and lay sources is inadequate for the task. Formulaic constructions of risk and statistics collected to predict danger with a degree of certainty and allocate resources to those deemed 'deserving' can be wide of the mark (Castel, 1991). Risk registers cannot predict the likelihood of disabled or other groups of children being abused. Nor do these controls protect workers from being blamed and subjected to a panoply of organizational and legal sanctions alongside media opprobrium if things go wrong, as Lisa Arthurworrey discovered when Victoria Climbié was murdered by her carers.

Failing children

Carers' failure to look after their charges appropriately is amply demonstrated by the abuse of children entrusted to their care. A number of scandals have exposed the appalling abuse of children physically, emotionally and sexually in both families and institutions responsible for promoting their welfare (Berridge and Brodie, 1996). Even highly vulnerable children such as babies and those with disabilities have not been spared abuse, while some have died at the hands of those providing for them. These appalling acts occur in the sanctity of the family setting with biological, foster and adoptive parents; within residential institutions (Waterhouse, 2000), schools, churches and hospitals (Carlile, 1994); and even on playing fields and the streets. The pervasiveness of child abuse, especially of sexual abuse, has been highlighted in a number of studies since the 1980s (Russell, 1984; Dominelli, 1986; Kelly, 1988; Bolen, 2002), and in the growing use of Childline and other helplines (Gillen, 2001b). Child abuse reflects the downside of dependency relations between children and adults. Adultist power relations have defeated many children who have protested and sought to get their voices heard. The failure of their challenge has left children to suffer in silence. Moosa-Mitha (2002) argues that children's rights are neglected because they have been construed as similar to adult rights instead of being conceptualized as different from the child's own vantage point.

Dependency is a key difference that skews power relations between adults and children and gives advantage to the former. Dependency relations can work to the detriment of children's welfare when care is carried out in secrecy and with little public scrutiny. It is hard to explain adequately the abuses of power perpetrated upon children by carers, but understanding a number of dynamics helps. Ideologies that construct children as less than human endorse their abuse. Aversion therapy is a form of behaviour modification that uses an economy of rewards and punishments to elicit appropriate behaviour. It can endorse extreme forms of physical deterrents that border on cruel and inhumane actions. Yet it is an approved professional intervention. Popular in the USA for work with children with difficult behavioural problems, it illustrates what for some constitutes institutionally legitimated child abuse. Tatchell (1996) highlights its abuse of young homosexuals, whereas Eysenck (1997) minimized its detrimental effects. These opposing discourses make aversion therapy contested territory, a point affirmed in a court case over its use on autistic children (Siegal, 1995). Its proponents have the power of naming both the problem and its solution and can exercise adultist professional power to continue treatments. This is unacceptable in a framework that values children as citizens.

Adultist power relations are evident in the ways that adults treat a wide range of children, including disabled children, children with learning difficulties, children with autism and those with attention deficit disorders (ADD). As some of these children have problems communicating in accordance with adult norms, practitioners have to acquire and use child-centred communication skills. Several voluntary organizations, including the Triangle Consultancy, the National Society for the Prevention of Cruelty to Children (NSPCC) and Rights of Children have developed a range of communication materials to assist social workers. These should be studied carefully for a child's view of the world to be heard and responded to appropriately. If children's voices were taken seriously, it is unlikely that practices such as those advocated in aversion therapy or the Pindown regime could have been so easily ignored.

The Pindown scandal in Britain indicates that poorly trained staff can succumb to the professional credibility of the form of aversion therapy represented by Pindown and condone abuses of power perpetrated by colleagues, not noticing the considerable harm caused to children in their care (Levy and Kahan, 1996). In other situations, parental poverty and stress can result in the emotional abuse and neglect of children (Aldgate and Tunstill, 2000). Sometimes, a frazzled parent lashes out at a demanding child. In others, abuse is systemic and organized to involve more than one family, as occurs in the trafficking of large numbers of children from poor countries to rich ones for the purposes of prostitution (Gillen, 2002). Child sexual abuse also highlights the importance of hegemonic masculinity in endangering children, whether by men previously known to them or not (Pringle, 1995; Cowburn and Dominelli, 2001; Scourfield, 2001).

The purchaser–provider split has fostered enormous growth in commercially run child care facilities which are ineffectually regulated. These can also become arenas where child abuse can occur (Laming, 2003). The murder of Victoria Climbié by her great-aunt and the latter's boyfriend provides an example of private fostering arrangements going seriously wrong. As it was a *private* agreement, neither carer was subjected to official vetting procedures regarding suitability to care. This state of affairs highlights the continued dominance of the sanctity of the family in public regulatory regimes, a feature that has contributed to the death of many children under adult care.

In Victoria's case, key actors, including the social worker assigned to the case, were black. The media's allegations of incompetence on the part of her social worker detracted attention from the institutional racism within a system of child protection that does not support black workers and line managers adequately. The absence of adequate resourcing to make this possible was compounded by the fears of white personnel overseeing their efforts. They were too frightened to ask questions that could safeguard the interests of a child with carers whose culture differed from theirs. Presented as anti-racist, rather than as the unacceptable politically correct form of practice that it is, this behaviour exposes white workers' collusion with racist policies, practices and attitudes. The fear of being labelled racist promotes the abuse of culture as an excuse for not adequately protecting black children and perpetuates racist dynamics. As Shama Ahmed (1978) said long ago, not everything is racism. White social workers and managers owe it to themselves and black clients to be able to distinguish which dynamics they are addressing at a given point.

The thirty-five government inquiries into the failure of British social services departments to effectively discharge their duty of care towards children since Maria Colwell's death in 1973 have severely dented public confidence in practitioners' ability to deliver the services necessary to meet children's needs and safeguard their well-being. The abuse of children indicates the failure of adults to treat children as human beings with their own inalienable rights (Franklin, 1995). It demonstrates how children are considered the private property of those who care for them rather than having their care vested in the community. The saying 'It takes a village to raise a child' suggests that society as a whole has to be involved in looking after the interests of children (Clinton, 1996).

It is ironic that children taken into care are now called 'looked after' children. The phrase hardly seems appropriate in describing what happens to children who hold that status. 'Looked after' children are more likely to end up in trouble with the police, homeless, unemployed, poorly educated and, if they are young girls, pregnant than are their peers living at home with their parents (Garrett, 1992; Saunders and Broad, 1997). At the same time, social workers sit in judgement over poor parents who live in fear of the knock on the door that will result in their children being taken from them (Callahan et al., 2000). Moreover, social workers acting as parent on behalf of the state are guilty of reproducing the same patterns of poor parenting from which they have allegedly 'rescued' children (Dominelli et al., forthcoming). These failures provide evidence that the inscription of poor families through the current technologies of control is failing to meet the needs of either the children or the families concerned.

In Britain, the Leaving Care Act 2000 provides a mechanism that practitioners can use to improve life chances for 'looked after' children and make long-term arrangements for their well-being and development. Its provisions entitle each young person to a personal adviser and a pathway plan which can be used to anticipate and respond to their specific needs when they leave care. These can be extended until the person is 21 years old. The Leaving Care Act requires social workers to ensure that young people participate fully in shaping their future lives. Thus, it contains an element of personal empowerment within it. To cover the range of young people's needs, practitioners implementing its provisions have to tackle obstacles that undermine their well-being at both personal and structural levels. Focusing on one to the exclusion of the other will not provide conditions that promote young people's growth across the board or their status as active citizens.

Child welfare work raises a number of significant questions that practitioners have yet to answer adequately. Addressing structural inequalities ranging from child poverty to silencing children's voices are key ones. Another focuses on who should work with children in difficult child sexual abuse cases. Research highlighting the importance of gender relations in sexual abuse situations queries the appropriateness of men undertaking such work (Pringle, 1995; Pringle and Harder, 1997). Pringle (1994) and Box (1987) follow the feminist position that men can do so under certain conditions (Dominelli, 1989). This qualified view is being challenged by some men: Christie (2001), for example, asserts that there should be no such limits on men social workers.

'Race' issues raise other crucial considerations, including gendered oppression. Black children face additional hurdles as a result of racist constructions of their identity when in the care of the local authority (Barn, 1993). Wilson (1993) claims that sexually abused young black women will not report their plight to statutory authorities because these are considered racist. Thus, institutional racism deprives these young black women of services that are necessary for their well-being. Mama (1989) argues likewise for black women victim-survivors of domestic violence (see also Bhatti-Sinclair, 1994).

Disabled children are three times more likely to be abused than others (Sullivan and Knutson, 2002). The abuse of children with learning difficulties and physical disabilities highlights the system's failure to protect them (McDowall, 2002). Other problems can stem from the setting – statutory or not, or whether the work is paid or unpaid. Ensuring practitioner accountability is harder to realize in sectors with few statutory controls. Limited control over care occurring in the private domain as a private arrangement contributes to the problem of policing carers' behaviour.

That mothers are berated for 'failing to protect' children from abuse by the men in their lives is well known: the women, rather than the men directly perpetrating the abuse, are held to account. Similarly, however, the position of (predominantly) women social workers who 'fail to protect children' is beginning to mirror that of their women clients. Child welfare workers are now being held responsible for 'failing to protect children'. In Nova Scotia and Ontario, social workers have been sued, sacked and gaoled if parents murder children in their care. In her research on domestic violence, Susan Strega highlighted the 'invisible men' – fathers absent in social work interventions. Interestingly enough, she found that social workers were extremely 'protective' of abusive men and did not encourage them to talk to others about their experiences (Strega, 2001)

Practitioners' failure to look after the interests of children in their care not only undermines public confidence in their abilities to discharge their duties towards children, but also diminishes the child's capacity to develop a relationship of trust with adults who hold power over them. 'Trust' is essential in facilitating the processes of feeling valued and understood. Schofield (1998) emphasizes a trusted relationship for children to talk willingly about their feelings or needs and experience the encounter as one of being listened to and understood. Their full participation in the processes of drawing up plans for their own future provides an opportunity for trust to develop.

Revitalizing communities: Approaching child welfare as a collective responsibility

The family as sole provider of children's welfare needs has been a persistent theme in British social policies (Fox-Harding, 1996).

Community approaches to child welfare provide important alternatives to individual and family-oriented ones. It is helpful to envisage both approaches in complementary rather than antagonistic terms. Children need to relate to their families and other significant individuals however these may be configured in a specific case. Furthermore, they have to be solidly grounded in a community where they feel they belong as valued human beings who can contribute to its collective present and future existence (Franklin, 1995).

As I discuss in greater detail in chapter 7, 'community' is a problematic and contested term (Wilson, 1977; Dominelli, 1990). Communities, being formed for particular purposes, are movable feasts and socially constructed. They may be based on geographical proximity, identity attributes or interests or combinations of all three (Dominelli, 2002a). A community's size is a matter for deliberation and determination, extending to the national and international domains if child poverty is to be eliminated globally. Communities have flexible, constantly shifting configurations that form and re-form through social interactions for specific ends amongst their members, and between their members and outsiders. An individual can belong to more than one community at the same time. Because 'community' constitutes and is constituted by those encompassed by its borders, the term is simultaneously inclusive of those who meet stipulated criteria and exclusive of those who do not.

By community approaches, I refer to the collective responsibility of all those living in a particular geographical locale to ensure the safety and well-being of the children in their midst whether or not they are biologically related or known to the child. Collective responsibility encompasses delivery of an ethic of care at different points in children's individual lives. An ethic of care is socially recognized as the right to receive and give care – the right to care for and about someone (Knijn and Ungerson, 1997; Sevenhuijsen, 1998). This ethic creates a *social* relationship without direct personal mediation having to take place. It is based on the idea of interdependence between generations and reciprocity amongst people who live in a particular locale and share the use of its social spaces and physical resources. Interdependence and reciprocity bind childless couples and individuals to contribute to the well-being of children who are not theirs. Rather than raising children, they support them in other ways: listening to what children say; helping them meet their aspirations; ensuring their physical safety; and paying taxes.

Reciprocity may be demonstrated largely by paying taxes to provide the services necessary to support children and enable their families to access child care, education, health care, housing and social services. This constitutes the 'giving' element of reciprocity. The 'receiving' aspect of reciprocity may take the form of living in a society at ease with itself, or it may happen later in life when those paying taxes or helping now experience the fruits of intergenerational solidarity by being cared for in old age. Through reciprocity, both yesterday's children and today's children contribute to building a better future for all.

The inability of children and their families to thrive without supportive communities is evidenced in urban areas such as those found in many British cities where so-called 'sink estates' engender despair and hopelessness because of the limited social goods that communities are expected to provide – jobs, housing, educational facilities, public amenities, health care provisions, social services that meet needs and a civic ethic of caring for and about others. Social workers have a task in reintegrating into mainstream society the people who live in these situations instead of leaving them outside it. Shifting official discourses, particularly the demonization of these estates and their residents, and tackling structural inequalities will be central to achieving this objective. Arguing for solidarity and mutuality amongst people within a framework of equality will assist practitioners in changing prevailing discourses.

Assimilation as exclusionary practice

The treatment of those defined 'deviant' as outside society and the lack of inclusive social support for families are evident in the experiences of formerly colonized peoples whose life support systems and communities were systematically destroyed through forcible policies of assimilation. The issues raised continue to bedevil social work. Initiatives detrimental to the well-being of those defined as 'outsiders' have included attempts to enforce assimilationist middle-class policies upon working-class people in Britain and indigenous[1] peoples overseas. These have devastated the family structures and traditional cultures of the First Nations peoples in Canada (Haig-Brown, 1988; Rutman et al., 2000; Bruyere, 2001), the Native Americans in the United States (Konstantin, 2002), the Maori peoples in New Zealand (Tait-Rolleston and Pehi-Barlow, 2001) and the aboriginal peoples of Australia (Thompson, 1994; Wilson,

1997), and have enforced slavery on peoples of African origins in the West (Gilroy, 1995).

Traditional heritages were destroyed when indigenous children were placed in residential schools and contact with their (extended) families and communities was severely curtailed. Measures were introduced to compel them to adopt the dominant Anglo-Saxon language, culture and way of life on the assumption that they would benefit from such interventions (Armitage, 1996). These included: the forcible removal of children from their homes; the rigid prohibition of indigenous languages and cultures; and cruel and degrading punishments for disobedience (Haig-Brown, 1988; Campbell, 1983).

In Canada, enforced stays in the Indian Residential School, and the systems of abuse linked to it (Haig-Brown, 1988), have damaged generations of First Nations peoples culturally, financially and emotionally (Maracle, 1993). Many of these abuses have only recently been discussed publicly through the sustained efforts of those affected to tell their stories (Churchill, 1998; Wiebe and Johnson, 1998). Maori peoples in New Zealand (Tait-Rolleston and Pehi-Barlow, 2001) and aboriginal peoples in Australia (Wilson, 1997; Gilbert, 2001) relate similar narratives of abuse through the welfare missions and voluntary agencies entrusted with their care.

Children of Maori descent in New Zealand, like First Nations children in Canada and black children in Britain, are over-represented in the child protection and juvenile justice systems (Barn, 1993). Racist ideas on which subsequent practices are predicated are reflected in social workers' constructions of these families as falling outside socially accepted norms and reinforce the notion that they are incapable of looking after their children. White settlers considered taking children into care an appropriate response in 'saving' children from parents who followed 'dangerous' cultures and traditions (Armitage, 1996). Indigenous people's narratives have exposed the negative configurations of their capacities promoted by mainstream social workers and highlighted their continued resistance to subjugation. The silences about social work's role are a shameful legacy that practitioners and educators have to address alongside policymakers and the general public in the countries concerned.

Rooted in assimilationist ideologies, practice with aboriginal peoples privileges expert voices and knowledges to clients' detriment. Its continued presence and dominance has generated resistance from clients and professionals in both academy and field. At the individual level, the story of the 'home children', discussed further in chapter 7 (Bagnell, 2001), and those of the individuals who have survived the Indian Residential School experience reveal how practice has oppressed and restricted growth in individuals and groups despite heroic acts of opposition to their treatment (Wiebe and Johnson, 1998). Collective resistance has built on individual opposition and engendered clients' refusal to call on social workers for services except as providers of last resort.

The struggles of colonized peoples to re-establish self-defined communities and cultures describe important processes of healing that individuals and communities have to undergo once they have been traumatized and damaged by colonization before they can reassert control over their lives individually and collectively. Each of their stories is different, and responses for promoting their well-being will differ by being tailored to their specific needs. Their struggles demonstrate courage and creativity when facing incredible odds. Their experiences provide sources of inspiration for other communities that need revitalization through the exchange of ideas about how such changes may occur. These are considered in chapter 7, and emphasize the significance of embedding families in vibrant cultural communities for social workers to respond to individual needs more fully. Investing in people requires intervention in their *social* circumstances, not just their personal ones.

I do not have space to detail the struggles of peoples reclaiming their rightful place in society by making known their histories of oppression by those caring for them and their contributions to developments in the broader world. As a considerable literature exists to which readers may refer, I focus briefly instead on several examples that have a direct bearing on child welfare. One draws on the experiences of First Nations peoples, another on the Maori peoples, and the last on black children in Britain today.

The removal of First Nations children from their families with the avowed assimilationist aim of improving their prospects in white colonial Canadian society subjected them to a series of inhumane treatments that had traumatic impacts upon the lives of children and their families (Wiebe and Johnson, 1998). The humiliation, degradation and awfulness of assimilationist strategies are evident in the following quote from a First Nations child in an Indian residential school. It exposes the racist underpinnings that lay at the heart of Canadian assimilation policies:

> Sellars spent almost nine years at this Catholic-run school, where he was not only sexually abused by a priest, but cut off from his family, constantly hungry, frequently strapped, and put down along with

> his friends as a 'dirty little Siwash', a cruel nickname he still does not understand. . . . There was also old-fashioned discipline which rarely let up. Girls were strapped if they were caught looking at boys across the segregated playground. Kids were punished by having their hair chopped off. Boys who wet their beds had to wear the urine-stained sheets over their heads. (Furniss, 1995, p. 10)

The dynamics of abuse evident in this extract are recognizable today and can be found in many children's lives, as this First Nations respondent makes clear:

> I kept running away and running away and running away. I mean I've been in homes where they grounded me and you know they would lock the basement door and the basement was all mine. I've been in homes where the foster parent would come home drunk and tell me in my face. I've been in homes where they just purely neglect [me] because of my race. (Dominelli et al., forthcoming)

The overall effect of abuse is to promote the adult carer's interests over those of the child. First Nations peoples resisted subjugating practices upon their families, particularly their children, often without success. Some responses were not directed at the abusers, but expressed as self-harm, including domestic violence, drunkenness and drug misuse (Campbell, 1983). Ultimately, the failure of the state to respond appropriately to their needs caused First Nations peoples to demand self-determination and the right to care for children according to their own cultural practices and customs. These were based on the community formed by the band or tribal grouping to which each Nation belonged. In provinces such as British Columbia (Rutman et al., 2000), Ontario (Hill, 2000) and Nova Scotia (Gilroy, 1999), several initiatives in band-controlled child welfare systems have materialized. These aim to heal First Nations peoples and encourage their active citizenship as self-determining beings with something to offer the wider society.

Maori peoples created alternative forms of practice to deal with situations according to their needs and cultural traditions (Tait-Rolleston and Pehi-Barlow, 2001). They responded to their exclusion from mainstream society by demanding their rights as equal partners in New Zealand's social order as provided by the Treaty of Waitangi (Ruwhiu, 1998). In asserting their rights to self-determination in the child welfare arena, they developed the family group conference (FGC) approach to child welfare. This model of family intervention has been copied in many countries in the West, including Britain (Jackson and Nixon, 1999; Taylor, 1999),

Canada, the USA and Sweden (Schmidt et al., 2001). A strength of FGCs is that practitioners draw upon the resources of the extended family to locate a child in a broader network of care and respond more effectively to his or her needs. In Western countries, this can reinforce biological links rather than the broader community ones that I referred to earlier.

FGCs have played an important role in challenging practitioner power in favour of parental power (Jackson and Nixon, 1999). They operate primarily within an adultist paradigm in which elders are presumed to know what is in the best interests of the child. The child can be asked to express his or her views, but the adults have the final say. The presence of a number of adults with varying interests is expected to prevent the abuse of adult power over young individuals. The empowerment of parents can occur at the expense of the child, and so practitioners need to ensure that this danger is averted. Additionally, social workers should be aware that in extending the network of caregivers, they can misuse FGCs to enable the state to wash its hands of troubled and troubling children during expenditure cuts.

Black children placed in care in Britain without due consideration of their heritage portray similar stories. Here is a quote from a young black person I interviewed:

> I was adopted by a white family when I was very young. I never knew anything about my real family until I'd left home. But what makes me upset now looking back is that my white family never talked about the fact that I was different – my black skin, my frizzy hair. Often it felt like I didn't exist. Just this other kid they had made up and I fitted into his shoes. It made my life difficult and lonely. I had to leave or I would have gone mad.

This treatment violates the black child's rights to his or her cultural heritage, which is endorsed by both the 1989 Children Act and the UN Convention on the Rights of the Child. Social workers could do more to support the realization of these rights through practice. Black people in Britain have rejected colourblind constructions of their situation and demanded changes in mainstream services to reflect this. They have insisted that black children are best cared for by black families who understand the racist nature of society and can teach black children how to survive its ravages (Small, 1984; Maxime, 1986). Others, such as Graham (2002) and John-Baptiste (2002), have built on the experiences of African-Americans (Asante, 1987) in asserting their own culture to argue that Africentred approaches to social work are more likely to provide appropriate services for black children of African origins and their families.

Each of these models – First Nations, Maori and Africentric – has been inspired to repair and resist further damage to its respective traditional culture and way of life by practitioners inflicting hegemonic technologies of control in family-based work. As mechanisms of survival, strategies endorsing their traditions have played key roles in reclaiming past heritages. Those defending traditional ways of life have had to endure what I call the 'ossification of culture' (Dominelli, 2000) – that is, the treatment of their heritage as if it were fixed in time and space. It seems that in relations of domination, only the privileged have the prerogative of experiencing and defining their culture as a living, changing entity. For those who are oppressed, interactional, dynamic growth in cultural traditions to take account of interactions with other peoples and cultures has been legislated out of living reality. Crucially, Canadian courts have perpetuated this condition. In the *Delgamuukw* v. *Queen* case, the culture of First Nations peoples was frozen at the moment of the European conquest (see Cassidy, 1992). Those protecting traditional values and norms in the hostile environment of hegemonic discourses are drawn into defensive strategies that reaffirm their heritage on these terms rather than setting their own. Social workers continue the 'ossification of culture' when they treat it as a fixed entity that is not developed over time through encounters with others.

The social work models formed through resistance to traditional practice described above are different from each other while having two threads in common. One is their emphasis on the extended family as a system of support for children in need. The other is gaining strength from rooting families in their cultural communities and, by this association, contributing to their further development. In these models a community's concern for children is vital in safeguarding their well-being. These approaches are in sharp contrast to the realities of the lost links between individuals, families and communities evident in the industrialized West (Wilmot and Young, 1968), a separation endorsed by the ideologies of possessive individualism (MacPherson, 1962), materialism and neo-liberalism (Brooks, 1996).

The case study below portrays the Gitxsan people's attempt to resist mainstream practice and provide more holistic, community-oriented interventions that both draw upon and develop traditional culture.

Case study

Ms G., a First Nations (Gitxsan) woman in British Columbia, engaged in substance abuse when pregnant. Arguments between her and child protection workers representing the state centred on the rights of the foetus to develop without harm in Ms G.'s womb. The practitioners claimed that the foetus' rights to protection superseded those of the mother to lead her life as she chose, so Ms G. was defined as an inadequate mother, incapable of looking after her unborn child. The 'child' was apprehended (taken into care) whilst still in the womb and Ms G. was compelled to undergo treatment for her addictions during the pregnancy. (Rutman et al., 2000)

Throughout this saga, social workers have pitted the rights of the child against those of the mother by conceptualizing them as in opposition or as antagonistic to each other. This approach is reinforced by the adversarial legal system in which Ms G. was judged. The case eventually reached the Supreme Court of Canada, which by majority decision did not uphold the lower courts' view that a foetus had rights prior to birth and referred this question back to the legislature for further deliberation.

Ms G.'s situation exemplifies the power of statutory social workers to intervene in ways that disempower mothers and uproot them from the supports that can be offered by their communities. In labelling the mother as inadequate and formulating her position in adversarial terms, both mainstream practitioners and the legal processes failed to connect her to her community, the Gitxsan people. Practitioners' individualized analysis and focus on the ailing mother closed alternative options for dealing with her situation and resulted in their being unable to utilize the resources of the Gitxsan people to explore how to safeguard the well-being of both mother and ensuing child in less destructive ways.

Approaching her circumstances according to different principles would require both social workers and the courts to ask why Ms G. is abusing substances rather than simply taking it as given, and support her to address the causes of her addictions as well as respond to symptoms. This would mean taking seriously the woman's rights as a woman alongside concern about the foetus. Sadly, traditional social work practice does not relate to women in their own right, but to their roles as mothers or carers of others. The treatment of

Ms G. in her mothering capacity is not exceptional in framing the interests of mother and child as antagonistic (Dominelli, 2002b).

Emphasizing healing, resiliency and support from other members of the community, the Gitxsan people have formed the Gitxsan Child and Family Services to link child welfare and protection considerations to traditional extended families and community support networks based on clan and house systems (Lundquist and Jackson, 2000). These seek to reconcile the different interests of those involved in any situation and help individuals and families who have difficulties through more holistic approaches that are consistent with the Gitxsan culture and worldview (Lundquist and Jackson, 2000) of valuing both mother and child as community members. In Ms G.'s case, substance misuse would be reconceptualized as a way of dealing with the psychological damage of the appalling treatment of First Nations boys and girls in the Indian residential schools (Haig-Brown, 1988). Repairing this harm in adult men and women would be addressed while meeting the needs of the foetus.

The resolution of Ms G.'s and similar situations would not be easy. The high numbers of mothers and fathers involved in substance misuse would test the Gitxsan community's limited financial resources for responding to the needs of its peoples. Their practitioners have to intervene on several levels. To address the financial problems, Gitxsan social workers are asking the Canadian government to change the funding formulas to provide financing for all Gitsxan children, not only those in care. If they are successful, they can develop good preventative services for all children rather than just those 'at risk'. This endeavour aims to change mainstream policies and practice, so it will require considerable skills in advocacy and lobbying and may take some time to realize. At the same time, First Nations practitioners are providing personal support such as counselling, healing circles and other appropriate services alongside responding to the challenge of securing structural change to meet the immediate needs of individuals and families in crises.

Some initiatives for improving their situations are not resource-intensive and will not require external financing. Changes under Gitxsan control can be implemented more readily, for example forming community partnerships. These can underpin changes that address short-term needs without losing sight of longer-term ones and form part of their holistic approach to social problems. The Gitxsan's more holistic community-oriented approach to children in need is exemplified in their welcome of a sick child and its parents after a lengthy stay in hospital. One of their aims is visibly to convey the message that caring for the child will not be an isolated and lonely act conducted in the privacy of the family home. To implement this ambition, Gitxsan community leaders organized a potlatch supper to receive the child and family back into their midst and invited all members of the community to attend. Through this action, both community links and intergenerational solidarity were (re)affirmed.

One participant in the welcoming ceremony summed up its purpose when he said:

> We'll go because this is part of building the family structure by showing the grandparents and parents that they are a part of a community and a family and they have an important place within that structure. We went . . . it was good to see the community rally around this family. (Lundquist and Jackson, 2000, p. 125)

This case also illustrates how cultures change and adapt to meet conditions of today whilst drawing on cultural knowledge, traditions and experiences of the past.

One lesson from these overseas examples that has relevance for the process of reinvigorating deprived communities in Britain and in Western countries elsewhere is that of seeing children as everyone's responsibility and not just that of their biological parents and families. Another highlights the significance of having professionals work closely and in partnership with the families of the children who have been brought to their attention. But, as Jackson and Nixon (1999) argue with regards to the use of Family Group Conferences in England, social workers may find parental challenges to their authority difficult to accept and have to work on developing skills in sharing power with those affected by their decisions before they embark on working in partnership with them.

Conclusions

Children are an important part of the web of interdependent relationships across generations. Adults may care for children today, but these children will care for older adults under appropriate conditions in the future. Recognition of this interdependence can become the basis for building intergenerational solidarity and challenging the dependent construction of childhood which deprives children of their rights as autonomous beings, and for ensuring that their voices are heard.

Child welfare professionals can add to the disenfranchisement of children by responding to them within a dependency paradigm. Adultist power relations play a large role in creating childhood as a dependent status. This construction denies children's voices and contributes to their abuse and exploitation. Developing child-centred forms of practice requires social workers to rethink childhood in ways that empower children and change the structural contexts within which they live as well as responding to their individual needs. This can be done by reconceptualizing children as a community responsibility which all adults share, ensuring that the Convention on the Rights of the Child is upheld in and through professional practice in the country in which the child lives regardless of citizenship status, and advocating child-friendly policies at local, national and international levels. Being sensitive to children's cultural heritage and the needs associated with this becomes part of the process of asserting children's position as active citizens.

SOCIAL WORK INTERVENTIONS WITH OLDER PEOPLE

5

Introduction

Adult men and women have few social services that are directed specifically to meeting their needs. This situation improves to some extent once they reach old age. However, social work with older British people has traditionally been considered a 'Cinderella' area of practice. It has been cast as low-status work to be carried out by unqualified social workers able to respond to the simple needs of elders for companionship and undertake practical tasks on their behalf (Barclay, 1982). Even the British Medical Association (BMA) decried geriatric medicine as 'a second-rate specialty, looking after third-rate patients in fourth-rate facilities' (BMA, 1986, p. 4). Small wonder, then, that white consultants have generally ignored the needs of older people and, in an interesting twist which exposes racist practices in the hospital hierarchy, left black doctors and nurses to minister to their needs (Rhone, 2001).

The decline in the status of older people in the West began in the nineteenth century (Cowgill and Holmes, 1972). Predicated on the idea that ageing is a biological process of deterioration, it carries the assumption that older people are a burden. Casting older people in these terms establishes a 'truth' that seems neutral and above power (Foucault, 1991). By conducting discourses within these parameters, it becomes easier for professionals to control what happens to older people who come into their ambit and define the conditions that impact upon those who do not. Discourses have this effect because they establish the reasons for doing things in a particular way and legitimate certain procedures for doing so (Foucault, 1991).

The lowered status of this aspect of identity can be considered part of ageism. Ageism is the oppression of people on the basis of age. For older people, ageism focuses on a body that is deemed to have outlived its sell-by date. Many older people have internalized ageist stereotypes and reproduce these in their own discourses. Ageist assumptions present older people as a homogeneous group and configure them as a weight that has to be borne by the work of younger people. In this worldview, older people are presented as dependent, incapacitated and incapable (Scrutton, 1989). Elders are in danger of losing their citizenship rights, among others, as well as their dignity as a result of ageism.

Ageist attitudes ignore the interdependence and solidarity that exist between people, young and old, and do not acknowledge the burdens that older people have borne for younger people in the past by seeing them through infancy, childhood and into adult-hood. As such, ageism underpins the loss of intergenerational solidarity and repricocity. Moreover, the linking of adulthood and independence with being involved in waged labour exacerbates ageist views of older people who have ceased or never had paid work (Phillipson, 1982). Constructing older people as not having a useful role in society because physical impairments limit their involvement in waged labour also draws on disablist stereotypes about the types of people that comprise society and is effective in promoting disablist discourses of exclusion. These discourses are crucial in reinforcing socially constructed images of older people as burdens who take from society without contributing to it and in medicalizing their condition. Thus, ageist attitudes contribute to the medicalization of old age and its unhelpful approaches to older people (Phillipson, 1998).

Negative images of older people are central to the medicalization of old age. These enable younger people to see decline due to ageing as inevitable natural processes that cannot be altered. They do not associate unflattering views of old age with the current (re)structuring of intergenerational relations and the lack of social resources for older people. The social exclusion of older people produces ageist constructions of old age and configures social relations to affirm these.

Challenges to dominant discourses on age arise from many quarters. Feminists have opposed negative configurations of age-ing and redefined it as a time of opportunities for further growth and development (Friedan, 1993). Black people have also treated

old age as a period when both men and women continue to contribute to the well-being of others (Patel, 1990). Older people are
aware of being defined as dependent burdens and have challenged
ageist constructions of their lives (Friedan, 1993). On the individual
level, many have refused services to demonstrate their capacity to
look after themselves without assistance and remain independent
(Scrutton, 1989). Large numbers of older people are well and do
not have health or other problems requiring social work intervention. In Britain, Higgins (1989) estimated that only 5 per cent of
older people come to the attention of social services. In Pittaway's
(1995) study of older Canadians, 17.6 per cent had not required
social services intervention.

Negative portrayals of older people are being challenged by ageing movie stars and pop icons who use what Foucault (1991) calls
the 'technologies of the self' to present themselves as retaining
their youth and vigour. These are evident in the practices of body
care exercised by older people who seek to defray the ravages of
time on ageing bodies through facelifts and other cosmetic procedures to keep the body beautiful. In subjecting themselves to
these measures, older people hope to remain encompassed within
discourses of youth. These attempts to redefine old age rely on the
advantages of class, that is, having extra finances to break with
part of the definition. At the same time, those engaging in these
practices reproduce the negative images they decry because they
collude with the opinion that older people are decrepit, even though
the awful day when they themselves will fit this description has
been successfully pushed into the future. They are challenging the
applicability of the label to them at this point in time rather than its
overall legitimacy. In participating in these activities, they reaffirm
youthism or discourses that value youth by disparaging old age.

The negative image of the older person as dependent and in
need of care portrays an ageist construction that treats every older
person the same by ignoring the specific needs of older individuals
and the contribution that older people individually and as a group
have made and continue to make to society. At the individual level,
older people who may need help in some areas of their lives are
likely to have skills and strengths in others, for example living in
poverty but undertaking voluntary work. Social workers should not
lose sight of this potential when intervening with people, whether
or not they are care managers utilizing assessment schedules.

Variations in how elders are depicted have not abolished ageist
constructions that portray old age as a time of social, physical and
mental decline. Part of the reason for this is that negative images of

old age have been and are being reproduced in many sites of social interaction. The media play a crucial role in (re)constituting unfavourable images of older people, although sometimes they support the view that elders are 'deserving' members of society and insist upon the appropriateness of younger people providing care and resources for them. Aside from variability in individual physical attributes, social resources and economic security, no one person's experience of old age mirrors that of another, so it is important not to construct older people as a homogeneous group (Pittaway, 1995). Ageing is further complicated by social divisions such as gender, 'race', class, disability, mental health and sexual orientation. The multiple dimensions which constitute the experience of growing old create a diversity of practices amongst older people's expression of their subjectivity.

Social workers replicate ageist representations of elders in and through practice. The images popularized through their interventions may not be those that older people themselves seek to establish. This happens if social workers request details of their nearest relatives when older people ask for help to remain in their own homes. Here is what an older woman told me when reflecting upon her treatment by social workers:

> When she [the social worker] came to do an assessment, she kept saying she'd have to go see my daughter-in-law and see what help she could offer. She took no notice of me saying she lives twenty miles away and has two little kiddies to look after. I thought it was a bit much really. She [daughter-in-law] is very good and helps whenever she can. If it were just a matter of getting her to help, I wouldn't have to go through a social worker. I'd just pick up the phone.

There is an element of arrogance in the social worker's handling of this situation. She does not listen to the woman, who is also questioning the practitioner's ageist construction of her. The social worker acts as if the problem were simply one of poor intergenerational communication rather than one of not enough caring resources for the daughter-in-law to cover the needs of the older woman and her own children.

Practitioners erroneously focus on the degree of unity of purpose and homogeneity amongst elders despite the diversity in their situations and range of social divisions found amongst them. This diversity is exploited during periods of public expenditure cuts by politicians who want to see the different fragments within the older people's grouping fight one another for the limited monies that are available. The politics of ageing are complex and require multilayered responses if the needs of a highly differentiated and varied group are to be adequately met.

Negative images of old age are not universal. In some societies, the strengths of older people are celebrated. Elders are revered by First Nations peoples in Canada as the holders of the wisdom and cultural traditions of the band to which they belong. Young people learn at their feet and are encouraged to enter into dialogue with them to find out for themselves the meanings of life, its mysteries and relationships between the person and society, the social world and the natural world, and between different groups of peoples, including those not in their particular band (Maracle, 1993; Bruyere, 2001).

In this chapter, I examine recent developments in contemporary constructions of old age, including the advent of community care for elders. I highlight both promising features and disadvantages in the present set-up. I also consider alternative ways of caring for older people by drawing on the experiences of countries which have traditions of promoting intergenerational solidarities, and ask the extent to which such approaches can be transplanted to the UK.

Mobilizing to challenge negative images of older people

Older people hold multiple dimensions to their identity and may not wish to highlight that concerned with ageing all the time. They may wish to assert their right to define for themselves which particular aspect of their identity they consider important at any given point in time and to which purposes they intend to harness their energies. They may exercise resistance to the way others define them in multiple arenas, in one or none, depending on their specific circumstances. Moreover, they have the power to alter their stance over time. Older people's resistance to negative social constructions of their situation are evident in the private domain of the home and the interpersonal relationships that occur within it, as well as those in the public sphere that involve their participation in social organizations of various types.

In Western societies, older people are considered free to organize themselves in pursuit of their objectives and mobilize the resources necessary for doing so. These activities are expected to take place in civil society and move from there to impact on the state and the policies it formulates. By organizing, older people exert their capacity to accept or reject their position as either subjects or objects of particular power relations. By destabilizing through their actions those terms that depict old age as a negative existence, elders show that words can acquire multiple significations and meanings and demonstrate that they can voice their own subjectivities.

Challenging cultural practices involves making claims about knowledge and contesting versions that are accepted as 'truth' (Foucault, 1979a). When positing counter- or alternative views of the world, this act provides a site of resistance. Resistance to established knowledge, including professional versions of the truth about older people, was achieved by elders making counter-claims based on their own experiences of old age.

Older people have been able to mobilize around identity, engage in collective action to question prevailing definitions of themselves as a group and demonstrate their capacity to act on their own behalf. Negative depictions of old age have been used positively by older people to advance their social position, even if these have ended up reinforcing off-putting images of them. Older people have also challenged accepted stereotypes of their status by selectively highlighting certain of its aspects in support of changes in policies that would enable them to retain financial independence. The securing of public pensions for older people in the United States exemplifies one such struggle.

In the 1930s, the Townsendites in America successfully argued for a state-assured income for older people on the grounds that they were a deserving category who had contributed to society in their younger years (Dominelli, 1991b; Pratt, 1993). The Townsendites subscribed to the medical model of ageing and used this understanding to get Medicaid provisions approved by the American government (Pratt, 1993). Thus, they drew upon negative images of old age and turned them to their advantage in advocating for crucial reforms in the way they were treated.

At other times, unflattering images of older people have been challenged in their entirety. In the 1970s, Maggie Kuhn rejected the idea of old age as a negative, unproductive period in an individual's life and organized older Americans to do something about it together (Kuhn, 1991). They formed part of a 'new' social movement of older people who reformulated identity politics to promote positive constructions of who they were. Members of the group that was created, known as the Gray Panthers, began to challenge ageism as a form of discrimination against older people and worked for the abolition of a mandatory retirement age through legislative changes to this effect (Doress and Siegal, 1987). In following their programme of action, the Gray Panthers became actively involved in reinterpreting the reality of old age and reshaping knowledge of it.

In challenging accepted boundaries around the status of the 'older person', collective actions initiated by the Gray Panthers raised the question about the age at which people become 'old'. Their questioning of accepted definitions unleashed a debate that highlighted the arbitrary nature of the distinctions that had been drawn in this regard and produced different understandings about the 'truths' associated with old age. Ultimately, such endeavours have exposed that the lay public, older people, policymakers, practitioners and academics employ varying definitions of old age. Some have proposed the defining age as 50, others 55 (Pittaway, 1995). Legal definitions based on mandatory retirement ages, meanwhile, have varied from 60 to 65 to 70. The cut-off has traditionally been gendered, with retirement forced upon women at a younger age than men.

In challenging definitions of old age based on biology, members of the Gray Panthers argued that what people can do should determine when they 'age'. The living biography of Dr Katherine Kendall, Honorary President of the IASSW, who is fully active in that organization and wrote her latest, well-researched book (Kendall, 2002) within a year at the age of 91, lends empirical support to Kuhn's view. There is no predetermined outcome to the ageing process. Ironically, by shifting the definition of old age away from an ageing process and onto retirement from waged work that is tied into an arbitrarily set chronological age, its biological basis is reaffirmed.

Linking definitions of retirement to waged work has rendered women's needs as older people invisible. The gaps that have been left by women's lower earnings potential in their waged working years are particularly evident in discourses about pensions and women's low incomes in old age. Ageist assumptions have also negated the contribution to the economy made by older women's unpaid work in the home. These contributions are substantial. Though not calculated on the basis of age, the Canadian government valued the contribution of women's domestic labour to the economy as equivalent to that of the manufacturing sector (Status of Women, 2001).

In creating their platform at the level of identity, the Gray Panthers engaged in redefining cultural practices and targeting civil society rather than either the state or the economy. Civil society occupies the terrain of 'the social', or the space where cultural practices are defined, contested and redefined. Organizations representing civil society link up with people's daily life routines and, in doing so, influence their thought processes, taken-for-granted assumptions and the choices they make.

By focusing on grassroots organization, emphasizing their role as active contributors to the social order and insisting on being treated within the bounds of social justice and fairness, the Gray Panthers established a different discourse about their situation. Their actions conveyed important messages about intergenerational relationships and manifestations of agency in a context that constituted older people as passive objects. These elders were capable of forming relationships with younger people while simultaneously affirming positive images of elders. They influenced intergenerational relations by linking up with younger people through a range of activities that enabled them to work together. These endeavours roused young people from their slumbers to make connections across age divides (Doress and Siegal, 1987).

The Gray Panthers' initiatives drew upon group solidarity based on age to configure their members as part of a collective struggle against domination constructed along age lines. By organizing, they tackled issues of personal insecurity, social worthlessness and financial penury. In gaining their voice as older people, they also undermined the stigma associated with old age as a marginal and unproductive period in life. Through these activities, the Gray Panthers highlighted older people's ability to act with purpose. Further, by displaying their militancy, ageing activists defined ageism rather than old age as the problem that society has to address.

However, older people's adoption of more positive and active images can be utilized to generate intergenerational conflict by pitting their interests against those of younger people, and fray to breaking point the threads of intergenerational solidarities (Walker, 1990). In recent discourses the media have played a pivotal role in (re)configuring intergenerational debates in oppositional terms. This has involved drawing upon ageist dynamics which play the interests of one age group against the other in an oppositional dyad that values youth at the expense of old age, a form of oppression I call *youthism*. Youthism takes place within the context of competing for both scarce resources and power to cast older people as unworthy winners and younger ones as undeserving losers.

Youthist (re)configurations of social relations across the generations have produced a new set of discourses. These disparage old age and are aimed at undermining the status of older people as 'deserving' of care and attention. In attacking older people's definitions of their realities, these new youthist discourses pit the needs of elders against those of younger people and treat them as antagonistic. For example, youth unemployment is attributed to older people's refusal to retire; housing shortages on their longevity and desire to remain living in their own homes. The media have advanced youthist discourses by depicting elders as 'greedy' for wanting to hang on to their jobs when poor pension provisions compel them to work longer than they would like and the economy is incapable of providing employment for all who want or need waged work. The media have also redefined them as 'wealthy' because they own their homes. Ironically, one reason older people give for wishing to retain possession of their houses rather than selling these to purchase care for themselves is to leave it to their children, an act which indicates that a show of solidarity across generations remains important (Dominelli, 2002b). Yet the media recast these acts as irresponsible and label older people 'voracious' for demanding more than their fair share of social resources if they ask for assistance from the public purse.

These representations of older people highlight fiscal concerns (Estes, 1989) and contribute to a declining consensus around older people as a 'deserving' group of deprived individuals (Walker, 1990). In the ensuing discourses, family members, especially adult women, are presented as failing older members by not responding to their needs. By framing responsibility for elder care as an intergenerational conflict, the issue is once more relegated to the private realm – a feature that is exploited by the current articulation of community care under conditions of inadequate funding. Discourses that focus on intergenerational conflict enable the state to avoid taking responsibility for providing services for the care of older people on a universal citizenship basis. Governments under tight public expenditure regimes endorse this framing of the matter because it shifts attention onto the family as the institution that is failing to cater for older people's welfare.

Walker (1990) argues that the declining consensus around older people as a deprived group is undermining their status as a deserving one. This reconfiguration of their status becomes a rationing device, and, hence, an instrument of governmentality. Social workers can play a major role in either affirming or countering these discourses. By challenging ageist constructions of older people, practitioners could affirm definitions of identity based on intergenerational solidarity and identify the positive contributions that older people make to society, in particular their contributions to child care. Turning social workers into advocates for older people, however, requires changes in current practice.

Elders' demands for more citizenship-oriented responses to their needs focus on their rights and entitlements rather than being treated as charity cases. This trend is likely to increase with the emergence of the 'baby boomers' as older people (Cork, 1998). As many in this grouping are well educated and have more money at their disposal than the current generation, their demographic composition and ideological predisposition are likely to impact upon both social policies and practice aimed at older people. In contrast to most analyses of older people, which emphasize their demographic features and assumed passivity while ignoring their ideological dimensions and agency, older people are in fact becoming an electorally active constituency, so politicians will have to heed their aspirations rather than take their support for granted.

Constructing the older person in social work practice

Social constructions of older people have a number of contradictory dimensions. One is that of identifying who constitutes an older person. If adulthood is the transition between adolescence and old age, at what point does old age start and when does it end? What further distinctions can/should one draw? Terms like the 'old older person', or even the 'very old person', fudge the inadequacy of using chronological age as a marker of this status. But this terminology is readily apparent in the lexicon of practitioners working with older people.

Adulthood is the period in which a human being reaches the peak of his or her powers. For social workers, identity in old age is fixed as a period in which a person has lost his or her physical prowess and social roles. This conceptualization of elders sets the scene for ageist views of old age as a period of physical decline, dependency and vulnerability, a disablist view of reality often challenged by older people (Priestley, 1999). Ageist constructions linked to the loss of one's place in the labour market (Phillipson, 1982) are likely to intensify with increasing early retirements and withdrawals of people from waged work as a result of economic restructuring and downsizing in a wide range of enterprises.

Class is an important dimension of the experience of old age (Phillipson, 1982; Scrutton, 1989). Middle-class and wealthy older people demonstrate that those with more resources at their disposal have a more privileged and less humiliating old age. They can purchase the personal social services and physical adaptations they need without undergoing demeaning means-testing or making do with inadequate services because cash-starved local authorities cannot supply those required.

The specific needs of ethnic elders in Britain have been ignored. Dietary requirements, religion, language, cultural practices, kinship networks and family forms have not been appreciated and specifically considered. Their small numbers have reinforced this neglect. Only a limited range of services are available to and accessed by older people from ethnic minorities (Patel, 1990). Black elders are also more likely to be poor and have less access to pensions and other contributory benefits (Blakemore and Bonecham, 1994).

Cross-cultural communication is important in working with ethnic elders. Different cultural practices may be significant in cross-cultural communication. For example, knowing that Chinese elders will not look people straight in the eye and orthodox Jewish women are not allowed to look at men (Pittaway, 1995, p. 55) will help social workers not to misinterpret their actions by judging them according to their own values. This should not be taken to mean that racist practices or institutional racism can be ignored by focusing on interpersonal relationships. It is important not to essentialize the relevant culture or treat each individual as part of a homogeneous whole in each of these illustrations. People's views of their own culture are affected by interactions with the dominant one. They can change or reaffirm it through these encounters. Cultures are interactional, not static entities.

For women, who constitute the bulk of elderly populations in Western societies, gender is a further complicating factor. If women have spent considerable periods outside the workforce, their position regarding income and social security rights in old age is worsened. The growing parity in labour market participation rates between men and women is not changing this situation because women continue to earn less than men, even in similar jobs. Moreover, women have more fragmented and intermittent work careers, particularly during child-bearing years. These inequalities in waged work are reflected in women's entitlements to benefits, especially contributory pensions later on. Women with poor contribution records and lower rates of pay than men will receive smaller pensions and live in greater poverty during old age as a result. Yet the gendered nature of social security provisions based on the insurance principle is rarely commented upon (Pascall, 1986; Fraser, 1989; Dominelli, 1991b).

Social workers play key roles in constructing and maintaining particular images of older people. Since they are enabled only to provide services to vulnerable elders, vulnerability becomes a crucial aspect in constructing the older client. Vulnerability implies incapacity to care for oneself or a dependency on others, and is used to configure older people as fragile or disabled beings needing assistance. Vulnerability coupled with disability encompasses the key image that social workers utilize to encourage close female relatives to provide care for older people. Resource limitations compound this portrayal of older people. The only older people who are eligible for public services are those who are really frail, without financial resources and other assets or people willing to care for them.

Such images encourage practice that treats older people as less than adults, that is, they are infantilized and denied autonomy. This disempowers them by reducing or taking away their right to make their own decisions. To avoid reproducing these oppressive relations, social workers need to question discursive practices rooted in daily routines and the subjectivities they take for granted, including their own. This critical questioning can destabilize accepted knowledge or what passes as 'practice wisdoms' and create new forms of knowledge that are based on the experiences of oppressed peoples. With regards to ageism, practitioners have to be reflexive and understand the specificities of age as older clients express them.

That people are living longer has implications for social work practice. One is that demographic changes will increase the numbers of older people who will eventually require assistance with health needs. Another is that older people will be caring for even older people. Older people can be called upon to provide care for grandchildren as younger women of child-bearing age put their energies into the waged labour market. This burden will fall largely on grandmothers caring for grandchildren, extending the base of kincare across a broader cross-section of the population, as black families have done for centuries (hooks, 2000). If resources to support kincare are not adequately funded and planned, however, the caring work done by older carers will become exploited and unsupported (Stogdon, 2000; Richards, 2001).

The problem of exploitation arises regarding the use of low-paid carers or volunteers to assist elders. Some authorities pay volunteers; others do not. These divisions can create tensions between paid and unpaid groups (Pittaway, 1995). Relying largely on volunteers can result in personnel shortages that prevent the office being staffed all the time. Having carers on the books does not guarantee availability or instant responses to requests for assistance, even if help is urgently needed to prevent various forms of abuse (Pittaway, 1995). The difficulties older people encounter in maintaining their independence and realizing their rights emphasize the importance of seeing them as an integral part of the community and a concern of everyone, not just their relatives. With only 13.5 per cent of elders having limited access to their own advocates (Pittaway, 1993), this gap in provision can create problems for elders wishing to realize their rights. Social workers can highlight patterns of uneven access to care and support and help people organize to redress their situation and obtain resources.

The lack of support for carers, despite legislation providing for it, has prompted discourses around the right to give and receive care. These have been initiated to ensure that those providing care for older people are valued and that provisions for them are rights-based and respect their status as citizens (Knijn and Ungerson, 1997).

Social workers also adhere to particular discourses about who should provide care for older people. An important element within these is kincare – the idea that women, particularly daughters and daughters-in-law, should be available as unpaid carers. This stereotype generates gendered relations that reinforce a sexist division of labour. Besides being insensitive to work undertaken by women, it also ignores the significant proportion of carers who are men. About 25 per cent of carers are men who look after their wives (Twigg and Atkin, 1994). Moreover, the assumption that family members can be counted upon for assistance, which determines the context within which social work in Britain is still practised, is not borne out by research, which indicates that family support only covers so much. In one of the few studies investigating levels of family care, Pittaway (1995) reveals that it is reliably available in only 11.3 per cent of cases and available on a limited basis for a further 35.8 per cent. A significant minority – 19 per cent – had no family help forthcoming (Pittaway, 1995, p. 51). Only a few older people or their carers were aware of the range of services that they could draw upon.

Working with older people within a family framework reverses the traditional relations of dependency that epitomize the early stages of the life cycle, in which children rely on parents, to propose instead that adult children parent their parents. Although not usually referred to as a type of kincare, this is what adult child carers provide. Children can feel uncomfortable with this reversal in their relationship. An adult child who had given up her job to care for her father following a stroke said in her interview with me:

I couldn't believe this thin slip of a man was my father. Where had the big, strong athlete of my youth gone? I couldn't bear to bring myself to bathe and wash him like he had me as a child. It seemed so unnatural.

This 'unnatural' relationship marks an important transition in intergenerational relations within the family. This woman had been working in an older people's home for some time, yet this had not prepared her for her new role as its emotional demands were different. As she said:

It's different looking after someone else's father. It's not the same as caring for your own. The relationship is less personal and doesn't pull on the heartstrings in the same way.

This woman claimed society 'was asking too much of her'. The emotional price she was paying was too great. And, in common with other adult carers providing kincare, the fact that she had sacrificed her own waged work and future pension plans remained largely unacknowledged.

Social workers become involved in managing this transition through discursive practices that aim to convince adult children that they can appropriately care for older parents regardless of an individual carer's actual wishes. Practitioners do this by engaging in a mutual dialogue that establishes the 'naturalness' of people being cared for within the family and treating its members as a whole unit without cleavages or fractures. If adult children share their assumptions, the social worker's task is simple. Keeping the range of disagreements that need to be resolved to a minimum may be a key reason why social workers are reluctant to challenge various 'myths' about the family, including the 'naturalness' of women caring for others. The importance of family care is pre-dicated on the view that older people require care from younger people because they are unable to look after themselves (Parker and Lawton, 1994). It picks up on negative images of old age that affirm older people's dependency and vulnerability (Priestley, 1999). Yet many older people do not require such care and find negative images of their condition offensive (Friedan, 1994).

Another ageist assumption is practitioners' belief that the general context of service provision that applies to other clients is also suitable for older people. Little attention has been paid to their specific needs as elders, or the desirability of questioning ageist stereotypes. In talking about the importance of adjusting counselling to the needs of older people Steve Scrutton (1989, p. 9) argues that their needs differ from those of younger people:

> Simple communication with the elderly is often not straightforward. Poor hearing may impair their ability to hold a serious conversation. Their eyesight may restrict opportunities afforded to the counsellor for body-language and other means of non-verbal communication. Their health may be bad, their morale low through loneliness and grief, and their ability to look enthusiastically at the future seriously reduced.

This description may accurately reflect the condition of some older people, but it relies on negative images to construct them as a deserving group and provide a rationale for accessing services that respond to their specific needs. It also propagates unflattering views of older people through practice routines that carry a danger of further medicalizing or biologizing their position. Although identifying the specificity of their needs, this construction of their case reaffirms the negative images it seeks to replace. Social workers have a key role to play in projecting positive images of older people's strengths and capacities alongside being alert to their needs for support.

Professional discourses have been dominated by the picture of downtrodden elders content with receiving an inferior service. This, however, has begun to alter. It has done so because groups of elders have challenged negative depictions of their position; social workers have become increasingly aware of the complex needs and range of problems encountered by older people, including those who have been physically, sexually, emotionally or financially abused by carers and others; and the levels of training amongst staff doing this work have increased. Policies that encourage market-based empowerment by aiming to give older people a choice in the quasi-market of their care, as has happened, for example, for disabled elders accessing direct payments, have also raised the status of this work (Hughes, 1995).

Community care

Community care caught the imagination of all political parties and professionals who supported the de-institutionalization of care or the movement to get older people out of residential care following the Griffiths Report (Griffiths, 1988; Bornat et al., 1997). Saving money was a key determinant of that policy. Another was that of opening the caring arena to the market, subjecting it to market discipline and having it become available as a source of capital accumulation. Community care became the mechanism through which the regulation of the market was imposed on care for older people, thereby introducing capitalist corporate culture into its ways of working (Griffiths, 1988). Initiated under the aegis of the National Health Service and Community Care Act 1990, these sought to remould the role of the state into that of a residual provider, installing quasi-markets and mixed economies to foster competition, contract out services and bring commercial management approaches into public sector management (Le Grand and Bartlett, 1993; Hunter, 1994).

Contractual forms of regulation provide the mechanisms through which the state as purchaser of services controls numerous agents charged with realizing its objectives on the ground. Legalistic contractual measures strengthen the power of the centre to dictate what sub-contracting organizations do and have confidence that contractually agreed targets will be met. This policy is also intended to prevent the inefficient, wasteful use of resources, and curb professional practices that by-pass direct accountability to managers and are unresponsive to consumer needs (Priestley, 1999).

The financial context provided by the market in community care has had the effect of sharpening competitive cost pressures on providers, exacerbating the rationing of services by local authorities and shifting the costs of services to consumers by charging user-fees for services rendered (Mandelstam and Schewr, 1995). It has also facilitated the rise of a commercial ethos within the context of a contract culture (Barker, 1996) in a system previously organized according to professional ethics and values but permeated by its 'Cinderella' status (Dominelli, 1997, 2002a).

The manipulation of policies to accord with the imperatives of market forces, and vice versa, has marked the provision of homes for older people. Policies promoting growth caused a blossoming of the number of homes that private providers built or purchased from the public sector. Expansion continued while the public purse paid the going rate for places, and profits were strong during the mid- to late 1980s. When these funds were capped, however, private providers faced large deficits (Batty, 2002). They demanded more public money to sustain provisions, and when this was not forthcoming, user-fees were introduced and homes closed. These actions placed the burden of privatization on individual older people and their families. Charging user-fees included means-testing that treated the roof over an elder's head as an asset that had to be sold to pay for care. Older people felt humiliated and bitterly resented these moves as they had contributed to national insurance schemes to avoid such predicaments (Dominelli, 1997).

Commodifying social work with older people

Social work with older people has been penetrated extensively by market discipline following the legal imposition of purchaser–provider relations through the CCA 1990 and the organizational restructuring accompanying its implementation. Community care has the specific aim of making the culture of social work more in keeping with commercial practices (Griffiths, 1988).

Community care has presented social workers with new opportunities and some of their greatest challenges. These have involved learning new skills in their roles as case managers, responding to budget-led policy frameworks, addressing disappointed customers and letting go of their desire to provide clients with a holistic service designed for each specific case in favour of acting as co-ordinators of packages of care that are delivered by others. In a full community care scenario, there is no need for a social worker to be involved in direct interventions with clients. As a result of these shifts, the case manager can be anyone because there is no requirement for a worker in this role to be qualified in social work. This change has been seen by some as signalling a decline in the influence of social work in the social care arena.

The development of market-driven community care requires serious examination. Research is necessary to establish the degree to which crucial needs are (un)met and whether client vulnerabilities have been exacerbated by such policies. Given the history of working with older people as the 'Cinderella' part of the profession, traditionally delegated to students and welfare assistants, it is not surprising that this was the area chosen for the new experiment that community care represented in the late 1980s. Any measures which promised to improve its status and the qualifications of those working within it would have been welcomed.

Ageism, sexism, personnel shortages and a demographic profile which suggests that rising numbers of older people would financially test the state's care system to the utmost in the near future have contributed to community care rather than residential care being the sought-after solution for elder care. However, the policy and attitudes that underpin community care continue to build on existing inadequacies in resourcing services for older people (Barclay, 1982). By rooting care for older people in their families and communities, policymakers hoped that (women) carers would fill the gap between what the state would pay for and what older people need. They assumed that care in the community would be cheaper than institutional care provided by the state because they expected women to furnish much of the necessary care gratis (Bonny, 1984).

This strategy is not proceeding according to plan. Other important demographic trends, including those that indicate that women are going into paid employment in increasing numbers, even if it is in part-time, poorly remunerated work, have produced a shortage of personnel in family-based or domestic caring. Meeting the demands of waged occupations cuts into the time, energy and resources that women can devote to unpaid caring duties. Labour mobility has further complicated matters, and women who are able and willing to care for ageing relatives do not necessarily live near them. Women have traditionally been the main providers of unpaid care for children and dependent older relatives, but it can no longer be assumed that they will shoulder this burden in future. Yet entering waged employment will not procure the resources necessary for women to purchase their own care in old age. They are paid too little. Of those paid the minimum wage (£4.50 per hour as of 1 October 2003), 70 per cent are women (Toynbee, 2002). Though a topic rarely making headlines, earnings derived from low-paid work are unlikely to provide adequate pensions or resources for buying the services women need in retirement.

Elder abuse

Social workers' assumptions about the family providing a safe environment in which caring work can be carried out has meant that elder abuse has only recently been acknowledged as a problem (Pritchard, 1992; Biggs, 1995). Elder abuse is the perpetration of violence against older people. It reflects the devaluing of age and the treating of older people as objects for other people's purposes. There are a number of different types of violence perpetrated against older people, including financial, physical, sexual and emotional abuse. Each form of abuse is supported by a particular construction of abusive social relations. Pittaway (1995) found that abuse and neglect were experienced by a significant number of elders. Physical abuse had been experienced by 28.6 per cent of her sample. Material abuse was evident in 26.6 per cent and neglect in 12.1 per cent (Pittaway, 1995, p. 55).

Violence against elders reflects the broader social acceptance of violence as a dispute-solving mechanism, and endorses a power-hungry response to conflict and disagreements in the broader society. Attacks on older people by youths indicate a lack of respect for age, and amongst other things expose the fragmentation of intergenerational solidarity. The gap between the institutional symbols of solidarity across generations and routines in everyday life is signified by signs on buses, trains and the underground that reserve seats for older people and personal behaviour that leaves them standing while youths occupy the seats. At the same time, these signs contrast with older people's perceptions of themselves by reinforcing negative stereotypes depicting them as frail and vulnerable.

Intrafamilial abuse involves people who know each other taking advantage of and abusing their positions of trust. It is displayed across a range of behaviours and includes sexual, physical, emotional and financial abuse. Relatives and carers who financially abuse older people engage in practices that can range from directly stealing their money to claiming a share of the older person's residence when it is sold. The motives behind financial abuse do not necessarily reflect financial need on the part of the abuser. In Pittaway's (1995) study, 43.5 per cent of abusers were financially independent of the older person, while 29.4 per cent were partially financially dependent on them. Sadly, many people do not acknowledge the abuse of older people by members of their families. Older people are afraid of their abusers and so will not report them (Pittaway, 1995). Holding power over others and keeping the abuse secret are potent weapons in the arsenal of the abuser (Biggs, 1993).

Not having money, especially in an urbanized and individualized society that has increased the need for financial resources to pay everyday bills, makes older people feel dependent and unwilling to accept offers of help from relatives (Pittaway, 1995) or feel content in residential care (Summerskill, 2002). Income hardship is another form of abuse perpetrated upon older people by an indifferent society that has neglected to mend fractured intergenerational bonds. As such, it constitutes a form of institutional abuse and can assume a variety of guises. Poverty is a key one, as it prevents older people from independently accessing the services they need. Leaving older people dependent on relatives without recourse to other social resources can be reconfigured as societal abuse of older people because being denied access to material forms of social solidarity becomes a form of social exclusion and a denial of citizenship. Other forms of abuse that reinforce this theme include giving older people little scope for making routine decisions. Examples of such treatment are: denying elders' sexuality; telling elders what to wear; refusing to respect their privacy; arranging physical surroundings to suit institutional priorities; preventing social interaction with others; belittling older people in subtle ways; undermining their confidence; and disparaging other family members.

Other forms of abuse deny older people the right to respond to bodily needs. Pittaway (1995) cites a case of a man being refused the use of the toilet when he had a prostrate problem. Treating people as instruments that function according to external command embeds people in abusive relationships. Alongside cultural ageism, this behaviour draws upon institutional and personal ageism and disablism. Community care policies and practice, by setting performance indicators with specified guidance on how and within what limits particular tasks must be completed by workers, contribute to institutional abuse if these guidelines disregard actual need, restrict the type of resources provided and the amount of time that a social worker can spend with each individual. In addition, interprofessional rivalries create abusive environments for older people when their concerns can be ignored or not taken seriously and responded to appropriately. Inadequate inter-agency communications complicate such problems (Bergeron, 1999).

Pittaway (1995) describes institutional abuse applying to First Nations elders by relating how First Nations youths in Indian residential schools were taught to disparage older First Nations people for adhering to their customary habits and language. Behavioural reinforcements ensured compliance; transgressions were severely punished. These practices created a lack of respect for elders in cultures that had revered elders for their wisdom and had carried band traditions across generations from time immemorial (Maracle, 1993, 2002). The abuse of children in Indian residential schools broke intergenerational bonds. In this, colonial practices mirror the intergenerational disrespect of disaffected urban youth.

Elder abuse has not reached the heights of moral panic attained by child abuse, but is becoming recognized as an issue that merits serious attention. British social workers' capacity to intervene in elder abuse is more limited than in child abuse as they do not have a similar range of legislative powers at their disposal. Legislative changes necessary to move practice with abused elders in the direction of child protection may be enacted in the future. Given critiques of child protection services, however, I am sceptical whether this way forward will safeguard elders' well-being. One concern I have is that in defining older people as vulnerable and dependent on others for their welfare, such a legal remit would intensify their infantilization and loss of autonomous rights.

Insecurity and loss in older people's lives

Older people have a number of different kinds of insecurity and losses to address. Some of these are associated with changing roles and increasingly complex transitions. These may be engendered through loss of status at work and in their community; financial insecurities; and emotional traumas. Shifting from being a parent to a grandparent entails both losses and gains. Older people who have looked forward to a period free of child care responsibilities may suddenly be called upon to rethink their plans. Having lost their parental role, grandparents may acquire another one with regards to their children's children and become involved in parenting their grandchildren, often assuming complete responsibility for their care.

Undertaking a new parental role can be particularly difficult in war-torn areas or when grandchildren have been orphaned through HIV/AIDS (Simpson, 2002). In these circumstances, older people as grandparents are required to adopt new roles just as they have relinquished old ones, and deal with a transition other than that anticipated. At the personal level, the loss of their own children may be extremely traumatic and they may need support to handle the grief of surviving those they meant to follow them into an afterlife. Dealing with the grief of grandchildren and enforcing kincare for siblings can be difficult. Social workers have an important role in ensuring that, where necessary, the transition from grandparent to parent is successful, and in assisting those concerned in the grieving process. Practitioners can promote the development of child care facilities that involve local communities in looking after these children so that the burden does not fall exclusively on grandparents, usually grandmothers.

Another form of loss can be linked to the transition from paid worker to retired one. The loss of status associated with paid employment is particularly relevant to men whose lives have revolved around their jobs. This experience becomes more problematic if it is accompanied by reduced financial prospects. With the loss of paid employment comes further loss – being deprived of social networks and friendships that have given the older person meaning, especially if these have drawn upon contact with workmates. These networks can be hard to sustain over time, and departure from a job and known routines can lead to isolation and loneliness. Depression can attend these feelings. Older people can develop new relationships through leisure activities in which they now have time to participate, but taking part in these will require money to facilitate and sustain them, and many older people will not be able to afford them.

For those with money, retirement can be an opportunity for growth and change as the drudgery of going to work every day is eliminated. Many older men regret this loss, however, and do not see retirement as progress. Low income, lack of leisure facilities and reduced opportunities to enter social relationships that require financial outlays lower the attraction of incorporating options for growth in their daily routines. Society has the responsibility of creating alternative ways of valuing people and supporting them financially once they have left paid employment. The majority of older women continue working in the home whether or not they have left paid jobs, and so the activities required for them to lead full and active lives will be different from men's. Social workers can articulate these needs and assist in the processes of defining forms of active citizenship that transcend benefit entitlements accrued through waged labour.

The departure of valued friends and spouses through death is another loss that older people have to deal with. Their going can be emotionally very difficult as they will miss their companionship and involvement in the activities that they have shared. It can also remind them of their own mortality, and they may be poorly prepared for this. Their reactions should not be taken as the basis for continued isolation or making decisions that cut the older person off from other networks of friendship and companionship that they have or can develop. Social workers promoting community-based networks that draw older people into their ambit could provide one strategy for moving forward.

Relationship loss can occur as a result of the abuse of an older person. This can be particularly problematic if their children are perpetrating it. Pittaway (1995) argues that such abuse can be self-imposed because older people increase their dependency by becoming over-reliant on their children, a view that seems harsh. Abusive interfamilial dynamics provide another reason for having the communities in which older people reside take an interest in their welfare and ensure that healthy relationships are maintained within the family as well as outside it. Having communities become responsible for elders does not mean that older people do not have the right to be supported by those outside these communities. Sometimes, it is absolutely necessary that this is the case.

The importance of external support is illustrated by what happens when a social worker wishes to 'rescue' an older person from the same-identity community by forcing him or her to participate in traditional activities because this is what elders do rather than enquiring into what the individual wants to do. If intervention means riding roughshod over older people's wishes, drowning out their voices on the grounds that professionals know best, or simply following a formulaic stance of their position, an older person's agency and citizenship is being violated by the person intending to care for them. Insensitive treatment can arise whether the social worker is looking for a place in a home for older people, providing residential care in a nursing home, seeking a placement in a daycentre, offering to staff a telephone help line for elders or advocating for an older person.

Young carers providing services for older people

Caring for older people has been shunted onto families in the community. But who are the carers in the community? Most of them are women, but there are also substantial numbers of others involved in providing care. As well as men who look after their spouses (Fisher, 1997), there are a large number of young carers (Twigg and Atkin, 1994), a particularly neglected group. Young carers usually care for disabled parents, but also for grandparents and siblings. Their work encompasses a number of tasks, including physical care, practical assistance and emotional support. The Department of Health (2001) estimates that there are 32,000 young carers in Britain, but acknowledges that this is a conservative guess. Young carers have to deal with a variety of issues in performing caring duties and can find that their own lives take a back seat. To begin with, they have to deal with their own feelings about 'role reversal', or providing care for parents instead of receiving it from them. Their emotional attachment to family may cause them to feel they do not have many options other than to care for parents or other family members. Young carers may keep their role secret. They may feel isolated and stigmatized if knowledge of their caring duties becomes public, especially if these involve parents (Undergown, 2002). They may become ashamed of what they do. Schoolmates may disapprove, and young carers may even be bullied because they do caring work, thus causing further emotional distress.

Caring responsibilities may impact badly on their performance at school (Shah and Hatton, 1999) and they may miss classes and extra-curricular activities. Sometimes, these absences occur because they are physically caring for parents; at others, parents may cause them to place their lives on hold by demanding that they cease attending school and look after them. Schools can take action against parents if their children skip classes to care for them, and some have been threatened with court action for unauthorized absences (Aldridge and Becker, 1993). If the young carers' grades drop, they may also endanger their future prospects.

Young carers also suffer from not having the parental support that their peers take for granted. This and the increased responsibilities that they shoulder will force them to grow up more quickly than would have been the case otherwise. Caring may make excessive demands on their physical capacities and lead to injuries, especially if they have to lift heavy adult bodies. Most young carers have not received training in how to do such work and may find out that they create more problems than they solve if they carry them out inappropriately (Frank, 1995). The mental health of young carers may also be disturbed as a result of the anxieties that they have to deal with (Becker, Aldridge and Dearden, 1998). They may manifest eating disorders and other forms of psychological stress (Nolan, Grant and Keady, 1996). The pressures of caring may also impact badly upon other parts of their lives by encroaching upon the time they have available for play, meeting their own friends and participating in peer group activities.

Young black carers face additional hurdles. If their parents do not speak English, the lack of translation and interpretation facilities often results in their being used as interpreters and translators for statutory providers and having to advocate on behalf of parents for their needs to be met (Shah and Hatton, 1999). This may leave them emotionally exhausted, place them in the embarrassing position of mediating between parents and official personnel or bodies of authority, and jeopardize family relationships when they have to handle sensitive information that is more appropriately left to adults. Pittaway (1995) reports that the lack of translation services for older people has resulted in desperate measures, including social workers calling embassy officials to help translate. Information about services available may also not be readily accessible to members of ethnic minority communities. A study by Bignall and Butt (2000) revealed that their sample of young British carers of Asian, African and Caribbean origins were not aware of direct payments that act as a gateway to independent living or the range of services that they could draw upon, whether these were from social services or the voluntary sector. A patchwork of informal family support filled the gap.

Young carers in Britain could receive support to relieve the burden of carrying out caring duties by being assessed as 'in need' under Section 17 of the 1989 Children Act. They could also have their needs assessed at the same time as those receiving care under the provisions of the Carers (Recognition and Services) Act of 1995. According to a survey conducted by Dearden and Becker (1998), few (11 per cent) young carers had been assessed. Of those that were, 43 per cent had been assessed under the Children Act, 35 per cent under the Carers (Recognition and Services) Act and 12 per cent did not know under which legislative provisions they had been assessed. The majority of adult carers are not assessed. A study by the Carers National Association (1997) revealed that only 18 per cent of carers had been assessed, but when they were, they found that help was forthcoming for most of them.

Conclusions

Old age is socially constructed in ageist terms and elder care is currently being commodified. Social workers' interventions into older people's lives maintain and reproduce negative stereotypes based on disablist, racist, sexist and ageist assumptions. These configure practice with older people around notions of dependency and vulnerability and depict them as passive victims with limited capacities for making their own decisions and requiring expert involvement in their lives. Older people have challenged negative depictions of their status and sought to ameliorate their position through endeavours that often reaffirm ageist stereotypes.

Older people may have medical problems that incapacitate their performance as agents. This should not become the basis for approaching them in ageist ways. Many elders contribute actively to society through voluntary work and parenting grandchildren. Seeing older people individually and collectively as having made and continuing to make important contributions to people and communities they know will enable practitioners to appreciate their strengths more fully.

When medical problems do incapacitate older people and they require the support of family members, it is vital that these carers are themselves supported. This, in turn, can promote the well-being of cared-for people. This can be particularly important for young carers, whose work can have a deleterious impact on their welfare as well as that of others.

Social workers have a crucial role to play in challenging ageist stereotypes of older people, including their intersection with other forms of oppression and discrimination centred on age, 'race', gender and disability. Although practitioners have to address elders' specific needs, which may be linked to having been abused and having had their vulnerabilities taken advantage of, they should do so in ways that affirm older people's citizenship rights.

SOCIAL WORK INTERVENTIONS WITH OFFENDERS

Introduction

Current discourses about crime in Britain are being led by two powerful sets of players: policymakers on behalf of central government; and the media. Coming from different positions, they act as key opinion-formers that foster convergent discourses embedded in authoritarian populism. These subject individuals to regulatory regimes that aim to make them conform to dominant norms, whether or not they make sense in their particular lives. Combined with growing public anxiety about safety and the fear of becoming a victim of crime, these discourses make 'law and order' a quality-of-life issue. By focusing on authoritarian populism, dominant discourses have unhelpfully politicized these debates and impeded the task of promoting positive life choices.

'Law and order' discourses are accompanied by competing ones which may or may not succeed in shifting the agenda on crime in other directions. Discourses around drugs on 'safe' sites, demands for the decriminalization of marijuana, and the provision of regulated 'hard' drugs indicate alternative discourses that are marginal to the mainstream position, although they engage with it, and occasionally cause it to shake (Lawrence, 2002). Professional voices have been more muted than those of policymakers and media pundits in shaping these discourses at present. Professional interests and opinions are amplified more when research findings and practice produce the kinds of results that politicians and the media think are needed.

Crime has been part of discourses about the fragmented nature of industrial society and legitimated the activities of the regulatory state bent on imposing discipline upon recalcitrant citizens and inculcating the work ethic within labourers unwilling to become factory fodder (Foucault, 1977). This approach to crime relies heavily on the 'technologies of self' being absorbed by individuals who regulate their own conduct to conform to prevailing norms. Discourses embedded in pathologizing individuals and demanding that they take personal responsibility for dealing with their failure to observe prescribed social norms are central to affirming the 'technologies of self'.

Offenders have occupied contradictory positions in debates that have polarized the question of what should be done with them – punishment or rehabilitation? Punishment aims to control deviant populations; rehabilitation to reintegrate offenders into society as useful citizens. Arguments around these two options have produced no clear victor. Social work with offenders has vacillated between these two poles of the continuum and become fraught with stresses that represent continuities and discontinuities in practice. The tension taking centre-stage is that of determining the end goal of intervention. In what has been characterized as the welfare versus justice debate in work with offenders, there have been swings in both directions as different governments, civil servants and practitioners align themselves on one side or the other of the arguments about its role and purpose (Smith, 1998).

The balance between incarceration as the ultimate in punishment and rehabilitation in the community as the opposite cannot be drawn in unambiguous either/or terms, despite the attempt to highlight it as such in official discourses about custody or diversion. Rehabilitating offenders who spend a spell in prison is an excellent practical example of blurring the boundaries between these two functions. Bauman (2000) challenges the Foucauldian analysis of prisons as disciplining institutions (Foucault 1977) by arguing that rehabilitation is irrelevant to contemporary societies because global capital no longer requires labourers indoctrinated with the work ethic, and the purpose of incarceration has shifted from producing factory fodder to immobilizing or warehousing people. This is part of the story, but Bauman ignores another role for rehabilitation: helping offenders relate to others as subjects in their own right instead of objects for their personal instrumentality and benefit.

Offenders tend to be part of the socially excluded population. They are more likely to suffer from structural inequalities and be poor, unemployed, homeless, suffer from ill health and to have been excluded from school (Devlin, 1995). These characteristics focus on a further source of conflict and contradiction in the 'law

and order' debate, one that revolves around the causes of offending behaviour. Are these rooted in the individual or embedded in
social structures and relationships? Mainstream discourses about
changing offending behaviour emphasize individual culpability
without looking at the social conditions which play a role in reinforcing or reducing it.

Responses to working with offenders have varied over time
(Smith, 1998), but have generally focused on individual pathologies
as the basis for criminal behaviour and the site for intervention.
Controversies over the role of social work in this process indicate
that official reactions on the subject are ambiguous. Ambiguities
are particularly evident in stipulations about the lines of responsibility and accountability for meeting specific goals in reducing
or terminating offending behaviour. What can be legitimately left
for the offender to address as an individual? In rehabilitating
offenders back into the community, practitioners treat them as
external to it – outsiders – rather than part of it, thus complicating
their reintegration. This externality is also apparent in practitioners'
attempts to balance the seriousness of an offence with protecting
the public by securing the willingness of offenders to comply with
specific sentencing options, particularly those diverting them from
custody.

Political discourses about 'law and order' have highlighted the
need of social workers and probation officers to prevent further
offending and ensure community safety. But these are conducted
in the absence of discussions about: causes of crime other than
personal pathologies; holistic approaches, which have to balance a
range of conflicting and contradictory aims and expectations about
the outcomes of any intervention; and the citizenship rights of
people to live in crime-free areas alongside the rights of offenders
to be helped to mend their ways. The public has an interest in
these developments even when it has not been directly affected by
offending behaviour because it pays for the incarceration and/or
rehabilitation of offenders through the taxation system, an expenditure consuming ever more money. In the United States, funding
for prisons exceeds that allocated to education, indicating a warped
sense of social priorities (*Net Briefings*, 10/5/98).

In this chapter, I consider the continued importance of the resolution of structural inequalities to the rehabilitation of offenders
and the work that is done with them. I also discuss the significance
of 'law and order' debates for probation practice and its transformation from a social work activity into a corrections-based one. I
ask what kind of probation practice can meet the contradictory

demands placed upon it. These include: rising expectations in protecting the public; increasing pressures to recognize victims' rights;
and populist discourses about punishment without a rehabilitative
dimension. These approaches sit uneasily alongside those in which
offenders demand recognition of their citizenship rights and social
workers express welfarist concerns in working with offenders.

(Re)configuring environments of crime and control

The question of which group of professionals should work with
offenders has occasioned controversy as society's responses veer
between punishing offenders and rehabilitating them. Today, there
are a number of stakeholders in the criminal justice system (CJS),
each of which plays a role in processing offenders from the point
of being charged to the implementation of their sentence. These
professionals engage in technologies of control that focus primarily
on individual offending behaviour while little is done to link it to
the social situations which contribute to it.

Probation officers and youth justice social workers have been
crucial to working with offenders who have not received custodial
sentences. Their work is marked by several tensions which complicate practice. These include: the uneasy relationship between
offending behaviour and its causes; the degree to which society
and/or the individual is deemed responsible for particular crime
waves; the dilemma between punishing offenders and rehabilitating
them; the difficulties in responding to the needs of both offenders
and victims; and the relationship between probation practice and
social work. Working with offenders provides the professionals
who undertake such activities with their own power base. Their
ideas may conflict with those who employ them and, in the case of
the Home Office, hold political power over them as well as controlling the purse strings. In the politically charged atmosphere of
authoritarian populism, power struggles occasionally erupt amongst
practitioners, policymakers and employers. The state seeks to
undermine professional power and destroy the legitimacy of
welfare-based approaches to offenders. In Britain, this saga began
to unfold during the 'nothing works' debates,[1] which the Home
Office later used to its advantage in the 1990s.

A preoccupation with issues relating to the CJS is never far from
public gaze as daily papers continually report crime and pronounce
on policies relating to it. Britain has one of the highest prison to
population rates in Europe (Young, 1999), reaching 139 in 100,000

population in 2002. A recent Home Office report demonstrates that rapes rose sevenfold from 1,255 to 7,929 between 1980 and 2000, while serious assaults such as wounding with intent and attempted murder increased from 4,545 to 15,737; actual bodily harm went from 90,654 to 201,290 during the same period (Rose, 2002). This growth in crime was not accompanied by an equal increase in conviction rates, which fell substantially in comparison. For example, convictions for actual bodily assaults fell from 53,648 to 50,966, with rape showing one of the highest rates of acquittal (Rose, 2002). The media's portrayal of the gap between rising crime statistics and falling conviction rates engenders widespread fear amongst the British populace. Whilst this response is understandable, the official crime figures do not warrant either its scope or intensity. This is because the chances of *actually becoming a victim* of crime are low, and in comparison with the position pertaining in countries outside Western Europe, for example the United States, which has the highest prison to population rate in the world (six times higher than that of Britain), the picture is less dramatic than it appears at first sight.

The public's response of heightened fear indicates the psychological impact of information that makes the unusual seem familiar by becoming embedded in people's everyday lives. Messages derived from crime statistics have spawned a 'law and order' debate in which the ideologies of mainstream political parties are converging around authoritarian populism as each seeks to outdo the other in demonizing offenders and seeking more punitive ways of curbing their behaviour (Young, 1999).

Crime can be a lucrative source of income and pleasurable lifestyles. Individualizing discourses about crime have moved the focus away from causes of crime linked to structural inequalities, including poverty, and reinforced those based on individual responsibility and personal behaviour. Politicians' comments ignore the close fit between areas of high crime and localities with multiple levels of disadvantage and deprivation (see Mirrlees Black, Mayhew and Percy, 1996). They also fail to engage with research studies that have identified links between poverty and crime for some time (Davies, 1974; Dominelli, 1983; Farrington et al., 1986; Field, 1990).

The identification of the career criminals or professional offenders who constantly commit crimes and spend the bulk of their lives moving in and out of gaol promotes behavioural explanations that are rooted in personality dysfunction and feature prominently in the discourses of authoritarian populism. In this, the idea that crime is a rational response to the limited range of options available to poor people is avoided. These discourses enable policymakers to argue that the individuals concerned are the problem and downplay the interface between structural factors and people's behaviour in specific social situations. The role that poverty plays in producing offenders in a constant stream of new adherents to criminal life-styles is downplayed by discourses that emphasize that not all poor people commit offences. These allow the enabling state to become the policing state, subjecting citizens' activities to close surveillance through technologies of governmentality. In electronic form, these technologies can easily encompass an entire population, not just criminal elements – a possibility highlighted in home secretary David Blunkett's 'snoopers charter' (Ahmed and Hinsliff, 2002).

In a rational choice response, some people (re)configure their understandings of situations to justify offending behaviour and obviate personal responsibility for it. Focusing only on either structural or personal grounds in the causal equation is unlikely to work, as recidivism rates show: 59 per cent reoffend within two years. Both individual perceptions and the social situations which support offending behaviours have to be changed. It is not an either/or matter.

Differentiated responses to offenders

Offending behaviour is differentiated across a range of social divisions: mental health, ability, age, class, 'race' and gender are key. These can permutate and interact with each other in ways yet to be fully understood. Crime continues to be dominated by men (Harvey et al., 1992), who comprise 94 per cent of offenders in the latest British Crime Survey (Home Office, 2002). Graef (1992) argues that one in three men are convicted of non-motoring offences by the age of 30, raising serious questions about the efficacy of criminalizing high proportions of them. The number of women offenders is rising at a faster rate than that of men: 11 per cent compared to 6 per cent in 2002. This growth can be placed in a non-alarmist and non-complacent perspective. The figures for calculating percentage increases are lower for women offenders – 4,400 compared to 67,912 men, making it easier to dramatize the rise in their offending behaviour, but harder to meaningfully compare it across the two genders.

Gender is affected by other social divisions. However, crime statistics do not feature their interactive nature: for example, the impact of mental ill health or learning disabilities. High-profile cases of mentally disordered offenders like Christopher Clunis, or those involving learning-disabled people like Stephen Downing, demonstrate that specific forms of oppression impact upon them.[2]

Women offenders

Women offenders are not seen as *real* deviants (Carlen and Worrall, 1987; Hudson, 1990). They tend to be defined as 'mad, sad or bad' (Worrall, 1990) rather than active agents who make deliberate choices about engaging in criminal activities. However, this depiction of women offenders in the literature applies primarily to white women offenders. As I indicated in one of the early studies on this topic (Dominelli, 1983), women offenders of Afro-Caribbean origins, by contrast, are cast as 'dangerous' rather than 'mad, sad or bad' and treated as if they have deliberately embarked on a life of crime, in a way denied to white women, who are assumed to lack agency in this arena (Dominelli, 1983). Constructing discourses about their behaviour in gendered terms amplifies the power of professionals over those of the women involved. As Annie Hudson (1990, p. 121) claims: 'the assignment of the "sick" role to young women in trouble reinforces the power of the professional expert at the expense of young women finding their own solutions'.

Discourses about women offenders endorse an undifferentiated view of gender, which research has increasingly shown not to reflect women's realities (Cook and Hudson, 1993; Dominelli et al., 1995). Traditional discourses do not take account of the seriousness of the offences and number of previous offences committed by women offenders, who are more likely to have committed offences involving prostitution (soliciting) and shoplifting (Dominelli, 1983). Men offenders commit higher-tariff crimes such as burglary and violent offences. Smart (1976) has termed these 'gender-specific' crimes.

At the same time, women, especially white women, are less likely to be stopped by police, more likely to be cautioned, and less likely to be sentenced to custodial sentences than men, particularly black men (Skogan, 1990; Home Office, 2002). Differential responses do not operate only on gender lines, but also (internally) on those of class, 'race' and age, thus young white working-class and black women are monitored more closely than other groups of the female population. Within this context, much professional input focuses upon young women's sexual activities, while those of men are ignored. By emphasizing areas of their lives that seem far removed from their own daily concerns, particularly the lack of decent jobs, incomes and housing, the systems professionals use to police young white working-class and black women create systems of ambiguity for them (Hudson, 1990).

Class-based offenders

Another social division that makes a difference to all offenders' experience of the CJS is class. Policing occurs primarily in working-class areas (Mathiesen, 1990), making poor, multiply disadvantaged communities where black minority ethnic groups live the most heavily policed areas. The bulk of offenders are from poor neighbourhoods and the class-based nature of the clientele of the probation service has been evident for some time (Mirrlees-Black, Mayhew and Percy 1996), although this aspect is discussed less frequently now than it was in the 1960s and 1970s. Working-class people are more likely to be imprisoned than their middle-class counterparts. Some theorists claim that greater surveillance of poor people, especially black people and their communities, and the ease with which middle-class offenders can escape detection leads to the over-representation of people on low incomes in the CJS (Mathiesen, 1990).

Research demonstrates that the need to increase income leads substantial numbers of men and women to commit theft and burglary to maximize money at their disposal (Dominelli, 1983). Similar trends are also evident amongst drug-takers who commit high levels of theft to finance their drug habits. Though useful, these analyses have failed to explain why only *some* people on low income will steal from others, primarily those in similar socio-economic circumstances.

Working-class crime is usually perpetrated by individuals or gangs upon others in their localities (Keida, 1994). Serious middle-class crime involves significant numbers of dispersed innocent parties as major examples of middle-class crime flout legal frameworks guiding corporate behaviour. A key one of these, the Enron scandal, began in a company based in the United States but has had worldwide ramifications. Enron's chief executive was able to claim Fifth Amendment immunity to avoid giving evidence that might incriminate him in lawbreaking. Aside from having well-paid lawyers argue his case, he differentiated himself from minor offenders by knowing how to protect himself within existing laws, despite the widespread repercussions of the malpractices that occurred (Carver, 2002).

Besides wiping millions off the stock market, leading to extensive redundancies, and endangering the future pension plans of millions of people, those involved in the Enron scandal have used 'accounting tricks designed to manipulate earnings and enrich top executives'. Malpractice in accountancy terms will 'affect insurance companies and pension funds' as the stock market falls (Pratley and Treanor, 2002). Civil charges may be brought against former executives by the American Securities and Exchange Commission (SEM), which can set fines, as it did Xerox, by fining it $10 million for its accounting irregularities. These responses, however, fail to assist the vast number of people injured by corporate offending behaviour. As in the earlier Maxwell débâcle over pensions, poor people have lost out (DTI, 2001).

Middle-class or white-collar crime exposes the inadequacy of the CJS to deal with offending behaviour that impacts upon the lives of substantial numbers of people. The spectacular collapse of Enron, WorldCom, Tico and Xerox as a result of various forms of financial fraud has led to a massive overhaul of the financial regulatory mechanisms or measures that protect small shareholders and pensioners whose earnings have been stolen and lives devastated (Pratley and Treanor, 2002). These scandals have highlighted the moral bankruptcy of corporate capital and the ineffectual controls that auditors of world renown have over them. President George W. Bush has resorted to pathologizing a 'few corrupt executives' as the 'bad apples' whom he holds responsible for this crisis rather than addressing the structural problems and systemic difficulties that these incidents represent. Who looks after the victims of such crimes? As the continued struggles of the survivors of the Bhopal disaster (Bhargava, 1986) and the Enron scandal indicate, the question currently has no adequate answer. Its absence has dented public confidence in a global capitalist system.

Racialized discourses on crime: Black offenders

Racialized identities feature in the dominant constructions of crime. Discourses on 'law and order' have been used to construct black people as criminals, particularly as muggers on city streets (Hall et al., 1978) and, later, as gun-toting drug-runners (Keida, 1994). Constructions of black people as offenders feed into racist stereotypes of their capacities and are reflected in the responses of those charged with administering justice. Black youths are less likely to be given police cautions (Cook and Hudson, 1993). These discourses have created a climate of fear where 'moral panics' around crime statistics legitimate authoritarian populist responses endorsed by the media. Black people are again feeling the impact of this through the (re)introduction of 'sus' laws where police have powers to stop and search people if they suspect an offence has or is about to be committed. The inadequacy of this approach is reflected in statistics that indicate that large numbers of those stopped are not charged, a feature also evident in its 1980s incarnation (Ahmed and Hinsliff, 2002).

The outcome of negative constructions of black people linked to crime is exposed in sentencing results. These indicate that black men and women are more likely to receive custodial sentences than white ones for similar offences and, consequently, are over-represented in prisons (Dominelli, 1983; Cook and Hudson, 1993; NACRO, 1994; Dominelli et al., 1995; Greenhorn, 1996). Home Office (1997) statistics show that 16 per cent of the male prison population and 26 per cent of the female prison population are from a black ethnic minority group. As they make up only 5 per cent of the general population, they are over-represented in custodial establishments. They are also serving longer sentences when compared to white offenders on similar charges (Home Office, 1994), showing a continuity with research undertaken earlier (Dominelli, 1983). These differentiated experiences indicate the gendered, racialized and classist nature of discourses about crime and how these are used to describe and orient responses to it.

Young offenders

'Moral panics' are created around offending behaviour (Hall et al., 1978; Cohen, 1980). Stanley Cohen (1980) formulated the term to encapsulate crisis responses to young offenders or delinquents. Young offenders have become targets of media frenzies on crime. The demonization of young offenders indicates an authoritarian populist response to troubled youths. It reached its zenith in Britain when two children murdered a toddler, James Bulger (Jackson, 1995). The 'moral panic' these discourses unleashed paved the way for more draconian measures against offenders, especially young ones. These called for: lowering the age of criminal responsibility, already at a European low of 10; increasing the stiffness of sentences meted out to them; and sending more young offenders to prison (Travis, 2001). These reactions fly in the face of evidence that indicates young offenders are more likely to break a 'career' of crime if they get intensive forms of one-to-one interventions provided in local authority secure accommodation units. Here, unlike in prison settings, the 1989 Children Act applies and the general welfare needs of young offenders, including education, can be addressed. In a prison milieu, they become more hardened criminals or commit suicide. Suicide rates for young offenders have risen to unacceptable levels (Pritchard, 2001b), being twelve times higher than in the USA (Preston, 2001).

The government's failure to deal with the high number of suicides amongst young offenders on remand in young offender institutions, when the young person's guilt has yet to be ascertained, is worrying. The protection of young children from abuse by adult offenders is also poorly handled. In one example, the police refused to take action against a 22-year-old man who sexually abused a 12-year-old girl because they considered the matter non-contentious. Their grounds for not taking action included the need to protect the human rights of the man concerned. In this framing of the issue, the police act as if the rights of the child or young person do not exist. Yet Britain, like many countries, has legislation that recognizes these to some extent.

The 1991 Criminal Justice Act symbolized an expanding system of non-custodial social regulation that brought more and more areas of social life under the disciplining gaze of probation officers. Despite controversies over its use, electronic tagging represents a fairly sophisticated system of control that blurs the distinction between private and public space. The use of such technology permits centralized control of individuals whose capacity to exercise self-regulation requires constant professional surveillance and direction. This contributes to blurring the boundaries between professional regulatory regimes (probation) and those exercised by the community (vigilantism). Keeping professional expertise within bounds requires more centralized and sophisticated forms of regulation. In community-oriented regimes the legitimation of particular kinds of knowledge and forms of control becomes more dispersed, and sometimes life-threatening: for example, when vigilantes (primarily men) attack suspected sex offenders to show loss of confidence in the CJS's ability to meet safety concerns.

Children's offending behaviour brings poor parenting under fire

The failure of the state to reduce offending behaviour amongst young people has meant that discourses about who should deal with the problem have been reoriented towards parents, particularly poor ones, and lone mothers. The idea that single-parent women produce young delinquents is not new, but the current technologies of control being used to bring them into line is focusing on an area not previously framed in this way: non-attendance at school. Truancy, as non-attendance at school is termed in popular consciousness, has linked increased rates of crime to poor parenting, especially the lack of male role models, and demands that parents be made responsible for the behaviour of their offspring. School patrols made up of multi-agency professionals including police and social workers have replaced education welfare officers, who earlier took over from truancy officers (Smithers, 2002).

The 'truancy sweeps', as these patrols have been called by the media, aim to catch young people who are out of school without good reason. 'Truancy sweeps' were introduced when research revealed that truancy is disproportionately represented amongst young offenders. Their operations have been conducted with considerable efficiency. In May 2002, police and social workers working in 900 school patrols in 34 English local education authorities found 12,000 young people on unauthorized absences from school (Smithers, 2002). Their activities have blurred private–public boundaries by shifting the focus from truancy to parental inadequacy in exercising authority in getting children to school. Defining the issue as parental deficiency avoids discussions about: the badly maintained buildings in which children spend large portions of their day; the poor quality of life at school; bullying and other forms of coercive behaviour that children endure; and the inappropriateness of the curriculum in developing well-rounded active citizens for tomorrow's world.

Authoritarian populism targets parents

The high-profile imprisonment of single parent Patricia Amos in Banbury, England, for not sending her two teenage daughters to school each day underlines the government's policy of authoritarian populism that intimidates people into conformity. The Amos case provides evidence that counters Foucault's (1979) view that coercive measures are not needed in modern societies. Coercive measures are drawn upon when self-control or professionally imposed forms of direct control fail. Spending time in Holloway Prison 'brought me to my senses', Patricia Amos claimed. But this intervention did not deal with the health and income difficulties that had caused the daughters to stay home to 'look after' their mother (Gillan, 2002).

Patricia Amos had kidney problems and drug addictions and suffered loss related to bereavement. She had recently lost the centre
of their lives and carer for her two children – her own mother, who
had died unexpectedly. The death of the children's grandmother
had devastated the two young women, and none of the remaining
members of the extended family, including their mother, had come
to terms with the grief of her passing. Another reason one daughter
refused to attend school was that she was being bullied. This family
was isolated and in need of preventative intervention to keep them
functioning adequately prior to a crisis point being reached. The
appalling lack of community support for this family was also
evident in the failure of the system to respond to the teenagers'
needs even when their mother was imprisoned. No social worker,
probation officer or police officer visited the house to tell them that
their mother had been sent down. Nor did anyone come to enquire
what help they needed to survive the period without her presence.
Help for Patricia Amos was provided via the prison service in the
form of bereavement counselling and assistance to break her drug
habit.

The family needed help on a number of fronts much earlier, but
the state justified the imprisonment of this woman on the grounds
of protecting 'the rights of the children to an education' and had
its professionals ensure that this opportunity was taken up. This
construction ignores the other rights children have and begs the
question of the quality of life at school and the education that
young people are receiving. It also sets up an oppositional view of
the situation in which the interests of children are pitted against
those of parents. In this family, the meshing of the interests of the
mother and two daughters and lack of external assistance were at
the heart of the interpersonal problems they experienced. In claiming that her daughters were not 'delinquents' or 'bad' (Gillan, 2002),
Patricia Amos also called into question the state's definition of
children who do not attend school as potential criminals.

When asked for views on the imprisonment of a mother for
her children's behaviour, the teaching profession was split. A
spokes*woman* for the National Union of Teachers thought it was
inappropriate to 'deprive these girls of their mother'; a spokes*man*
for the National Association of Head Teachers felt that imprison-
ing Patricia Amos was appropriate 'in extreme circumstances'
(Gillan, 2002). Gender and status differentials seem to produce
differing discourses. The two young women themselves felt responsible for their mother spending time in Holloway Prison and
decided that they would go to school and not skip it again (Gillan,

2002). As a technology of the self aimed at improving self-control, this strategy has worked.

Besides sending parents to gaol, the state is threatening to withdraw child benefits for persistent truants (Travis and Hopkins, 2002). This response would create the loss of benefits as a further weapon of compliance. This proposal, like the other, misses the link between poverty and truancy. Aggregating finances as endorsed in familialism, it ignores the *child's* right to a decent income. If implemented, this policy would exacerbate difficulties arising from low and inadequate incomes in poor communities and cause further offending behaviour as people seek to maximize financial resources.

Punishing offending behaviour by hitting people in the pocket has antecedents. For some time, social security administrators have been able to deny offenders who fail to comply with community supervision orders the whole of their job seeker's allowance and 40 per cent of their income support. Additionally, courts have had powers to fine parents whose children do not attend school since the 1996 Education Act. In the event of a default in payment, these fines can be withheld from parental earnings or welfare benefits through a court-imposed attachment order. The Education Act 2000 doubled the maximum fine that can be levied against parents to £2,000. Parents can be compelled to attend court or risk arrest if they do not respond to a court summons. This provision tackles the problem of 80 per cent of parents not turning up for hearings under the previous Act (Travis and Hopkins, 2002). Social workers could find out about and help deal with the causes of such disaffection.

The 1989 Children Act can also be used to reinforce parental responsibility regarding children's education. Under its provisions, a local education authority can apply to the family proceedings court for an education supervision order if they suspect parents of failing in their duty to send children to school. Parenting orders can be used to assist parents in managing children. These require parents to attend classes to improve parenting skills. These measures are technologies of governmentality that supply social workers, probation officers and police with extensive powers to enforce conformity in behaviour *without* addressing the limited resources of those most affected by them. Many of these parents, like Patricia Amos, are lone mothers living on benefit or low incomes. Further depriving them of meagre finances would impose considerable hardship upon children. These policies are likely to exacerbate the exclusionary forces already operating in their lives and contradict the government's goal of social inclusion.

Risk assessment and risk management

Uncertainty of outcomes has been another theme that has persisted in work with offenders. Attempts to break this through 'what works' initiatives have relied on the measurement of 'risk' as the way of targeting interventions on offenders whom practitioners have thought most likely to reoffend and thereby constitute a 'danger' to the public. The 'risk society' involves the individual management of risk and has prompted a preoccupation with managing risk rather than ascertaining what causes offending behaviour (Giddens, 1998a). In moving the spotlight away from causes, this represents a departure from welfarist approaches to work with offenders. It accords with more bureaucratic forms of intervention and is a powerful symbol of the bureau-technocrat operating in probation practice.

Risk assessment techniques have become crucial instruments in controlling the behaviour of individual offenders. Under risk management regimes, the risk that each offender poses to society is measured and his[3] dangerousness to others identified so that his potential victims can take care of their own safety. This approach marks a shift in the state's approach to crime – offloading its responsibility for dealing with the causes of crime to promote the view that individuals look after their own safety. Thus, public discourses on 'law and order' focus on the role of the CJS in managing individual offenders. And so, probation officers have joined other professionals, including social workers, psychiatrists and psychologists, in using risk assessment tools to increase their capacity to predict 'dangerousness' in particular individuals.

Despite being treated as reliable sources of knowledge and information, research shows that risk assessment instruments are notoriously suspect tools of prediction and highlights their inadequacy under most conditions. In assessing one group of practitioners who rely on these tools extensively, Limandri and Sheridan (1995, p. 10) conclude: 'Mental health professionals in general, have a poor track record of validly predicting violence amongst the mentally ill ... individual psychiatrists have not been very successful in predicting this danger.' Improving predictability regarding the behaviour of a given individual is difficult. According to Quinsey (1995), risk assessment tools are unreliable because these measure a narrow range of indices. To make more useful forecasts, he suggests that a wider variety of factors have to be taken into account. Feminist scholars and others have questioned this approach completely for its failure to: contextualize crime especially that inflicted upon women and children; link offences to contexts and social expectations around masculinity; and acknowledge unreported crime as significant to resolving the problem (Cowburn and Dominelli, 2001).

The much publicized murders of innocent bystanders at the hands of mentally ill individuals, such as that of Jonathan Zito by Christopher Clunis in 1992, have further undermined public confidence in professional competence in these matters.[4] Ironically, the media's faith in accurately calculating risk remains. This has been achieved by blaming the professionals concerned for incompetence rather than evaluating the (in)adequacy of the tools for the task.

The identification of young people 'at risk' of offending with some degree of certainty (Farrington, 1990) has diverted probation energies towards crime avoidance strategies and ways of focusing on group-based rather than individually based forms of intervention. A key rationale behind group-oriented strategies has been to avoid stigmatizing young offenders as it might be counterproductive in preventing future crime (Findlay, Bright and Gill, 1990). These strategies are useful in reducing the costs of providing probation services to individual offenders on a one-to-one basis. The wisdom of this policy is suspect, however, given that research indicates that intensive work with offenders on a personal basis is more successful at reducing recidivism (Smith, 1998).

Alongside the demand that offenders' behaviour is controlled through audits of their behaviour by management drawing on quantifiable technologies came that of containing, disciplining and predicting professional conduct. The managerial tools of performance indicators and risk assessments are expected to assist in these two tasks and provide the basis through which managers can subject both probation officers and offenders to surveillance and keep track of them.

The 'what works' debates favour cognitive therapies for treating offenders (Ross, Fabiano and Ewles, 1988). The optimism of this position is misplaced for sex offenders, who continue to reoffend despite such interventions. Cognitive therapies benefit offenders whose *thinking* can be changed. For some sex offenders, the problems lie not in what they think about their behaviour, but in what they *do*, and the excuses they use to legitimate actions that they *know* to be unacceptable and even wrong. Their rationality is constructed around discourses that draw on publicly sanctioned norms such as those endorsed in hegemonic masculinity (Cowburn and Dominelli, 2001; Dominelli, 1991a) and the knowledge that adultist power relations sanction their 'power over' children.

Without strategies that link individual behaviour with socially approved forms of abuse such as those contained in masculine discourses, probation practice is likely to continue to focus on one-to-one approaches that individualize offending behaviour and reinforce personal responsibility whilst the broader causes of crime remain unaddressed. Community approaches to offender rehabilitation and crime reduction, by contrast, have the potential to transcend individually based causes of offending behaviour.

In developing alternative strategies, communities cannot be viewed as homogeneous singular entities. Nor should offenders be seen as being outside their communities (Currie, 1988). Offenders are usually members of the communities in which they offend. Most crime in disadvantaged areas is committed against poor people by others like them. This insight is the opposite of the one underpinning schemes such as 'Neighbourhood Watch'. These assume that communities need protection from 'outsiders' and are unable to deal with the thorny issue of the home-grown offender (Rosenbaum, 1988). This externalizing of the problem is also evident in child protection strategies which emphasize 'stranger danger' in child sexual abuse and ignore that perpetrated by known others who live in their midst, often holding trusted positions of power over them (Cowburn and Dominelli, 2001). Community ties hold no magical powers for safeguarding people or providing crime-free spaces. Integrating offenders back into the social order through a reciprocated citizenship approach provides a firmer base for realizing this objective.

Probation is crucial in facilitating community approaches to crime reduction (Geraghty, 1991). Its role is strengthened when policy-makers want to tackle the public's fear of crime, as exemplified by New Labour's 'law and order' initiatives. These emphasize the management of crime rather than dealing with its causes. In failing to tackle both personal and structural factors, these are like fig-leaves covering the paucity of the programmes on offer.

Managing crime statistics

Overall figures of *reported* crime decreased between 1992 and 2001 (Hough, 2002). This picture has been reversed recently as crime against the person, street crime and theft of mobile phones has risen. Robbery rose by 13 per cent between 2000 and 2001 (Walker, 2002). These figures fuel public fears about the pervasiveness of crime.

New Labour's angst over the public's growing anxiety about crime even when official figures depict a decline has intensified a punitive approach to offenders and prompted other responses like changing the presentation of crime statistics and intensifying managerialist control over professionals in the CJS. Public scepticism about claimed reductions in crime had David Blunkett pleading with chief constables not to publish separate crime statistics, but to endorse instead an increased frequency of centralized official reports published once every three months instead of yearly (Travis, 2002). He hoped this move would stem the upward trend in people's fear of becoming victims of crime by reducing the 'drip, drip' effect of constant publication as each police authority produced its own set of figures (Travis, 2002).

New Labour's focus on bureaucratic representations of crime ignores people's experiential responses. Their scepticism about 'official' crime figures feeds on their knowledge that much crime that impinges on everyday life is not reported, often because victims do not believe that the police will do anything about it (Travis and White, 2002). The shunting of responsibility for managing the risk of becoming a victim onto the individual means that the fear this is predicated upon never goes away. A person is constantly conscious of having to take deterrent action and is aware that he or she has to do this on his or her own. Moreover, people know that they or others close to them have not reported crimes, so they will be suspicious of publications that claim it is declining. In addition, people's negative experiences of how the system handles reported cases intensifies their disbelief (Tapley, 2002).

The aggregation of crime statistics to reduce overall numbers undermines the public's faith in the system. Aggregation results in an offender who has broken into ten cars in one vandalism spree being recorded as one crime. But ten individual victims and their families and friends will have been affected by and know about 'it'. Similar points can be made about unreported speeding on the roads, theft, burglary, drug abuse, sexual abuse, domestic violence, assault or rape. People's awareness of these cannot be swept under the bureaucratic carpet. The government's failure to deal with the *experiential basis* of crime means that people will continue to feel its impact and fear becoming another victim. Also, by individualizing risk management, the collective dimension of caring for and about one another's safety becomes submerged and ruptures people's faith in the system to look after their needs.

Besides toughening its stance on offenders, New Labour has drawn upon the tenets of new managerialism to enable the government to tighten its hold over professional behaviour and ensure that workers in the CJS work together in 'getting to grips' with the 100,000 most persistent adult offenders. Professionals in the CJS have been given performance targets, with threats of sanctions for non-compliance, thus subjecting them to the technologies of control alongside clients. Each professional grouping has been given specific orders. Lawyers have been threatened with fines if they deliberately slow down court proceedings, and each police force area has been given local crime reduction targets to meet. By 2004, the government expected: a 30 per cent reduction in car crime; a 25 per cent cut in burglary; a 14 per cent decrease in robberies, and a diminution in the fear of crime (Walker, 2002). The government also aimed to achieve: a 5 per cent cut in reconviction rates for those on probation; a 5 per cent cut in the numbers of young offenders; a 50 per cent increase in qualifications for prisoners in gaol; and no Category A prison escapes (Walker, 2002).

The crime and disorder partnerships initially brought into being under the 1998 Crime and Disorder Act aim to foster joint working by the police, doctors, probation officers, schools and local authorities in developing a crime and disorder reduction strategy. These partnerships have the task of making the streets safer by ensuring that offensive and offending behaviour generally is curtailed and that there is improved victim satisfaction with the services provided by the CJS. Funding for any projects that these partnerships may devise has to be approved through a cumbersome and time-consuming bureaucratic process which saps recourse to it. Probation officers, like police officers, spend a large proportion of time filling in forms and writing reports for meetings. A police officer claims he spends 60 per cent of his time on such activities (Hopkins, 2002).

The top-down authoritarian populist approach to crime in which the government thinks it knows best is not the only possible road to crime reduction. A different avenue has been followed in France. Here, community approaches have linked the social problems that cause crime with mobilizing the population on a local basis to find solutions. These involve local people in working with a range of agencies to bring about its realization (Bonnemaison, 1983). This handling of the issue has had a degree of success for recorded crime has declined in deprived areas of France, while it has risen in similar communities in Britain (Pitts and Hope, 1998).

Anti-social behaviour orders are a recent initiative on youth offending. These aim to tackle abusive and irresponsible anti-social behaviour on housing estates, and are supported by interim anti-social behaviour orders that enable the police and others to take immediate action to protect the community at an alleged offender's first court appearance pending a full hearing. Dominant discourses around 'anti-social behaviour' focus on young offenders and fan the fires of intergenerational hostility. The media play a key role in reinforcing the view that young and old people who share the same geographical community are at loggerheads with each other, with the former filling the latter with fear of crime.

Recent headlines in local papers have claimed that 'a gang of youths aged 14 to 17' are intimidating older people who are 'living in fear after being subject to a cocktail of problems including drug abuse, arson, vandalism and crime' (Harvey, 2002). 'Yobs' and 'louts' are terms used to describe young people living on Dryden Road in Sheffield. They have stopped it from being the 'beautiful place [in which] to live' remembered by its older residents, thereby further reaffirming their demonized status and the antagonism between young people and elders. The response to these worries is higher levels of community policing. The headlines on the first page of *The Star* on 23 May 2002 which preceded this story were 'High impact. Police launch new team to blitz Sheffield street crime.' This initiative saw seventy officers join the new Impact Squad that was going to clear the city's streets of offenders. Such coverage promotes externalizing discourses that define offenders as not of and from the community, although they clearly are.

Similar headlines have been found in local media coverage of young offenders in southern England. For example, *The Fareham and Gosport News* on 15 May 2002 highlighted the case of Maxine Jeans (name and photo included) who was given an anti-social behaviour order. Referring to the same young person, another local newspaper, *The News*, gave as its front-page headline that day: 'She's just 16 but she has already committed 125 crimes. She has assaulted 40 police officers. She is a "nasty and hate-filled" menace. She is the girl . . . FROM HELL' (capitals in original), before devoting three pages to covering her story.

It applauds police action in curtailing her behaviour without asking why 'three spells behind bars' and social work support through the Persistent Young Offenders Project and the Wessex Youth Offending Team failed to turn her away from being a troubling and troubled teenager. Nor does it ask why she is in this position in the first place. The freely distributed paper with national circulation, *Metro*, also distributed on the same date, headlined her case on page 5 with 'Girl of 16 who's a curse on her city'. This coverage also lambasted the bureaucratic nature of police work with the headline 'Eight hours to process a single arrest' and claimed that only 17 per cent of an officer's time is actually spent on patrol, thus implying that paperwork is a waste of time and detracts from rather than contributes to the *real* work of the police – catching offenders.

Even younger children have been subjected to similar treatment, without their names being released. *The Evening Herald* in Plymouth on 9 May 2002 led with '4-YEAR-OLD TERRORS' (capitals in original) covering the entire front page to focus on a 'gang of vandals aged between four and seven who went on a rampage' to cause 'thousands of pounds of damage'. The boys were branded a 'menace' and the paper 'blamed the parents for a lack of responsibility' in allowing very young children to engage in such acts. Their condemnation was followed up on page 10 under the headline 'Parents of "mini yobs" must pay for crimes'. Again, the 'causes' of crime amongst people living on estates experiencing multiple forms of deprivation are ignored.

Discourses around youth offending have also focused on a small group of persistent offenders who have committed the majority of offences. But all young people are treated as if they are potential lawbreakers. In a recent pronouncement on crime, Oliver Letwin, then Tory Shadow Home Secretary, was quoted as saying that 'many youngsters were forced to a conveyor belt of crime by the age of four' (Wintour, 2002), thus adding to a discourse that constructs the inevitability of a criminal career for young people unless the government intervenes to stem such developments.

A range of other people have been drawn into the net of authoritarian populism, including refugees and asylum seekers, who, whether young or old, have been redefined as criminals rather than people in trouble and subjected to detention for asking for a place of safety when fleeing their own afflicted countries. Discourses in which people in either difficulty or need are framed as criminals both affirm and perpetuate an authoritarian populism which has become a hallmark of New Labour's approach to 'law and order'. It is part and parcel of punitive welfarism.

In casting young offenders as demons, the state becomes deeply implicated in promoting the politics of hate, a treatment also meted out to asylum seekers and refugees. New Labour's punitive approaches to crime undermine its commitment to the social inclusion agenda, for many excluded people appear before the courts. Anderson (1999) argues that this contradiction is particularly apparent in relation to youth crime, where young people who offend are effectively excluded from its remit.

Support for the police and other professionals who work with young offenders on these problems comes at the expense of demonizing the children's parents. But other than demanding more police on the streets and punishing parents for not fulfilling their duty of raising good citizens, no other solutions are proffered. This is a pity, because the structural problems which cause the alienation of young people on these estates and ensure their disconnection from others are ignored. Without a mix of personal and social action that involves parents, children and 'law and order' professionals taking joint responsibility for tackling the causes of crime, it is hard to see how success in reducing future offences can be achieved. Young people need to feel they belong to and are part of society if they are to show respect for communities and those who live within them, regardless of age. Strategies aimed at meeting this objective are likely to resolve intergenerational tensions.

To carry out its programme of curbing youth crime, New Labour has initiated a series of legislative and organizational changes that have restructured this part of the CJS so that it is more in keeping with the imperatives of the new managerialism and centralized technologies of control. The Crime and Disorder Act 1998 and the new Youth Justice Board (YJB) created in September of that year have been central to its more interventionist project regarding young offenders. The remit of the YJB covers England and Wales and the government intends that local Youth Offending Teams (YOTs) follow the policy, philosophy and practices that it sets, giving youth justice work a distinctly top-down feel.

Its implementation has not been monolithic and there is variation amongst YOTs in these two countries. A major reason for this variety has been the exercise of professional discretion to take account of local contexts and individual situations. The use of discretion provides a creative tension with, and at times a challenge to, central control. The scope for such diversity may be whittled away as research undertaken on behalf of the YJB identifies 'best practice' initiatives. These are likely to favour YOTs that follow national guidelines more closely than those that do not.

Youth justice issues are extremely contentious. Young people are more likely to have their interests safeguarded when professionals can demonstrate the negative consequences of inappropriate interventions. During the 1980s, social workers and probation officers played a key role in promoting innovative ways of dealing with young offenders by arguing that addressing their welfare needs yielded encouraging results and reduced offending (Haines and Drakeford, 1998). Most approaches to youth crime have not involved young people in examining the causes of crime, or in defining appropriate responses to those committing offences. In other words, the CJS's responses to young offenders occur within adultist paradigms.

Persistent young offenders have been targeted by a Home Office (1988) keen to see their numbers reduced, even though they constitute a small proportion of the entire prison population. The media hype around young offenders when they do commit serious offences is cause for concern because it neglects the citizenship rights of young people. Media coverage of the two young boys who murdered James Bulger treated all young offenders as if they were on a full-blown career of crime, when the majority of them 'grow out of' their offending behaviour (Graef, 1992). Following the 'moral panic' around these few, the government proposed major changes that promote punitive approaches to all offenders.

Punitive disposals have been advocated in recent years to secure populist electoral advantage (Pitts, 2000). The youth justice politics of both Conservative and New Labour parties have converged around punitive policies. As the issue has become highly politicized, justice for young offenders has turned away from the welfare orientation of the 1980s, when targeted intensive supervision and low rates of custodial sentencing were used effectively with the 'heavy end' young offenders (Haines and Drakeford, 1998). For New Labour, this punitive approach has been central in managing public perceptions of crime. At the same time, this agenda has been anti-child and in conflict with its social inclusion ambitions (Anderson, 1999).

Managing offending behaviour

Ironically, for a government committed to the ideals of empowerment and inclusion, authoritarian populism has become part of New Labour's 'modernizing agenda'. This approach picks on themes familiar to the Victorians – punishment, retribution, personal pathology and individual responsibility. By promoting self-regulation while the state provides the regulatory codes whereby this is to be done, these ideas have been clothed in modern garb. Under neo-liberalism, the state provides the legislative remit for controlling personal behaviour. In ensuring its implementation, private responsibilities become subjected to public surveillance, thus blurring the boundaries between private and public domains. Although he has back-pedalled on the idea after a public outcry, Blunkett's so-called 'snoopers charter' is a symbolic representation of this trend. His desire to ensure that all public bodies could access private telephone calls and emails was about controlling the private sphere. This element is in marked contrast to the Victorian position, in which domestic privacy was more readily safeguarded.

Opening up the private realm to external scrutiny is crucial in a state that is realigning its responsibilities towards managing private behaviour through public regulatory codes and redefining its relationship with citizens who have been excluded from full participation in public life. As the state relies on professionals to enforce these codes, it has to change its relationship with them too. Reducing professional autonomy and increasing managerial control have become essential to sustaining this part of the state's project. Fragmentation and individualization have become important vehicles for containing resistance to the state's neo-liberal programme of change. As a result, a government that is keen to strengthen social cohesion, which is about bringing people together, is implementing policies that are driving people further apart. Further, the ties that bind individuals, families, communities and society together are coming under severe strain, and in some cases have burst asunder.

The state's handling of issues of care and control has varied over time in response to professional views of 'what works', public anxieties about crime and the attitudes taken towards offenders by prevailing political ideologies. In the 1980s and early 1990s, both Labour and Conservative administrations were committed to diverting young offenders from custodial sentences and were successful in doing so through the use of cautioning and other diversionary sentences (Haines and Drakeford, 1998). These were to shift towards the more punitive 'boot camp' approach admired by Conservative Home Secretary Michael Howard in the mid-1990s in response to media-orchestrated 'moral panics' about young offenders (Jackson, 1995). They have resurfaced in another guise recently with Blunkett's demand for lowering the age of responsibility for children.

A new emphasis on welfarist approaches to the needs of young offenders became evident in the early 1980s. The Department of Health backed this initiative by allocating £15 million for voluntary organizations to develop 'intermediate treatment' facilities that would keep young offenders in the community. The police used cautioning to divert non-persistent young offenders from prison. These discretionary powers were differentially applied, and black young people were cautioned less frequently than their white counterparts. This response confirmed popular stereotypes that cast young black people as more likely to commit offences than young white ones (Hall et al., 1978). Configuring black people as threats to public safety through crime statistics subjected young black men to intensified racist biases within the police service and CJS more generally, a point affirmed years later in the Macpherson Report (Macpherson, 1998).

In a parallel to the increased surveillance of offenders, Section 95 of the 1991 CJA requires a closer monitoring of the CJS and the regular reporting of the analyses of sentencing options as applied to women and black people. Scrutiny of their work aimed to assist practitioners in not discriminating through their practice, including when writing pre-sentencing reports (PSRs). This objective has had limited success.

Between 1982 and 1991, punitive approaches were reflected in discourses about the 'seriousness of the offence'. These sought to ensure that imprisonment was reserved for offenders who committed the most serious crimes, usually associated with violence against the person and repeat offenders. The welfarist tradition in work with offenders sits uneasily alongside the much older one of seeking punishment and retribution which was also evident during this period. The tensions between them have been explored historically within the context of the prison by Foucault (1977).

New directions in crime management aiming to integrate offenders more firmly within families and communities emphasize young offenders. Like any other socially excluded group, integrating them links to a feeling of belonging somewhere and playing a full part in the life of the community concerned. Young offenders are likely to have truanted from school and do not engage in meaningful daytime activities (Haines, Jones and Isles, 1999). Many have never had gainful employment and are unlikely to acquire it. To counter their social exclusion, initiatives such as the Cue-Ten Project in Scotland exemplify more inclusionary approaches to young people in trouble. It seeks to reintegrate young offenders into their community through education and training aimed at improving their chances in securing gainful employment. Such measures should emphasize stimulating and well-paid work that makes people feel valued, but usually focus on low-paid jobs.

Reparation schemes or projects linked to restorative justice aim to get offenders to think about victims' views of offending behaviour in a bid to help them move away from lives of crime. These initiatives promote an understanding of the consequences of one person's behaviour upon another and draw on the principles of empathy and solidarity. Restorative justice initiatives seek to (re)integrate offenders into society. These can involve young offenders in meeting their victims to appreciate the impact of their behaviour upon them. Such approaches are also known as victim–offender mediation (Smith, Blagg and Derricourt, 1988); a more recent version is 'reintegrative shaming'. Reintegrative shaming has been developed to return an offender into the community from which he stems (most offenders are men) by combining restitution with rehabilitation (Braithwaite, 1995).

A key attempt at integrating young offenders within supportive community networks, particularly their extended families, has come through family group conference (FGC) models of youth court work developed initially by Maori peoples in New Zealand and later adopted elsewhere (Jackson and Nixon, 1999; see also chapter 4 above). FGCs have extended worldwide the theory and practice associated with reintegrative shaming and ethnically appropriate practice.

FGCs engage those with a direct interest in a young person's offending behaviour, including victims and family members. According to Braithwaite (1995), FGCs provide the opportunity for 'reintegrative shaming' whereby the offender's behaviour is condemned at the same time as he is helped to make reparations to victims and learn more acceptable ways of behaving. The potential to reduce recidivism rates amongst offenders undergoing this process has contributed to its use as a preventative strategy. The dynamics of FGCs are considered effective in bringing about change at the personal level. They also indicate continuity with the practice commitment of separating the person from his behaviour. The attempt to build up the offender's confidence and treat him with respect rather than contributing to his further humiliation is a positive step forward. By not attempting to further humiliate offenders, as initiatives such as the 'boot camp' approaches favoured by Michael Howard do, FGCs are a positive step forward that focuses on treating each offender with respect and building up his confidence. Thus, FGCs model alternative ways of relating to youths, but have been criticized for not encouraging young people to express their own decision-making capacities and relying too heavily on the skills of the FGC co-ordinator to bring an FGC to a successful conclusion (Taylor, 1999).

FGCs refocus discourses on the causes of crime away from its structural dimensions and governmental responsibility. They individualize the issue of crime by pathologizing the individual family for failing to keep its members on the straight and narrow. They also reinforce young people's dependency on parents, making controlling young people's anti-social behaviour a parental matter that they may or may not be able to handle.

The United Nations' Standard Minimum Rules for the Administration of Juvenile Justice (the Beijing Rules, 1985) can be used to promote the well-being of young offenders even though they are not binding on Britain. The UN Convention on the Rights of the Child (1989) has been ratified by all countries except Somalia and the United States. It applies to young offenders as it does to other children under the age of 18. Probation officers could use the provisions in Article 3 to promote the best interests of young offenders, including their being treated with dignity, being well educated and being helped to acquire the skills they need to turn their lives around and integrate back into their communities. This would mean treating young offenders like all other children, not as little demons. Recent developments in Britain are running in the opposite direction, as specialist programmes for young offenders emphasize offending behaviour and ignore their links to the community (Hope and Chapman, 1998; McGuire, 2000). Community-based sex offender programmes in Canada (Dominelli, 1991a; McGuire, 2000), by contrast, indicate that communities can play an important role in reducing offending.

Working with offenders: Changing roles and directions

The police, prison officers, probation officers and social workers are involved in working with offenders. Their roles have varied over time, but until recently, they have revolved around two main themes: preventing the commission of further offences and, through that, promoting community safety; and ensuring the welfare of offenders once the justices have passed verdicts on their behaviour and determined the appropriate sentences. Now, however, they are also required to consider the welfare of victims (Home Office, 1990).

Any consensus around work with offenders has been shortlived, with constant challenges emanating from both within the CJS and without. During the 1990s, the social work role within the CJS came under attack. One reason for this was the failure of social work interventions to either rehabilitate offenders or contribute to crime reduction (McIvor, 1990, 2000). Other reasons have included the rise of professional power and the growing gap between professional ideologies and those of policymakers. The desire to respond to critiques of being oppressive through sexist and racist practices has convinced professionals in the CJS, particularly those in probation, to implement equal opportunities policies and schemes for monitoring their activities with respect to their achievements on this front. These controls became particularly relevant in social enquiry reports (SERs), later called pre-sentencing reports (PSRs), which research had demonstrated had contributed to the over-representation in custodial sentences of black offenders (White-house, 1986) and first-time women offenders regardless of ethnic origins (Dominelli, 1983).

The involvement of the police in performing social work tasks has become another area of ambiguity in roles that has produced conflicting loyalties amongst serving officers as they become embroiled in the care–control contradiction. This tension has been heightened considerably as police officers' duties have further encroached into the social work arena through the requirement to take account of the human rights of people that they investigate for criminal activities.

Further role conflicts have emanated through the new information technologies. These impinge upon social relations, and as more activities are conducted through the internet, new sites for the per-petration of crime open up. The growth of internet-based paedo-philia, pornography, sex trafficking, racist hate crimes and credit card fraud are prime examples of this. The use of the worldwide web, the internet and mobile phones by offenders enables them to transcend national frontiers and the boundaries of time and space to network with other offenders and transmorph their identities. These possibilities make it more difficult for law enforcement agencies to detect and track their activities. Responding to these challenges requires further developments within the CJS. These include: new or adapted roles; additional legal structures to curtail criminal behaviour; new technological equipment; and political structures of co-operation across national borders.

Such initiatives are evident in the European Union, where drug trafficking, people smuggling and terrorist activities are being brought under the surveillance of multinational organizations that share information. Some of these initiatives involve transatlantic co-operation. Since the 11 September 2001 attacks on the World Trade Center in New York and the Pentagon in Washington, these have highlighted crime control with an emphasis on terrorism and drawn the general populace into its net. Responses to the 'terrorist threat' are eroding key tenets of liberal democracy such as the pre-sumption of innocence until proven guilty as security considerations supersede civil liberties and other rights. These measures have fragmented citizenship rights at the individual level and focused more on personal culpability, whilst the social causes of terrorism are ignored. They have also brought vastly different political regimes together to ensure their own security and survival. The ensuing loss of civil rights is a social work concern.

Probation: The link with social work

Looking after the welfare needs of offenders has been an important thread running throughout the history of the probation service. From its beginnings as work undertaken in reformatory schools for young offenders (Carlebach, 1970) to the police officers working in the Court Missions to the present day, the concern to change the behaviour of offenders has been linked to looking after their needs. Responding to the welfare needs of offenders whilst keeping them out of prison was highlighted during the 1980s in legislation stretching from the 1982 Criminal Justice Act to the 1991 Criminal Justice Act. This latter Act attempted to increase the range of sentencing options at the disposal of the courts and reduce the rigidity of parole conditions. Decisions about disposals drew on PSRs. These provided information that evidenced probation officers' recommendations and were required for all offenders under the age of 21 if considered candidates for a custodial sentence.

Changes in the probation service have wrought a number of alterations in probation practice for court-based criminal work. The introduction of National Standards in 1992, revised in 1995 and 2000, constituted management's attempt to bring procedural predictability into the work done by individual probation officers. These developments have been intensified through Occupational Standards (Home Office, 1992). Along with National Standards, these have had considerable impact on the labour process in probation by reducing individual officers' capacity to exercise professional discretion and intensifying the drive towards managerialism and its attendant bureaucratic forms of control.

Probation practice in court-based criminal work has been altered in other ways. Its officers, once almost exclusively white men, have become a more diverse group, with white women beginning to approximate the numbers of white men at basic-grade level; more black people are also joining them (Dominelli et al., 1995; Cook and Hudson, 1995). A glass ceiling still bars white women from promotion prospects, however, for although some have become chief probation officers, they remain a minority (Home Office, 2002).

Black officers at the senior levels of the profession also continue to be few and far between, despite equal opportunities and anti-racist practice becoming commonplace, at least in departmental rhetoric. For the few who have made it into maingrade ranks, promotion to its higher echelons remains scarce. The devolution of responsibilities to probation service officer (PSO) level has resulted in tasks formerly undertaken by probation officers now being performed by them.

Politicians have undermined the role of social work with offenders by using rising crime figures to claim that society cannot afford to be 'soft' on criminals. Espoused by Michael Howard as Conservative Home Secretary, this line chimed with earlier professional discourses that challenged the appropriateness of social work intervention with hardened offenders and lent credence to the 'nothing works' hypothesis (Martinson, 1974; McIvor, 1990) popularized through the media. Claiming that 'prison works', Howard built on discussions about the ineffective interventions of his immediate predecessors within both the academy and policymaking to shift discourses onto terrain that left social work out on the margins as an ineffective, meddlesome discipline that had no basis for inclusion within the CJS.

A weakness of the 'what works' approach is the failure of programmes to develop networks and layers of support that embed changes secured in offending behaviour over the long term (Raynor and Vanstone, 1996). Practitioners' inability to link individual changes with community-based reinforcement and structural change to sustain these beyond short-term gains undermines the effectiveness of arguments favouring 'what works' initiatives (Raynor, Smith and Vanstone, 1994).

The 'what works' debate has created discourses leading to new directions for practice. At the heart of these has been a changing perception of prison, which, rather than being seen as 'an expensive way of making bad people worse' (Home Office, 1990), is now applauded for its efficacy as the principal instrument for working with offenders. Incarceration became the 'be-all' and 'end-all' of policy and practice during the 1990s. These developments downgrade rehabilitation, strengthen managerialism through bureaucratic mechanisms of control of practitioners' activities, and increase pressures for probation officers to conform to rational bureaucratic definitions of their work.

Michael Howard's endeavours and the authority given to his ideas in the media seriously undermined the credibility of both social workers and probation officers (Smith, 1995). Following this,

Howard promised to remove any trace of social work knowledge from probation officers' repertoire of skills (Dews and Watts, 1994; Sone, 1995). He also threatened to replace social work 'do-gooders' with hardened army men who would inculcate proper discipline into unruly offenders, especially the persistent few committing the bulk of offences (Sone, 1995). A general election intervened and prevented Howard from implementing his promises, but his approach was endorsed by his New Labour successor. Jack Straw set about altering the status of probation in the CJS, and severing the link between probation and social work.

The break in the longstanding association in joint training between probation officers and social workers in England and Wales occurred in 1998 when Straw ensured that probation officers would no longer indulge in social work, but in corrections activities that control offending behaviour and protect the public. He did so by training probation officers away from the contaminating influence of social work knowledge, skills and values. Although Straw has moved on, his successor, David Blunkett, treads in his footsteps.

Discourses of 'law and order' link offending behaviour to fears about public safety and the desire to keep society free from crime and violence, turning probation practice into a politicized activity. Engaged in their creation and reproduction, politicians use these discourses to legitimate interventions in probation practice through constant changes in legislative frameworks and policies (Downes and Morgan, 1994). Discourse change occurs readily when politicians reinforce discourses that concur with public anxieties (Cohen, 1980). The rapid switch from diversionary practices to incarceration during the early 1990s when Michael Howard replaced Douglas Hurd as Home Secretary exemplifies a classic shift of this nature. Swings in policy also reflect the contested nature of 'law and order' discourses. Various interest groups redefine their position to line up along different fault lines and engender changes in the existing set-up. In probation education and practice, these shifts indicate how easily prevailing discourses can be countered when there is a concerted attack upon them by people who wield power, have resources, get the ear of opinion-formers in the media and access dissemination networks.

The phenomenon of focusing largely on punishing offenders and seeing incarceration in and of itself as a sufficient response to their needs, as popularized by politicians in a range of countries, has begun to be challenged by practitioners, offenders and others who argue for the abolition of a punishment-focused system: for example, feminists have called for measures to improve offenders' behaviour.

They have insisted anew that work be done with convicted violent men in prison to prevent their attacking women and children (Dominelli, 1989, 2002b).

Breaking the link with social work

Different professions have appropriated roles previously performed by social workers; others have been shed by the profession itself. The loss of fields of expertise to other professionals has caused a rethinking of the boundaries that have demarcated social work. At the end of the twentieth century, working with offenders in England and Wales had been removed from social work's remit and punishment replaced rehabilitation as the main goal in work with convicted criminals (Sone, 1995). Probation continues to be part of social work in Scotland and overseas, however.

McGuire's (1995) and Pritchard's (2001a) research indicates that social work with offenders can be effective in reducing offending behaviour. Raynor, Smith and Vanstone (1994) have argued that it is possible to predict which interventions are more effective than others. This view has not been shared by a number of their contemporaries (e.g. Neary, 1992), particularly those critical of the failure of work with persistent offenders, especially sex offenders. Studies by Quinsey (1995) also shed considerable doubt on practitioners' ability reliably to predict 'dangerousness' and thereby 'protect the public'.

Market incentives

Social workers' perceived poor track record resulted in losing the remit to work with offenders in England and Wales. In achieving this shift, the training of probation officers has been decoupled from the Diploma in Social Work (DipSW). This process began in 1994 when some probation training was transferred to the workplace. It peaked in 1998 when the Home Office assumed complete control of it. Probation trainees now receive a Diploma in Probation Studies (DPS). Under this model, employers commission training from providers that form consortia to bid for contracts, thereby locking probation training into the purchaser–provider nexus.

With market discipline penetrating the criminal justice training arena, tendering for the DPS has encouraged a bevy of freelance consultants and university departments to compete against each other. Some consultants are redundant university lecturers who have become self-employed to continue the work that they have the skills to undertake in another guise. Others with little or no previous experience in probation teaching, but able to offer low-cost training, became experts overnight. There has been little incentive to monitor the qualifications of such experts and ensure quality exists in the unregulated arena of the private trainer, or even the private agencies that either employ them directly or choose them as employees for state jobs. Ironically, management and accountancy firms, concerned with balancing ledgers, and having little or no knowledge or experience of social work education or practice, have played major roles in this development. For example, Price-Waterhouse was given a Home Office contract to train managers for the probation service (Dominelli and Hoogvelt, 1996b).

The mixed economy of provisions in the CJS has both preceded and accompanied developments in probation practice. Its growth acquired a considerable boost with the introduction of private prisons, some of which had been commissioned to overcome the shortage of prison places once magistrates started issuing more punitive sentencing. This was compounded by the impetus given to non-state providers during the early 1990s when the Home Office dictated that a certain amount of a probation service's budget had to be spent in the voluntary sector (Home Office, 1990). These changes have resulted in the growth of commercial and voluntary providers in a range of services from prisons to community safety and victim support groups. These developments have emphasized the importance of effective inter-agency working and partnership as advocated in the 1996 Woolf Report.

Alongside these moves, parts of the probation service such as family court work and community service have been separated off from its core business – criminal court work. At the same time, the Criminal Justice and Court Services Act (CJCSA) of 2000 has restructured the probation service by abolishing the fifty-five local probation services in favour of a centralized national probation service of forty-two regions with boundaries coterminous with police force areas. This move has reduced the number of autonomous probation areas, and increased central control over local services. These events are beginning to alter the face of probation practice.

The CJCSA has re-enforced the surveillance and monitoring dimensions of probation work by extending the use of electronic tagging in tracking offenders on orders and licence. The state has also tightened up on breach proceedings, limiting the number of violations of a particular order to one in a twelve-month period; demanding stiffer sentences for those labelled persistent offenders; and requiring that all released prisoners be subjected to a period of mandatory supervision. A contradiction remains within these provisions: the supremacy of incarceration. It projects a rise in the prison population within a prison system that already has severely stretched and extremely overcrowded facilities (Woolf, 2001[5]).

Privatizing parts of the criminal justice system

The Home Office has facilitated privatization processes in the CJS since the early 1990s, allowing the construction of private prisons and dictating that a certain amount of a probation service's budget be spent in the voluntary sector. Voluntary agencies have played key roles in 'Safer Cities' programmes that support victims of crimes. Large multinational private sector corporations like Wackenhut and Sodexho now provide correctional services, particularly prisons and detention centres.

The nightmare scenario of a substantial growth in the prison population has assisted the privatization of prison services (Woolf, 2002). The increase has followed policy changes commenced under the 1993 Criminal Justice Act, promulgated following hostile pressure from magistrates opposing the 'leniency' of the 1991 Act, which had become operative in October 1992. Begun by the Tories, greater use of incarceration has continued under New Labour. Consequently, the prison population in England and Wales rose from 44,552 in 1993 to 67,054 by 2001 (Hough, 2002).

Private prisons were introduced to Britain in 1992 when HMP Wolds opened in West Yorkshire. There are now seven private prisons in Britain, with ongoing negotiations for more, including a facility in Middlesex for 450 women offenders, making this the first private facility devoted to women prisoners. The Private Finance Initiative (PFI) has been extended to the prison service to expedite the building of new prisons to absorb the increase in prisoners more economically and speedily than under state-run facilities. The first PFI-financed private prison, Fazakerley, now Altcourse, was opened in Merseyside in 1997. Private prisons have been enormously profitable for entrepreneurs (Hencke, 2001). They have also placed pressure to improve standards on the prison service as a whole.

Prison privatization is being challenged in a number of quarters. For example, insurance companies are unwilling to provide cover for some facilities. Lloyd's Syndicate 962 refused to insure immigration detention centres after 2001, when rioting and fire caused £97 million in damages and closed the Yarl's Wood Immigration Centre in Bedfordshire run by Group 4. If the government has to provide cover, the costs of privatization to the taxpayer rise. The insurance of Fazakerley (Altcourse), which was initially the responsibility of government, has been undertaken by private operators in subsequent contracts. Reducing costs in running and maintaining a criminal justice system, particularly the prison service, has been a major factor driving government policy in this arena. It is imperative, therefore, that public expenditures are reduced. However, with the staggering projected rises in the prison population and the necessity for building ever more prisons, this objective may prove elusive, even if buttressed by an increase in the number of community-based sentences for offenders committing less serious crimes.

Meanwhile, the trade union UNISON has argued for employees in private prisons to enjoy the same rates of pay and conditions as those in the public sector. UNISON's concern to improve working conditions and the rights of workers are being set back by New Labour's opposition to a European Union draft directive that gives new rights to temporary or agency workers because it endangers profitability. UNISON demands an end to privatization because those running Public–Private Partnerships (PPPs) lack probity. It cites five accountancy firms that advise the public sector on £54 billion worth of contracts as simultaneously auditing many of the builders (Maguire, 2002).

UNISON sees conflicts of interest in forty-five cases where subsidiaries and consultancy firms have been used. It argues that

[t]hese companies are running the government's privatisation agenda and charge massive fees as advisers and auditors. There must be a huge question mark over the independence and impartiality of the advice these firms are giving on PFI and PPP. (Maguire, 2002, p. 10)

The commissioning state exerts power through financial means, primarily by the mechanisms associated with contract government, which have been used to encourage growth in commercial and voluntary providers. Contractual arrangements specify the type of service to be provided and number of offenders to be covered. By controlling supply and demand, the commissioning state curtails local autonomy to facilitate the provision of additional resources and services.

From a social work activity to a corrections-based one

The 'moral panics' around 'law and order' played a key role in bringing about the demise of the direct ties between social work and probation training in England and Wales. The link remains in the value orientation of the two disciplines, but their implementation in practice varies considerably. These changes have failed to deal with the basic contradiction at the heart of probation practice: what to do with convicted offenders. How can they be reintegrated into society or the communities from which they came? How can they learn to live in a society that insists on certain standards of acceptable behaviour? These questions reaffirm the tensions between rehabilitation and punishment. Probation officers have a longstanding commitment to helping offenders become full members of the community – a goal that easily comes within the remit of the social cohesion agenda of New Labour. Their position is reflected in serving probation officers' continued support for alternatives to prison.

The government's concern to increase the use of custodial sentences for offenders who could respond to other measures has had interesting unintentional effects. Willis (1985) suggests that this has resulted in more serious offenders being given community sentences. Thus, probation officers now work with offenders who have already been convicted of offences and may have more difficult personality problems to be addressed. This trend is reflected in probation caseloads as the number of offenders with no previous convictions fell from 25 per cent to 13 per cent between 1980 and 1989 (Raynor, Smith and Vanstone, 1994). Vass and Weston (1990) claim that probation has become more integrated into corrections discourses and moved away from its association with welfarist ones. Raynor, Smith and Vanstone (1994) make the counter-claim that such developments can be interpreted as a more enlightened approach to offenders because it has taken out of the prison network people who would have been sent into its embrace earlier. The failure of prison to work in the long term is evidenced by high recidivism rates. A recent report reveals that former prisoners commit 18 per cent of recorded crime – 900,000 offences a year at the cost of £10.8 billion, without the ongoing costs associated with their lifestyles (Travis and White, 2002).

The rise of victims' rights

A further key criticism of probation's incapacity to deal adequately with offenders and issues of 'law and order' has been its inability to reduce substantially reoffending or recidivism. Another was its preoccupation with the rights of offenders, which the media and policymakers have asserted deny victims' rights to justice. Feminist voices had added to the clamour for change earlier by demanding rights for women victims of male violence and victim-survivors of child sexual abuse. Their activities have challenged the probation service's failure to take seriously the needs of women and children at the receiving end of much of men's offending behaviour.

The shift to victims' rights received a further impetus during the early 1990s when a plethora of Citizens' Charters indicated consumers' right to specified standards of service and having their concerns addressed. Amongst these was the Victims Charter. It targeted victims and articulated the rights and services they might expect from employees of the CJS when requesting assistance. These pressures have given rise to victimology, or the theory and practice that responds to the needs of victims. With it, the culture of probation with regards to victims has begun to change (Tapley, 2002).

The challenge of victims' rights posed problems for an offender-oriented probation service and it took some time for it to become sensitive to the new demands being made of officers (Rock, 1990). At the same time, offenders have to be treated with fairness and due process to ensure that they are justly dealt with. Despite several versions of the Victims Charter, each aiming to improve the relationship between victims and CJS, this objective has not been met. Joanna Shapland's work with her colleagues (Shapland, Willmore and Duff, 1985) and Jackie Tapley's (2002) subsequent study reveal how much further there is to go for victims to feel justice has been done. Although the charter approach has had the advantage of highlighting victims' needs and legitimating their concerns, it has turned victims into consumers to do that.

Tapley's (2002) investigation of victims' responses to their treatment under the provisions of the Victims Charter demonstrates that victims continue to feel bypassed by the system as a whole. More recently, widely publicized cases, for example the murders of Stephen Lawrence and Damilola Taylor in London, have highlighted the negligence of victims' rights to appropriate services despite the presence of the Victims Charter and the government's attempts to bolster its implementation. However, this has been undertaken with limited funding dedicated to the purpose of improving services for victims. As a result, support services for them are provided by under-resourced voluntary sector agencies like Victims Support. Whilst appreciative of the work done on their behalf by Victims Support, victims prefer a statutory agency to deal with their concerns (Tapley, 2002). They see the voluntary and under-resourced nature of the services provided as reducing their status in comparison to offenders, who have the bulk of CJS resources spent on them.

Victims are subjected to the 'technologies of governmentality' and (re)inscribed as they are processed by the system (Tapley, 2002). The Victims Charter focuses on victims primarily as consumers of the services provided by the CJS according to bureaucratic routines. Hence, victims are treated as citizens only when not making demands of it. The over-demanding victim is treated as an 'undeserving' client and so less entitled to professional support (Tapley, 2002). Tapley (2002) calls for a well-resourced statutory body to look after their interests, alongside Victims Support and the Witness Service.

Other forms of intervention have included the community as a stakeholder in the work of the CJS. Victim–offender mediation schemes have sought to bring offenders and victims together to get offenders to appreciate the impact of their actions on victims and agree reparation to either individual victims or the community more generally. These initiatives have focused on what offenders can do to change their behaviour and not on what changes are needed in the community to develop conditions that are less likely to support criminal activities. Nor do they provide victims with the vast array of services they might require – counselling, adequate compensation and, in some instances, life-long support, to itemize a few.

Discourses around the rights of offenders and victims have been conducted in binary oppositional terms which pit the interests of meeting the needs of one group against those of the other. This configuration of the matter is unfortunate since both sets of people have legitimate concerns that have to be addressed if the long-term goal of reducing crime and dealing with its aftermath are to be achieved. Dealing with the causes of crime, rehabilitating offenders to make positive contributions to society, and enabling victims to feel that their interests are being upheld are all necessary for improving the climate in which people can feel that crime no longer has a negative impact upon their quality of life.

Citizenship and offenders' rights to rehabilitation

Offenders experience a loss of rights under punitive regimes. Traditional conceptualizations of offenders have revolved around the idea that they have abrogated their rights as citizens by committing an offence and being convicted. Constructing offenders as being outside rights-based regimes once they have been sentenced, the state's concern has been to control and manage offenders' behaviour to reduce their dangerousness to other members of society rather than to enforce their citizenship rights. This approach has emphasized risk management and risk assessments as the main instruments for dealing with their recalcitrant behaviour.

Anti-offender discourses are concerned with preventing offenders from exercising their citizenship rights. Key to these discourses has been the loss of the right to vote – *the* symbol of political citizenship – during periods of incarceration or for life in parts of the USA. Discourses of citizenship have tended to ignore the rights of offenders. Besides negating offenders' rights of citizenship, these discourses have limited their right to be rehabilitated or assisted in changing their behaviour while serving custodial sentences.

This attitude has begun to unravel recently as concern for offenders' citizenship rights have become voiced by those imprisoned. Some offenders have articulated a worry about being unable to reintegrate into communities. A group of sex offenders in Kingston Penitentiary sued the Canadian state for not meeting their needs as prison inmates by not providing rehabilitative interventions during their time in prison so that they could be better people when released. The courts concurred that the state was neglecting its duty to care for them. This failure is dangerous in that in the absence of care, the prison setting easily becomes a 'university for criminals' (Boyle, 1977).

Attempts to be more inclusive of offenders are difficult, with outcomes depending on the offences committed. Sex offenders have not been welcomed back into their communities because they are deemed to continue posing a threat to the safety of children. Public campaigns against sex offenders expose the failure of professionals to convince ordinary people that 'prison works' and that those who have served their sentences are sufficiently reformed to no longer endanger the lives of other citizens.

A community-based ethic of care that reintegrates offenders on the basis of their citizenship rights is more likely to promote long-term change than one that suggests that there is nothing redeemable in an offending person. A citizenship approach would require a display of solidarity and connectedness between offenders and the communities in which they live. Practice would focus on establishing reciprocal relationships that combine individual responsibility with social responsibility to ensure that structural causes of crime are addressed alongside personal ones. Pursuing this would embed probation practice in notions of social justice as well as seeing that justice is done vis-à-vis condemning and punishing offending behaviour. In addition, it is more in keeping with social work values of showing respect and dignity for the person whilst condemning unacceptable behaviour.

Conclusions

Work with offenders is a contentious part of social work practice located within the CJS. Discourses about its effectiveness have varied from endorsing the prison regime as the ultimate in 'what works' to moves to rehabilitate offenders and respond to their welfare needs. Under the new managerialism, practice has undergone a number of changes to:

- control professional discretion;
- ensure professional accountability;
- transform the nature of professional work;
- change offending behaviour and public perceptions about it;
- redefine parental responsibilities;
- alter relationships between individuals and the state; and
- shift relationships between the public and private sectors.

The new managerialism is complemented by a punitive populism that endorses the pathologizing of individual offenders but ignores the structural causes of crime. Dealing effectively with the challenges of offending behaviour requires that *offenders take responsibility* for their actions and that the *social causes of crime* are addressed. Offenders are part of the community, not outsiders to it. Their needs and rights have to be upheld alongside those of non-offenders who wish to see their communities freed of crime if crime reduction strategies are to work and rehabilitation is to support offenders in becoming law-abiding citizens.

SOCIAL WORK INTERVENTIONS IN COMMUNITIES

7

Introduction

Community work has had a chequered history in British social work. During the 1970s and early 1980s it was considered one of the three key settings in or methods through which interventions occurred (Mayo and Jones, 1974) and was taught in social work programmes in universities. The other two were working with individuals on a one-to-one basis or casework and groupwork (Younghusband, 1978). Community work's subsequent loss of place in the social work curriculum can be attributed to three major factors: the decline in recognized jobs, which has impacted negatively on numbers interested in training for practice; the ideological positioning of community work within the discipline of social work in the academy; and, from the late 1980s, the refusal of the CCETSW to recognize and fund such training.

Ironically, whilst community work was losing favour in Britain, it was being practised as a key method in several other nations. In industrializing countries, it is linked to social and human development (Kaseke, 1994). In southern Africa and India, it became a major way of dealing with poverty and educational disadvantage. In the United States, the Association of Community Work led a campaign for recognition as an important part of social work and was admitted as such into the Council for Social Work Education (CSWE) at its Annual Programme Meeting in Orlando in 1998. In the international domain, community work is an accepted part of social work (Garber, 2000).

Community is a 'golden glow' word that conjures up images of unity, solidarity and goodwill. But communities are also where exclusion, war and hate thrive. How do people make sense of these two antagonistic images of the sites in which and through which people become who they are? How do people promote inclusivity in communities? And what role do social workers play in bringing this about? I examine these questions in this chapter. While doing so, I consider some of the history relating to the shifting place of community work in the British social work curriculum. I argue that under globalization the integration of societies and the attendant decline in the infrastructure of local communities make it imperative for social work practitioners to be aware of community work methods. They have to become proficient in mobilizing communities if structural inequalities are to be eliminated or their impact on individuals and social environments is to be mitigated.

Rothman (1970) identified four key models of community work: community care, community organization, community development and community action. Community care revolves around good neighbourliness or people using resources at their disposal to provide services to people in need. Community organization schemes seek to improve communication links between different service providers, eliminate waste and avoid duplication in existing resources. Community development endeavours to integrate people more thoroughly into capitalist economic relations through projects that enhance access to resources. These three models rely heavily on self-help initiatives to make good the gaps in existing service provisions and endorse the status quo. Unlike the other two models, community development initiatives are foreseen as having the possibility of promoting social change. Rothman (1970) argues that once this happens, it becomes community action. In his schema, only community action can mobilize people to change existing social relations. Elsewhere (Dominelli, 1990), I have extended the latter category to include identity-based forms of community work: class-based community action, feminist community action and community action from black perspectives. To this, I now add the disability movement's social model of disability, and the anti-globalization movement's networking within civil society. These are change-oriented models of community work and aim to alter the status quo by tackling oppression experienced through targeted social divisions. A major limitation of each of these models is the inability to transcend the boundaries of its own self-defined community and link up with others to secure broader social change.

I now explore the meaning of 'community', examine its use in social work theory, policy and practice, and consider how community relations might be rethought to become more inclusive of diversity, celebratory of difference and involve social workers. I refer to social workers in the broad inclusive sense of practitioners who are interested in promoting human well-being and bringing about social justice in their local patch whilst assisting international developments to bring this about elsewhere.

(Re)defining communities

What does 'community' mean? Its definition is highly contested and varied. In the 1970s, Bell and Newby (1971) found ninety-eight different usages of the term. Abercrombie, Hill and Turner (1994, p. 75) claim that the word ' "community" is one of the most elusive and vague in sociology and is now without specific meaning'. They go on to suggest that it has three characteristics: 'a collection of people with a particular social structure'; a sense of belonging or community spirit; and 'all the daily activities of a community'. For popular usage, the Collins Dictionary defines 'community' as 'the people living in one locality; a group of people having cultural, religious, ethnic or other characteristics in common; similarity or agreement'. The assumptions of homogeneity and unity that form the basis of a community are evident in the framing of public discourses around it.

Wanting to clarify the term, Toennies (1957), in his influential studies of rural communities, draws a distinction between *Gemeinschaft* (community) and *Gesellschaft* (association). He argues that communities are self-contained entities, united by kinship and share a sense of belonging. His work has established a tradition that has shaped thinking about communities as unifying forces. It remains prevalent in today's discourses and has been authoritative in both social policy and social work practice. Popular discourses about communities focus on its inclusionary elements – the unitary community associated with a particular group that invests all its energies in it. Its enforced unity becomes exclusionary.

Toennies' conceptualization of 'community' has several drawbacks. It idealizes communities; establishes divisions between people according to whether they are insiders or outsiders; and promotes totalizing and exclusionary social relations. Those drawing on his thinking to define communities become embedded in exclusionary processes and do not speak to the experiences of *all* those living in a particular 'community'. Consequently, white men in dominant power-wielding positions promote discourses that talk about *their* community and marginalize those considered outside it, for example white women, black people.

By focusing on unifying forces within a community, those adopting Toennies' framework ignore fragmentation in communities and suppress recognition of the range of diversities apparent within any given community, including fractures that occur along age, class, gender, 'race' and religious lines. Toennies' formulation is unable to deal with change in how communities are (re)defined and (re)delineated. Particular configurations of community alter over time as people interact with one another and negotiate the spaces within which they are located. These negotiations are conducted through day-to-day interactions across and within social divides and contribute to the shifting and fluid nature of communities during both daily routines and moments of massive social upheaval.

Communities provide spaces in which people seek and gain approval, are reaffirmed in their interests or sense of who they are and what they stand for, participate in key decisions, and negotiate with others around issues of change and stability. A community to which an individual belongs is where he or she expects to be treated with dignity, show solidarity with others, experience the interdependent nature of relationships between human beings, and work with others in mutually beneficial ways. Dignity, reciprocity, interdependence and solidarity provide the ties that bind communities and disparate people together.

Post-war community work in Britain

Britain's most recognized experience of community work harks back to the experimental Community Development Projects (CDPs) of the late 1960s to mid-1970s, although the British state had imported community development models to former colonies earlier (Marsden and Oakley, 1982; Kwo, 1984). Managed by local authorities, CDPs began as traditional community work projects focusing on community organization models of bringing people together to improve co-ordination amongst agencies delivering services to the locality. CDPs' incisive analyses of the social problems caused by economic decline in twelve small neighbourhoods scattered throughout Britain rapidly turned community work into radical community action. In it, activists, whether paid or unpaid, organized and mobilized communities to challenge officialdom in the local state for failing to meet the needs of local citizens.

Local authorities managing CDPs were major providers of services – housing, education, personal social services and employment opportunities. Local councils came under activist fire, especially in housing, where council tenants were supported to protest unmet housing needs and being allocated housing unfit for human habitation. In seeking to remedy these deficiencies, CDP workers engaged in direct action alongside residents and embarked on a collision course with local authorities employing them. These conflicts led to the closure of several of the most actively oriented CDPs and ultimately the whole experiment (Loney, 1983; Dominelli, 1990).

Local employers in CDP areas were already feeling the pressures of globalization, although these were not acknowledged as such. The de-industrialization of working-class communities in the industrialized West took hold as local and multinational companies relocated jobs to communities in the industrializing South. The British state has worked closely with employers to protect jobs, but has been unable to halt decline in inner-city areas or substantially revitalize old industrial heartlands. The forces of globalization have intensified since CDP days. The penetration of the local economy by global forces and the interconnections (or lack of them) between global and local developments have now been recognized. Meanwhile, care in the community has become its commercialized variant – community care – and been integrated into global networks. Under the impact of globalizing forces and legislative frameworks linked to community care, the local state has become an enabling state. Instead of acting as a direct provider of services, it commissions these from the voluntary and commercial sectors and controls their activities by applying the strictures of 'contract government' (Greer, 1994) and its massive purchasing power.

In Britain, community work has disappeared primarily from the social work curriculum in the 'old' universities. It remained a subject taught in polytechnics prior to the 1992 reorganization which converted them into universities. The Federation of Community Workers has continued to offer a Diploma in Youth and Community Work, but this has not been recognized by schools of social work in universities. Outside these, community work education and training continues to flourish.

Contemporary community workers are less likely to organize around protecting housing and jobs than environmental issues ranging from opposing the construction of roads, airports and housing developments in ecologically sensitive areas, to resisting the spread of genetically modified (GM) food. These continue to be concerns of everyday life, but differ from objections to the closure of factories, schools or nursery places that featured strongly in CDP workers' repertoire.

The concern to maximize income and development in communities continues, but is addressed differently. Schemes to promote community economic development within a sustainable physical and social environment, the social economy and local credit programmes such as credit unions and micro-credit projects provide examples of community initiatives that seek to create social relations outside the capitalist nexus (Shragge and Fontane, 2000). Avoiding capitalist relations is difficult in the context of globalization, and these have begun to impact on these initiatives in negative ways. McKinnon (2001) identifies key barriers to their independent development and the loss of autonomy arising through interaction with the broader capitalist system and from constraints on community-centred initiatives emanating from renewing capital for reinvestment purposes.

The Desjardins schemes demonstrate that there is considerable mileage in following community-based development (Shragge and Fontaine, 2000). People can acquire jobs that lift them out of poverty, even if only marginally, and exercise greater control over their lives through community-based economic developments. These provide examples of community action endeavours that have organized beyond the borders of local or even national communities and begun to challenge the hegemony of capitalist global relations (Prigoff, 2000). Grameen Bank enterprises and the Desjardins schemes, considered successful examples of these initiatives, have, however, been unable to eradicate poverty or draw into their ambit all of the poor populations in the areas where their projects exist (Burkett, 2002).[1] Other attempts to eliminate global poverty, such as Jubilee 2000, have also been unable to meet this objective.

Reconfiguring community work in Britain

The British government has usurped community work methods for its own purposes. These have included facilitating the growth of job-creation schemes and mobilizing poor communities to look after their own needs (Finn, 1985). Beginning with the Youth Training Schemes (YTSs) promoted and monitored by the

Manpower Services Commission (MSC) in the 1980s, community-based job-creation schemes have offered employment-based community work with limited training in its techniques and knowledge base. Those enrolled on these programmes learn skills on the job and are inadequately trained in community work methods. Programmes have taken the form of short courses which have not been recognized beyond those providing them.

The theoretical basis of community work, knowledge of the latest research findings and familiarity with examples of best or innovative practice elsewhere are rarely found on in-house courses with a practical orientation. Their absence can diminish the advantages of learning that can be derived from knowing how others beyond the immediate locale do things. This feature is essential in ensuring a broad student-centred learning experience. As a result of inadequate training, the knowledge base of community workers often mirrors the self-help one. This may limit capacity to offer leadership in new directions and jeopardize their role as innovators when problem-solving, organizing campaigns or beginning other initiatives.

The self-help principles promulgated in YTSs by Thatcherite administrations have continued in a modified way to the present under New Labour's 'New Deal' and community regeneration programmes (Blair, 1999). Work and community-based self-help schemes have become the Blair government's preferred policy options for pulling people out of poverty (Craig, 2001). Blair's initiatives have been linked to the social inclusion and modernizing agendas and drawn on self-help ideas that people's own capacities can be released to overcome disadvantage. These schemes have focused limited resources on younger generations in disadvantaged communities through programmes like 'Sure Start'. Blair's endeavours have depoliticized community work and drawn it into the ambit of bureau-technocrats and competence-based appraisal schemes. Its crucial weakness is relating to residents as excluded people without engaging in the necessary structural changes, particularly the polarization of wealth. Countering income inequalities has been a persistent theme in community work, though largely neglected by mainstream social work (Jones, 1998). Reflecting upon the position of the major 'client' group with whom social workers interact – poor people – can enlighten the profession on insider–outsider forms of exclusion and facilitate analyses that focus on structural change.

Social workers and community workers rarely deal with the multidimensionality of complex and fluid community dynamics. In practice, community workers tend to work in geographical communities based on neighbourhoods with fixed boundaries. These have distinct interests or problems that residents wish to solve. In industrializing countries, many community endeavours focus on everyday difficulties like the provision of food and clean drinking water that are linked to poverty and deprivation experienced by those living in these locales. Key actions in Western countries include environmental degradation, lack of employment, poor housing, inadequate public transport arrangements, low levels of provision for playgroups and insufficient child care facilities. Community concerns have been divided into 'hard' and 'soft' issues. 'Hard' issues have been associated with men's interests in the public domain, 'soft' ones with women's preoccupations in the domestic arena (Dominelli, 1990).

Community work has been gendered, with practice conventions designating specific areas as appropriate for men community workers and others for women (Mayo, 1977). In this division of labour, men assume leadership roles and women supporting ones. Although the community is the location where women dominate, they are sidelined into doing the day-to-day organizing and caring dimensions of community work (Mayo, 1977; Dominelli, 1990). Community work has been (re)conceptualized as men focusing on public matters and women on personal issues centring on family or interpersonal relationships and needs. Consequently, working in the community becomes an extension of work women do 'naturally' in the home. Care in the community acts as a buffer zone bridging private and public domains. In the fluid and shifting borders of communities, women's work oils the wheels that keep relationships turning.

In my own writings (Dominelli, 2002a, 2002b), I have focused on three different bases on which people form community affiliations: identity, geography and interests. I argue that each is multidimensional, interactive and fluid. Identity I define as who the person is or the attributes that each person perceives as providing a sense of self when engaging with other people's perceptions of who he or she is when interacting with them. This makes identity a formative, negotiated, interactive process in which a person defines while being defined. These definitions of the self and other person(s) are not complete or total. Each individual holds a number of roles and attributes that make up his or her identity. Which of these is revealed to a particular audience at a specific point involves the individual making contextualized and negotiated choices about which features are brought into the public domain from the private one and when. Certain attributes are *selected* as germane to the interaction and activated by being brought into the interaction when the person deems it appropriate to do so. Others are disregarded.

The self is bounded by a person's body. Bodies provide terrain which is inscribed by both the self and others. Inscribing the body is an action statement about identity and displays the impact of a number of different identity communities that a person draws upon to emphasize his or her own uniqueness. By borrowing from other distinct cultures, these inscriptions bring the global to the local at a very personal level. In addition, the borrower adapts or transmorphs them to accommodate different circumstances. In today's society, body piercing and tattoos are physical embodiments of inscriptions which require interaction with others to materialize as significant cultural statements carried out at the individual level. On the collective one, the return to traditional dress codes, as, for example, the covering of the body by Muslim women, and/or the use of ancestral clothes, names and rituals by those of First Nations, Maori, aboriginal or African descent, represent powerful group statements that assert and reclaim their own unique pasts and heritages and imbue these with new and current symbolism. In the process, each has become the embodiment of a culture that stretches from the present into the past and forward into the future, thus uniting today's generations with those who have been and those yet to come.

Identity can be glocalized in a unique blend of the local and global. It can be generational as well as gendered, racialized or structured according to other social divisions such as class, disability and sexual orientation. Geography is becoming fluid as images and traditions from different countries are adopted away from their source. This process is intensified by aeroplane travel, the new computer technologies and internet-based communications, which have undermined traditional distinctions of time and space.

This fluidity in identity creation and re-creation suggests that the geographical sense of community with its fixed notions of identity that was previously utilized in professional discourses needs to be rethought. Mobility within local areas and across national borders involves the constant (re)negotiation of the boundaries that differentiate these attributes and their meanings (Brah, 1996). Such movements also indicate their permeability, as well as their constancy. The fluidity of a community's borders causes angst for some and delights others. Thinking of these borders as static and to be defended against incursion from others may increase inter-community conflict and makes it difficult to revel in the idea that encounters with others who are different can be a source of enrichment. Static conceptualizations of others become problematic in professional interventions by preventing those preoccupied with them from either responding effectively to others or engaging with them to redraw community boundaries in more inclusive terms.

Communities are also formed on the basis of interests. Those drawing on common interests involve a collection or group of people coming together around a matter that arouses their interest, concern or curiosity. It can be an issue, hobby or sport. People may belong to more than one community simultaneously. So, a person with a passion for history may enjoy playing tennis and belong to 'communities' that form sites for engaging in historical pursuits or sports activities or both. This person may join other communities based on interests that have nothing in common with either of these. As interests change, a person's involvement in a particular community may shift or end.

No one should feel that he or she has to choose to belong to only one community and be restricted to an all-encompassing and limiting life within it. Each person may hold membership of several communities, some with overlapping borders. Thus, each person becomes multiply positioned, although he or she may choose to emphasize one community more than another at a particular point. These communities may stretch from the local to the global (or vice versa); they may be intensely private or very public and shared with many others. People create communities as they negotiate with one another through interactions which simultaneously position the individual concerned as he or she engages in positioning other people.

People may be both insiders and outsiders in one community. This occurs when they are theoretically members of one community but excluded within it, or when those categorized as being outside society are within it. African-Americans living under segregationist 'Jim Crow' laws in the United States illustrate this point. Being 'outside' the mainstream community, African-Americans protesting their racist treatment engendered further forms of exclusion as part of the process of resistance. This exclusion was partly based on creating an area free from white interference and protecting a space that 'black people' could call their own. At the same time, supremacist white groups sought to (re-)entrench their privileges by containing the activities of black freedom fighters and further excluding them from mainstream society (Kinsella, 1998).

Exclusionary community relations

Discourses about communities exclude as they include. Communities are grounded on features that provide unity amongst members. This unity may be 'fictitious' insofar as specific myths of unity are developed to enable people to join forces for specific purposes. Those who do not fit given criteria are left out. Most definitions of community embodied in unifying discourses treat community as a fixed static entity to which an individual either belongs or does not. The communities of these discourses are geographically bounded and have an ahistoricity or timeless quality about them, existing out of time rather than in it. Postmodernists would call this approach to community essentialist. Essentialist conceptualizations of identity allow for an infinite range of communities, but these exist in opposition to each other, pitted against each other in binary dyads of exclusion and inclusion. A person is either in or out; part of 'them', or part of 'us'. Postmodern critiques of essentialism are inadequate because they lose sight of the unifying elements which people create to bring disparate groups together into a community which those involved self-define as well as have defined for them. Additionally, postmodern formulations of essentialism buy into the very binary dyads that they purport to oppose. Thus, they fail to appreciate the 'centredness' in identities that give people meaning.

As long as communities think of themselves in dyadic terms, they automatically exclude those who are different from the group, asserting its power to define itself and in doing so define others. Dyadic formulations of community relationships do not encourage one part of the dyad to take responsibility for the well-being of the other. Nor do they promote the formation of bonds of solidarity and the development of platforms that could unite them despite differences between them.

The conceptualization of relationships amongst people claiming ownership of a particular community space in an antagonistic them–us dyad is important to 'othering' processes. 'Othering' targets those who are different to exclude them. Hostility to the 'other' provides fertile terrain for the elaboration of oppressive relations that control those who are different. It promotes the demonization of the 'other' because they are different and is central to rupturing ties that could bind together people living in communities, regardless of difference. This in turn enables those who belong to the 'superior' or included group to see the 'other' as incomplete, having deficits, inferior. Demonization casts the 'other' as less than human and legitimates violence to control their aspirations and activities. Relations of dominance being perpetrated upon them confirm these controlling dynamics.

Dyadic conceptualizations of community submerged in relations of dominance are inappropriate in the pluralist contexts of multicultural societies in which people want to both celebrate difference and hang on to their own sense of uniqueness rooted in a unity that draws on overlapping values and centres on a shared geographic space. To move away from the 'them' or 'us' mentality, people have to think differently about communities and explore continuities and discontinuities amongst and within them. The continuities allow for some aspects of identity to be maintained across time and space. The discontinuities represent changes, adoptions and accommodation that occur through interactions within and across communities. These encounters produce change within those communities.

These understandings facilitate thinking about communities as dynamic, fluid entities, constantly in a state of flux as each person interacts with others who are within his or her community and outwith it at the same time. The challenge is to conceptualize communities as constantly in the process of formation and re-formation, and sites where people position themselves as actors for particular purposes. Breaking the singularity of communities and thinking of them as having permeable borders which bring about change within both a particular community and those interacting with it are critical in promoting social cohesion.

People in communities are linked together through a variety of ties and networks that bind them to each other. These ties may be based on a variety of features and cover a range that includes romantic, kinship, friendship or national affiliation. Ties that bind are likely to centre on what people hold in common. These are largely taken for granted and invisible. People may understand how these manifest themselves and provide the threads that knit their relationships with others together.

There are other ties of which to be aware. These are the ties of interdependence, mutuality or reciprocity, and solidarity. They underpin people's entitlements and responsibilities as citizens and are experienced at one remove. Although they impact upon daily lives and routines, these link people unknown to and different from each other, counter the fractured nature of modern existence, and add to people's stature as human beings. They do so by acknowledging and valuing difference and encouraging people to accept responsibility for one another's well-being. To incorporate these ties in their lives, people have to think differently about difference and diversity. Rather than fearing what is not under-stood and focusing on the difficulties of connecting with differ-ence, people have to welcome or cherish these to more readily embrace and celebrate them. By interacting with and dialoguing across difference, people's fears will disappear and they will feel safer about retaining their own unique existence.

The intolerance of difference has contributed to people reaching the twenty-first century in a world with increasing disparities in wealth, the homogenization of cultures, the militarization of societies, violence within and across borders, distressful migratory movements and ecological degradation. These negative trends are counteracted by positive ones: the celebration of difference, particularly at the level of civil society; an acknowledgement of the interdependence between people and societies; the assertion of people's desire for a better quality of life within sustainable economic development; and the wish to be part of meaningful, self-defined communities. How will we reinforce these positive aspects in a world riven by inequalities?

For an individual to enjoy his or her own well-being, it is import-ant to work for the well-being of all and live in a world without fear. To address scarcity, isolation and alienation and eliminate avoidable inequalities such as poverty, people need to endorse the peaceful resolution of disputes and conflicts rather than rely upon war. To achieve these goals, they have to find ties that bind them together across and within communities regardless of type with-out overlooking any differences that might exist between them. Seeking unity within diversity will not be easy. It requires a leap of faith into better relationships locally, nationally and internationally and social change that transforms existing social relations and patterns of wealth and resource distribution into egalitarian ones. Though not an easy task, social workers can facilitate change pro-cesses in this direction.

Control or liberation?

Social workers concentrate upon specific settings and methods that differ from those in which community workers dominate, although there are overlaps between them. Community workers often view social workers with suspicion. A key rationale for this has been the perception that social workers control people and compel them to adjust to the status quo with its unequal power relations while community workers empower people by helping them to challenge existing social arrangements and take control over their lives. This configuration of community work discourses is naïve and simplistic. Depicting community work as only liberating ignores the use of the technologies of control within this domain.

A critical examination of the history of intervention undertaken in both arenas reveals that controlling and empowering activities are conducted in both. The exposure of sexist and racist relations in community work and social work indicates the existence of oppressive relations in both at least with regards to gender (Dominelli and McLeod, 1989) and 'race' (Ohri, Manning and Curno, 1982; Dominelli, 1988, 1990). Critical analyses have highlighted the different dimensions of oppressive social relations that occur in various practice settings (Fook, 1993). Commonalities in the dynamics of oppression or processes whereby oppression is perpetrated exist alongside differences in the oppressive dimensions promoted in and through the specificities of practice in both. Oppressive social relations focus on control issues – ways of confining people to choices and options that are not of their making.

Control is also exercised by defining who belongs to a particular community and enforcing exclusion from it. Communities may be extremely oppressive in patrolling their boundaries and controlling the permeability of their borders to curtail access by outsiders severely. Those encompassed by a community are expected to reproduce relations that signify its particular boundaries, attributes and status. On seeking inclusion, the adherents of a particular community may subject entrants to rigid requirements and rituals which must be met to expunge attributes that mark them as different. Acquiring citizenship status to belong to a specific national community exemplifies such practices. Some countries are more restrictive than others about the conditions which must be met for citizenship to be granted. Citizenship communities are also exclusionary. One example of this is citizens' reaction to those excluded from their midst by the label (im)migrant. Discourses referring to them are hostile, depicting them as strangers who abuse welfare rather than as contributors to the social and economic life of the country. These images reinforce their position as those who do not belong. Yet (im)migrants help to make a country what it is.

Totalizing and unitary discourses are useful in binding particular groups together, creating myths rooted in past glories to affirm strengths in people or address nostalgic yearnings. Unifying discourses may be powerful enough to submerge or transcend differences amongst participants if they are prepared to put these to one side or temporarily suspend them for a particular purpose.

Traditional unitary discourses tend to control or submerge differences and diversities in their midst, usually to promote an otherwise
non-existent unity.

The totalizing notion of Britishness to encompass Protestant
people of English, Welsh, Scottish and Irish extraction for the Act of
Accession in 1703 embodies such a creation. A product of unifying
discourses, this Act ignored distinctive differences in the identities
of the four specified groups in bringing them together and sup-
pressed the needs of segments of the population that did not fit
within these categories, for example Catholics. Discourses about
the homogeneity or unity within a community population do not
have to result in negative experiences, however. Now that people
are no longer willing to accept the submerging of difference, this
unitary conceptualization of Britishness is being (re)critiqued
and (re)modified. New forms of community interaction are being
developed to celebrate difference and address any difficulties that
diversities might pose.

Changing notions of Britishness have found formal expression in
phrases such as 'Black British', 'Anglo-Asian' and British Muslim,
and, for the four founding nations, in devolved structures of governance that give pride of place to distinctive national cultures,
even though these are largely in the process of being (re-)created
as I write. Each of these categories can be refined to highlight
differences within it, including those of religious affiliation, 'race',
ethnicity, class, gender, disability, age and sexual orientation, as
people begin to celebrate multiple heritages and identities. These
are positive developments as they will redefine Britishness so that
it becomes less totalizing and dismissive or submersive of difference than has hitherto been the case.

Communities in social work

Why should social workers be interested in how we celebrate
diversity within communities and promote equality and the liberation of peoples from oppressive relationships? Although contentious, my answer is simple. Social work is the profession that is
responsible for ensuring people's well-being and for integrating
outsiders to society. This can be done to include difference or exclude it. For social workers, society represents the broader national
(and sometimes international) community in which practice is
situated. Social workers' interventions both create and are created
by prevailing discourses about communities. Social workers

operate within the boundaries of communities as defined by the society in which they live.

To discharge their responsibilities, social workers draw on ties of solidarity or belief of the collective grouping that those who are less well-off and vulnerable should be helped. Solidarity is a tie that bridges the gap between insiders and outsiders. When integrating outsiders through helping interventions, social workers use legislation that establishes welfare entitlements. These are predicated upon and embody the value of solidarity to justify social workers' involvement. In Britain, legislation has been formulated within a framework of residualism and holding individuals responsible for their predicaments. Below, I use a social worker's casenotes to examine this approach in work done with a disabled mother caring for a child with mild learning difficulties:

Case study

Donna[2] is the 29-year-old mother of 8-year-old Tricia who has mild learning difficulties and bladder control problems at night. They live on the sixth floor of a high-rise flat in a shabby part of the city. Tricia is aggressive, has few friends and frequently skips school. Tricia's father, Alan, left the family shortly after her birth and has not been in contact since, leaving Donna as Tricia's sole carer. Donna suffers from depression and a twisted spine which causes her chronic pain and limits her mobility. Donna lives near her parents, Jessica and Charles. Both are in their late sixties and in poor health. They help her whenever they can, mainly in the form of 'being there for her and Tricia'.

The family came to the attention of social services four years ago when a neighbour reported red marks on Tricia's arms and bottom. Donna finds her situation extremely stressful and complains she cannot manage Tricia's behaviour, which includes 'dangerous' forms of play such as climbing over the edge of the balcony to the flat and going into the street in her pyjamas in the early morning when her mother is still asleep. On one of these forays, she upset neighbours by constantly ringing doorbells. Donna has recently attempted to overdose, an action which raised further child protection concerns.

Both Donna and Tricia are described as having 'poor self-esteem'. Donna is seen as 'depressed', 'mentally disordered', 'lacking motivation', unable to 'make decisions or carry out

her daily work', and in 'deteriorating physical health' exacerbated by 'poor diet'.

Donna attended a review of the case supported by her social
worker. It was agreed to transfer Tricia from her mainstream
school to one for children with special needs and its attendant
support services, provide her with a psychologist, and submit
a request for respite care and a family support worker. The
family is on a waiting list for the last two items and it
is unclear how long they will have to wait. Meanwhile, the
social worker is asking Donna's parents for more support.

This family has been labelled as unable to cope, but deserving
of help. The assistance provided builds on personal resources without addressing structural inadequacies: poverty and discrimination. Neither Tricia's nor Donna's difficulties are linked to her social
and physical environment. There is no investigation of the causes
of Tricia's 'aggressive behaviour'. If it is a response to being ridiculed
as a learning-disabled child, oppressive and discriminatory relationships are a cause. Psychologizing her efforts as 'poor self-
esteem' only highlights symptoms. A holistic approach that builds
self-confidence and deals with discriminatory attitudes amongst
those in her social networks would be a more positive way forward (Priestley, 1999). No support is offered for Donna's own needs
as a woman locked into 'caring for others' when she needs care
herself. This is evident in the inadequate responses to being a disabled woman and depressed (Barnes and Oliver, 1998). Depression
is often rooted in being a mother caring for a child with multiple
needs under extremely constraining conditions exacerbated by
a lack of resources (Barnes and Maple, 1992). Both personal and
structural issues have to be tackled if Donna and Tricia are to be
supported into long-term growth. The father's lack of involvement
with his daughter can be considered both a structural and a personal matter (Dominelli, 2002b). In dumping sole responsibility on
Donna, he is enacting socially accepted ways for men to relate to
their children. The absent father is embedded in and legitimated
by hegemonic masculinity (Connell, 1995).

This case reveals that entitlements exclude those not meeting
specified criteria and include those who do within narrowly
defined parameters. Waiting lists become instruments of controlling demand. The actions of social workers intervening to protect
vulnerable people may cause considerable pain, for example taking children into care. This outcome would have been even more

difficult for Donna and Tricia, given the many layers of intersecting oppressions they encounter – poverty, gender, disability, mental ill health. These 'isms' and shortage of resources to support Donna and Tricia are social problems that the community in which they live has to address collectively. That this is not happening indicates the individualizing of social problems. In this, the removal of children or threat thereof becomes a coercive technology of governance intended to assist mothers and fathers in becoming better parents through professional interventions rather than providing resources for them.

By ignoring the specific significance of gender, disability, learning difficulties and mental ill health, the social worker in this case has accepted dyadic framings of 'communities' and endorsed professional discourses that depict these as static, fixed entities in which conformity reigns. The social worker presumes the community is a seamless whole rather than a site where identity is enacted. By framing community in singular terms, the practitioner submerges difference. Identity is treated as singular, immutable and totalizing.

Practitioners are often pushed in the direction of totalizing identities by social policies that cast communities in oppositional terms revolving around the dyadic construction of 'deserving' and 'undeserving' people that is embodied in residualism. In this, the 'bad' or 'undeserving' group over there is a threat to the 'good' or 'deserving' one over here. Professionals separate people into these two groupings to manage and control them through the distribution of assistance (or not). Rationing resources intensifies divisions that arise from treating each group differently within an *in*egalitarian framework of thought and (re)action.

The 'undeserving' group is further subdivided into those who are redeemable and those who are not. Those who can be helped through outside intervention are considered potentially 'deserving' and separated off from those labelled unworthy of assistance – the totally 'undeserving', who are ruled out of the helping relationship. The 'deserving' ones are able to benefit from acquiring white middle-class heterosexual norms and enabled to access resources to guide them in this direction. This division endorses a socially sanctioned welfare apartheid that splits the 'undeserving' from the vulnerable, 'deserving' person, who becomes an object to be pitied and thereby entitled to be helped. This binary dyad is evident in the discourses of welfare recipients themselves. In these, the 'deserving' differentiate themselves from the 'undeserving' (Dominelli et al., forthcoming) and thereby affirm the paradigm.

Divisive binary constructions of people in need become an essential part of what Foucault (1979) calls the 'technologies of control' that both enable practitioners to do their jobs and justify doing it in particular ways. As in the case study, these draw clients into strategies of self-regulation. Binary constructions privilege those holding resources and power. In worker–client relationships, this privileging of the ingroup – professionals – over the outgroup – clients in need – is a form of exclusion that lies at the heart of social work. The challenge for social workers in transcending this deeply entrenched view of the world is to move discourses away from 'deserving' and 'undeserving' clients into ones about active citizenship. These allow every individual to: experience being treated with dignity in having their needs met; acknowledge interdependency amongst people; and show solidarity through reciprocal and mutually beneficial relationships. To transcend binary divides in their work, practitioners have to rethink communities as dynamic interactional entities.

There are many examples of social work practice that assume homogeneous and totalizing concepts of community in their encounters with difference. In these, a person's own sense of community is disregarded in favour of assimilationist versions aimed at integrating difference into a hegemonic view of community that favours the status quo. Assimilationist endeavours may have been conducted with the best of intentions, such as improving the life chances of the person concerned by making 'them' one of 'us'. However, paternalistic disdain and presumed superiority ensure that those deemed 'deserving' of attention to improve their lives are treated in ways that promote oppressive relations in and through practice, as illustrated in chapter 4.

The social work profession covers a wide terrain, but its variety is a source of fragmentation. Social workers add to this by handling communities within a larger one as discrete entities lacking connection to the greater whole, thereby losing the complexities and dynamics of interconnection. Fragmentation becomes evident in practitioners' work with communities, where they deal with each one in isolation from the others and find it hard to focus on commonalities that are shared across different divides. Their action may increase competition between different segments of a community and by-pass working collaboratively on behalf of all. Unhelpful competition occurs when small community organizations waste resources by vying against each other for limited funds or control over similar concerns. Collaboration requires imaginative approaches in forming networks that produce benefits for larger populations. In collaborating and engaging with what they have in common, they have to ensure that they do not ignore differences between them. Neglecting difference can exacerbate tensions amongst community members (Naples, 1997).

Vulnerability: A factor in oppressing diverse communities

Social workers' understandings of the ties of reciprocity or mutuality are less well developed in the area of identity, although they exploit these ties to free up self-help initiatives in deprived communities. This is largely because social workers configure their clients as people lacking in expertise or skills in living as 'good citizens'. The 'good citizen' identity is a white middle-class construct that they appropriate for themselves. By positioning themselves as superior and independent, social workers rarely deem clients equals who can offer them something, let alone acknowledge that they are professionally 'dependent' on them for their salaries. For if there were no clients, there would be no need for social workers.

In the 1970s social workers attempted to transform their relationships with clients by moving away from dependent characterizations of their abilities and argued that their job was to become redundant by ensuring that clients acquired the skills to look after themselves. The inadequacy of positing relationships in dyadic terms couched in notions of dependency/independency is overcome by (re)positioning workers and 'clients' as interdependent. Framing their interactions as interdependent emphasizes mutuality in configuring each other through their relationships. Interdependence increases the likelihood of practitioners valuing the expertise that clients hold. By reframing their situation in mutual terms, practitioners and clients can both contribute to the relationship and take from it. Reciprocity arises because social workers will be giving and receiving alongside clients and the subjectivity of both is (re)affirmed.

Vulnerability as dependency legitimates treating people as incapable and denies their agency. Characterizing clients as vulnerable casts them as dependent on practitioner expertise and goodwill. This lays the foundation for denying clients' citizenship status and for abusive or oppressive relationships which strip them of dignity. A dependency framework sets preconditions that can be exploited and abused by unscrupulous individuals who take advantage of individual vulnerability. Their denial does not prevent their agency from being exposed on disclosure. Acting as subjects provides the antidote to vulnerability. Respecting the dignity of and valuing the person are essential to forming non-oppressive relationships with others. Without these, the ties that build networks and links between people can be abused by social workers, other paid professionals and other carers. Horrendous examples like the Pindown scandal (Levy and Kahan, 1996), the Clwyd Child Abuse Scandal (Waterhouse, 2000) and others (see Berridge and Brodie, 1996) stand as testimony to the abuse and oppression that professionals can wreak on vulnerable people.

Child abuse scandals and the murder of children by parents, relatives and known others highlight the disastrous consequences attending the exploitation of dependants by family members and known carers. The casting of parenting as a private activity controlled by mothers and fathers with little external accountability also contributes to child abuse. If parenting were a public community-based activity, the entire community would be involved in caring for each child and it would be easier to hold individual carers accountable for their behaviour towards vulnerable ones. Community involvement in caring for children would ease the formation of intergenerational links between community members of different ages.

The duty to care for vulnerable people in trouble or need can be violated through indirect abuse. Social workers' concern to integrate people into the society within which they live can fit this pattern. The most obvious example is that of treating people in need as victims who must respond to expert advice and do what the experts say. Although evident elsewhere, this attitude is prevalent in work undertaken with adults and children with disabilities. Clients' ways of knowing, particularly experiential ones, are disparaged rather than valued (Morris, 1991) as a result of the dogmatic application of positivist logic and thinking which privileges professional expertise about disability (Wendell, 1996).

Direct and indirect discrimination are also perpetrated against individuals and communities of people with learning difficulties (Philpot and Ward, 1995; Booth, 2000). The failure to acknowledge their needs for sexual expression, active consensual sex lives and parenting (Booth and Booth, 1998) are indicative of such discrimination. Established professional nostrums about them are challenged through experience and research. The dangers of perpetrating stereotypes of incapacity through evidence-based practice that reaffirms these by ignoring experiential evidence should be noted (see Sheldon, 2000).

The belittling of client knowledges is an abuse of professional power found in attempts to assimilate people with different cultures into dominant (white) English norms and lifestyles (Wiebe and Johnson, 1998). Assimilation in the history of British social work has assumed many forms. Some have been linked to 'normalization' endeavours that seek to integrate people with disabilities or learning difficulties into mainstream society, but *not* on their own terms. Others have endorsed assimilationist escapades overseas; or handling difference as a 'deficit' (problem) in Britain. In these situations, professionals attempt to obliterate 'difference' and replace it with mainstream English ways of thinking and doing, by having people adopt white (Anglo-Saxon), Protestant, middle-class, heterosexual and able-bodied lifestyles. Several instances of this were discussed in chapter 4.

Although I focus on the 'home' children below, their experiences of being abused and having their specific needs ignored resonate with those of other oppressed groups. The lack of community commitment to and disrespect towards other people's children is illustrated in what happened to British working-class children who were sent to homes in Commonwealth countries. These children were transferred abroad by their national community, which then took no other responsibility for their welfare. Although begun earlier, a key wave of migration occurred under the auspices of Dr Thomas Barnardo, when 'orphan' children were sent abroad for a better life. Those removed to Canada from 1869 to the 1920s were not allowed to maintain links with relatives and friends back home; nor was appropriate care assured (Bagnell, 2001).

Known as the 'home children' (Bagnell, 2001), these young people were placed in surrogate families on Canadian farms. Here, their new lives were shaped by isolation and abuse for they were often cruelly treated by their hosts/carers. Social workers failed to protect them even when their plight was brought to their attention by the children concerned on inspection visits (Bagnell, 2001). They suffered in silence because both professional and host communities failed to intervene in the private domain of the families where these children's daily lives were enacted. The recent spotlight on the 'home' or migrant children has exposed the inadequacy of professional surveillance over those committed to their care in both Canada and Australia (Humphries, 1997).

The misery of their existence is exemplified by the sad story of Fred Treacher, who complained about cruel and abusive treatment, but was disbelieved by both Dr Barnardo and the inspector whose duty was to see to his care. Having found no support for being treated with love and respect amongst either officialdom or the substitute family, Fred found the courage to leave his tormentors:

> ... still abused and beaten, [Fred] got up very early one morning, his only possessions the clothes he wore, and like so many boys of his kind and time, ran away ... to a farm near Belleville, and there too he found only pain. It would be only the First World War that would rescue him from despair and give him the dignity that his childhood did not have. (Bagnell, 2001, p. 163)

Wilson (1997) documents similar atrocities vis-à-vis the 'stolen' children in Australia. Fred's abuse by carers portrays a pattern of practice that has been difficult to eradicate. Its present-day variants are witnessed by a catalogue of inquiries into the physical, emotional and sexual abuse of children by both professional and lay carers (Berridge and Brodie, 1996; Laming, 2003).

Other situations of community-based ill-treatment affected aboriginal peoples in Australia, New Zealand and Canada (Armitage, 1996). Children were taken away from parents and put in residential schools where carers denied them the right to their indigenous culture, language and family life in order to inculcate English language and traditions into their daily regimes. The overall aim was to form the homogeneous society believed to epitomize the height of civilization. The state often delegated these actions to religious institutions who ran residential establishments set aside for this purpose. Beatings and other forms of abuse used to enforce carers' injunctions made a mockery of social work's claim to care for vulnerable children, even if its intentions were good. The end products of these interventions were sites of abuse where children's rights were violated daily. The ties binding indigenous people to their own identity-based communities were sundered in the process of enforcing links to another community – the hegemonic one that was deemed superior.

Despite subscribing to the values of equality, respect for others, valuing people as unique individuals and self-determination, social workers become caught up in the ideologies of their time, including those that reproduce oppression on a massive scale. Shocking as it may seem, Lorenz (1994) cites the complicity of social workers in Nazism's attempts to create a superior race. Averting these dangers requires constant vigilance on the part of professionals.

The over-representation of black children in care and custodial settings in Britain reveals the abuse of difference today. Social workers' failure to denounce the oppression of vulnerable groups by rich and powerful people and lack of courage in speaking against the many injustices – classism, disablism, homophobia, racism, sexism, mentalism, ageism, poverty and deprivation – endured by large swathes of the world's population indicate their distance from the suffering endured by clients every day. Social workers seem to have lost their vision of a better world and do not recognize that they are part of the communities they live and work within rather than being outside them. They can actively advocate for personal and communal well-being supported through individual and collective endeavours.

Western social workers have not always been this removed from community issues. They played key roles in rebuilding societies throughout Europe under the Marshall Plan after the devastation of the Second World War. In Britain, as noted above, Clement Attlee (1920), a social worker, even became prime minister. Compare the activities of his post-war Labour administration in the welfare arena to the silence of the twenty-one social workers currently sitting as MPs in the House of Commons. Also compare the quiescence of these with the activism of social workers in other countries, for example South Africa and India. Community and social development initiatives in southern Africa and Asia provide practice models that Western social workers can draw upon to improve their knowledge of and confidence in utilizing skills that make them more client-centred within a context of globalizing communities and structural change (Sewpaul, 2003).

Social workers in the West have difficulty addressing the structural problems that bedevil communities because they have become enmeshed in a web of competence-based approaches to social work advanced under the new managerialism. Competence-based approaches have intensified social work's bureau-technocratic dimensions and downgraded its relationship-oriented ones. Managerialist regimes promote quantitative performance criteria and outputs at the expense of direct work in empowering clients in their environments. Bureau-technocrats cannot deal with the multiple complexities of modern life. Moreover, in not building a relationship based on mutual trust and respect, it is easier to lose the humanity of people and treat them as bureaucratic instruments that can be more readily inscribed with the technologies of control. As a young mother in our study put it:

> You just get a number and half the time you don't usually have the same person [as your social worker]. So you gotta explain your thing over and over and over again. (Dominelli et al., forthcoming)

Reifying people makes it easier to perpetrate bureaucratic rationalities that engender bureaucratic violence against clients. This treatment leads to incomprehension and frustration that legitimate the expulsion of clients from services they need and yield physical or verbal violence against social workers. Hence, solidarity and the ties of citizenship between these two groups are lost. As the weight of the state is brought down against clients, they are left with nowhere to go. The dynamics of reification and bureaucratic rationality draw social workers into supporting repressive regimes.

Fortunately, some social workers continue to play a strong role in the life of communities in Britain and elsewhere. They continue to fight for social justice, at times being threatened with imprisonment, as in the case of Satieh Fariman Fariman (1996), or being put to death for acting upon their beliefs, as happened to numerous social workers in Pinochet's Chile. The 'disappearance' of Chilean social workers has been recorded and protested locally and internationally by the Chilean Association of Schools of Social Work in a dossier of cases several inches thick. Social workers' responsibility to speak out and defend human rights is also being enacted internationally through the Joint Commission on Human Rights, involving the IASSW and the IFSW. It advocates on behalf of specific cases brought to its attention.

Social work educators and practitioners are denouncing the growing inequalities and disintegration of communities caused by globalization. Globalization has impacted upon working relations, private lives and the relationship between the individual and the state as well as bringing about widespread economic change. A key failure of globalization is its inability to deliver the 'trickle-down benefits' that were expected to reduce world poverty rather than widen the gap between rich and poor both within countries and between them (Wichterich, 2000). Today, there are 1.3 billion people living on less than $1 a day, and a further 1 billion living on $2 a day eking out an existence on the margins of a global world. At the same time, even before the advent of the dot.com millionaires, 387 individuals, mainly men, owned 45 per cent of the world's wealth (UNDP, 1996).

Most of the world's poor people live in industrializing countries, but they also exist elsewhere (Osberg, 2002). Britain has its own homegrown variety of poverty, which is unevenly distributed. In Sheffield, 40 per cent of children live below the poverty line. This is higher than the national average of one child in three. Most of these children are with one or more parents on income support. The government has promised action on this point by offering tax credits, increasing child benefit and by setting the target of halving child poverty by 2020. Though laudable, this marks a retreat from Britain's international commitments vis-à-vis its children. When it signed the 1989 UN Convention on the Rights of the Child in 1991, Britain, like the other signatories, agreed to eliminate child poverty within its own borders by the year 2000. Successive British governments have failed miserably on this target. Given this record, a question with the 2020 date is whether the resources necessary for implementation will be released. Another is that this strategy leaves generations of children growing up in the interim without hope for improvement. What will happen to them and the remaining 50 per cent after 2020? Who will speak out for the missing generations that this approach is producing?

With the fourth largest economy in the world, Britain is a rich country and can devote more resources to its children. The political decision to make the necessary allocations would be easier if British people accepted responsibility for the care of all children, not just those with biological ties to them. Accepting this challenge requires a solidaristic community response that is hard to achieve. Even Sure Start, which professionals consider a huge success, is problematic because it is inadequately funded and targets the needs of only the poorest of poor children. In a recent interview I conducted in a local community in 'affluent' southern England, residents commented upon the inadequacies of such targeting. On this subject, I quote a young mother of two small children who was on income support. She had a husband on a disability allowance:

> Sure Start is good. I wish I could go on the scheme. But I can't as I'm over the threshold. But I really want [small son] to go to nursery school. Although I can't get help, I'm one of the lucky ones. Somehow, I'll manage. I'll find the £7.50 a session to send him to [nursery school]. I want [him] to go twice, so it's £15 a week. That's a lot of money. But I'll find it. I have a husband on disability allowance, we'll manage. But what will happen to those others, especially the single mums. How will they do it? That's what I want to know.

This woman's comments are interesting. She is demonstrating solidarity with other poor women living in her community. She wants their children to have access to what she considers a crucial opportunity to improve their life chances as much as she does her own child. There was no punitive 'deserving'/'undeserving' divide for her.

Practitioners are well placed to obtain information that identifies the negative impact of policies aimed at helping those in need.

Social workers can use data collected through their work in poor communities to lobby for change based on knowing what is happening to people living in these areas. Even the personal advisers on whose shoulders fall the New Labour government's modernization agenda and responsibility to promote social inclusion can begin to advocate for deprived communities using the data they collect locally. Practitioners can draw on the commitment to self-help evident in this woman's thinking. She is an active person, capable of analysing her situation and that of others. She is not a victim who has to be told what is going on. Social workers should listen more to women like her and act on their insights.

Practitioners need to value what clients say about their lives, acknowledge their resourcefulness and engage in relationships of reciprocity with them. Practitioners can show empathy or put themselves in another's shoes and have 'clients' experience this too. Working to raise the status of the profession and the people they work with would put reciprocity into the relationship. The idea of social workers as community change agents has to come back into fashion. This means speaking out against the demonization of poor people and communities. Without such an approach, social workers collude with the undermining of poor people. If society denies the humanity of those on the margins, it cannot be surprised when excluded people retaliate by dehumanizing others and committing criminal acts against them. More importantly, a society that demonizes others denies its own humanity.

Client resourcefulness raises complex ethical questions for community workers if they engage in illicit income-generating activities such as selling contraband to supplement incomes. Research on local areas exposes such ingenuity (Pattison, 2002). These skills could be utilized in more appropriate enterprises if those involved were encouraged to reorient their talents constructively in furthering their welfare. Meeting the needs of excluded people, including men who no longer have roles or jobs, is important in revitalizing communities and building a hopeful future.

Poverty is a key issue in deprived communities. Social workers fail to assist people in taking responsibility for their behaviour when they do not model it in their interactions with them. This happens when social workers blame victims for the structural inequalities that destroy their lives. They know that white middle-class individuals would be unable to meet all their needs on $1 per day, or even the weekly benefit payment. A businessman would spend their weekly allowance on one lunch and think the amount a snip. If he is entertaining a 'client', he can claim this as an expense and deduct it from his company's profits. This is a taxpayer sub-sidy, as is charging Prince and Princess Michael of Kent £70 per week rent instead of the £50,000 obtainable on the open market. These cases exemplify different types of exclusion. The first example is based on poverty, the other two on exploiting taxpayers' generos-ity from which poor people are excluded. Only those caught in the first category see their personal growth stunted through society's failure to eradicate poverty.

Social workers can shift the focus of practice to show inequalities along various social divides as well as respond to individual need or pain. They can argue against the targeting of services on only the poorest of people and demand universal services available to all as a right at the point of need. This would remove the stigma of social work interventions and make the realization of citizen-ship, human rights and social justice the centrepiece of practice. It would also strengthen the community-focused elements in a social worker's role.

Universalism in the personal social services is not a new idea. It was promoted by Beveridge before the Treasury trimmed budget-ary allocations to the welfare state (Kincaid, 1973). Getting clients involved in political processes may facilitate movement in creating unstigmatized universally accessible social services. But excluded people are unlikely to vote. If social workers were to take a leaf out of the American civil rights movement and encourage social work clients to flex their political muscle by voting, it might make politi-cians quake or at least pander less to the worst prejudices of middle England and consider more seriously the solutions to social problems suggested by those living in deprived communit-ies. Social workers can promote change in people's behaviour by appealing to their best instincts and ask that they show solidarity with those worse off. Solidarity was more evident in Britain in the 1970s when redistributive measures reduced income inequalities to a greater extent than now. Social workers could encourage the implementation of redistributive initiatives that are not rooted in charity, paternalistic arrogance or residualism.

Conclusions

Communities are an important aspect of social life. They are the sites in which individuals (re)configure the relationships and networks that (re-)form their identity and make them social beings. It is cru-cial that social workers understand communities and acquire the skills necessary for working effectively within them. This means knowing about inclusionary and exclusionary dynamics and how these privilege some groups at the expense of others through day-to-day routines enacted in community settings and within the relationships that these encompass.

To work effectively within communities, social workers have to shed their individualistic orientations and look seriously at community mobilization and collective action. For this, they have to rethink practice and engage with 'clients' as co-partners in revitalizing deprived communities. They also need to challenge their own professional practice – the valuing of expert voices and professional ways of knowing to the exclusion of 'client' ones. In addition, they have to promote user-led agendas aimed at eliminating the structural inequalities that destroy communities and marginalize people. Practitioners can contribute to this by reconceptualizing communities as fluid, multidimensional dynamic entities that are constantly being reconfigured through interpersonal interactions. Finding ways of including difference by valuing diversity within unity is an important element of this. Finally, practitioners need to understand how macro-level forces and meso-level policies impact on daily life routines and address these in their work. To engage with all these areas, social workers have to link up with others and form alliances with other professionals who share the overall objective of enhancing individual and community well-being to promote social justice for all.

NEW DIRECTIONS FOR SOCIAL WORK

Interdependence, Reciprocity, Citizenship and Social Justice

Introduction

Social work in Britain is currently fighting to ensure its existence as an influential profession that can make a lasting contribution to improving people's well-being. This seems a decidedly modernist project. In an academic world enchanted by postmodernist thinking, supporting its endeavours and defending its modernist direction is a brave position to adopt. Social work, with its traditional commitment to the individual within his or her social context, is well placed to balance postmodernist concerns which celebrate individual identity and empowerment with modernist ones rooted in the idea of universal rights that support the realization of social justice and personal development. In my view, both dimensions are necessary for social work practice to provide a profession worthy of the name and live up to its clients' expectations for a better life.

Practitioners have to develop new paradigms for practice in partnership with those who have a stake in their activities: service users, community activists, practitioners, policymakers, business leaders and academics. They will have to begin working from the assumption that clients, whether marginalized or not, are citizens with social, political and economic rights that need to be argued for, defended and upheld. By adopting a humanitarian approach rooted in the realization of human rights and citizenship, social workers could work in ways that acknowledge the interdependence that exists between different groups of people in society and facilitate the implementation of reciprocity in their interactions with them. They also have to recognize differentiation within and between groups alongside the significance of various cleavages in an individual's identity. These should be treated with sensitivity and within a framework of equality.

At the micro-level, rising to the occasion requires social workers to treat clients as active citizens and agents who contribute to practice as well as obtain resources from it. For this to happen, client–worker relationships have to be redefined as interactive negotiated situations in which social workers support clients in acquiring the resources necessary for playing an equal role in decision-making processes and becoming full members of society. In this context, interdependence becomes reflected in the aim of pursuing social justice by recognizing that 'differences' in status, resourcing and power differentials have to be consciously addressed at the beginning of a working relationship and not be anticipated simply as outcomes at the end. The processes, or how something is done, have to be taken on board while working to meet agreed goals (Dominelli, 1996, 2002a, 2002b).

In the relationship of social giving, society responds to unmet welfare needs through the social worker, and, in accepting contributions to their welfare, clients acquire an obligation to contribute to society. Helping relationships will be meaningless without reciprocity and a commitment to securing social justice evident on both sides. Combining interdependence with reciprocity and social justice provides the basis for a holistic approach to social work practice that deals with both personal and structural issues. Furthermore, it legitimates social workers' role as change agents committed to social inclusion at both the individual and societal levels.

In this chapter I focus on how social workers can endorse citizenship and social justice through reciprocity and interdependence exercised in and through practice. These are rooted in social workers' commitment to human rights and values that are underpinned by respect for the person and entitlements to welfare resources without preconditions. Working for this challenges social workers to engage in structural change by arguing for personal social services as a universal service tailored to individual needs, available to all when required without stigma, without labels and without first having to appear with either a chequebook or the deeds to one's home.

Social workers would also act as catalysts to help clients take responsibility for their behaviour and assist them in the process of releasing their potential by focusing on the strengths that enable them to take control of their lives and give back to their communities. The practitioner would also endeavour to ensure that society's responsibilities for meeting the needs of individuals and communities are fulfilled. Key to this would be providing the resources necessary for achieving both personal and structural change. The aim of the social worker's task would be to integrate the individual with his or her communities in ways that uphold their human rights and access to social resources. Ensuring that these are realized requires them to question the inegalitarian social arrangements that currently exist. Safeguarding cultural diversity and respect for the human rights of the least powerful party would be essential. Conflicts would have to be resolved using just processes as well as arriving at just solutions. Defining what these might be will be contentious and fraught. Practitioners can play key roles in ensuring that people keep talking to each other through these difficulties. Social workers would have to act as society's conscience, challenge unjust social arrangements and promote definitions of welfare articulated through discussions with client groups.

Social justice and citizenship

The realization of an active citizenship (Lister, 1997) amongst socially excluded people is crucial in a society endorsing human rights within a framework of social justice because it provides the basis from which to justify claims to social resources necessary for well-being. Social workers, as professionals concerned with individual and collective well-being, should be aware of the theory and practice of citizenship and operate within its remit. They also have to be critical of society's failure to guarantee its actuality for all inhabitants on a daily basis. In other words, social workers can identify the gap between theoretical and actual citizenship. The commitment to social justice enables them to locate individuals within collective entitlements and obligations, and ground their interventions in this arena.

Citizenship involves an individual's status in society – his or her sense of belonging and being part of a greater whole. As such, it contributes towards social integration and stability. Citizenship has traditionally been associated with nationality and ethnicity tied to a particular geographic area. Limiting citizenship status to those within particular geographic boundaries, however, is inadequate in today's fast-moving socially configured spaces for human agency and belonging. Diasporic elements of populations have undermined static notions of citizenship by settling in graphic locations while retaining their ethnicity, natio............ culture of origin. These are groups of people who have spread across the globe historically as a result of adventure, colonization, dispossession and a search for security or a better life linked to the desire to maintain key aspects of their identity intact (Brah, 1996). These citizens are now called 'dual' or 'hyphenated' nationals.

The denial of citizenship rights to individuals merely because they have crossed borders from one country to another has also been challenged through mass migration. The substantial movement of people across boundaries has undermined the rooting of citizenship in the nation-state and produced the concept of a 'global citizenship' to replace it. These challenges emphasize the exclusionary potential of citizenship and highlight the importance of rethinking citizenship to make it more inclusive. The idea of global citizenship has its attendant difficulties, especially in relation to who confers the rights associated with this status, who pays for the entitlements attached to it, and what administrative system is necessary to run it.

Citizenship is a contested concept. Currently, being acknowledged as a citizen yields a status that accords an *individual* certain rights. Associated with T.H. Marshall's (1970) claim, modern citizenship covers three sorts of rights – political rights, civil rights and social rights represented through the welfare state. In his writings, Marshall envisaged citizenship as a progressive development process in which an individual acquired more rights. Citizenship in modern Britain has been linked to the addition of more and more rights or entitlements to individuals who reside within its borders and meet certain stipulated criteria. Since the 1981 Nationality and Immigration Act, however, citizenship status has been tied more closely to immigration status and controls, so that people who have been born in Britain no longer automatically qualify for citizenship status. They have to have at least one parent who is already a British citizen.

Marshall's view of citizenship has been critiqued for being overly simplistic and optimistic (Bulmer and Rees, 1996). Many people have been excluded from its entitlements, particularly those associated with post-war social rights. Citizenship has been gendered to deny women access to benefits in their own right (Williams, 1989; Dominelli, 1991b; Lister, 1997), racialized by privileging those of white British origins (Gilroy, 1987; Williams, 1989; Dominelli, 1991b), and linked to an imperialist project (Gilroy, 1995). Discrimination and oppression have limited the expression of citizenship status amongst many members of a national grouping and exacerbated its exclusive potential. Citizenship has been criticized as a Western concept imbued with individualism and fragmented bonds of solidarity (Jordan, 1996). As a result, the *independent* individual citizen who operates within a social order that coheres around a person receiving entitlements that are not accompanied by a set of mutual obligations is being countered with the *interdependent* citizen. In this, the collective provides the space wherein individuals flourish. Reciprocity ensures that the individual contributes to the collective good as well as receiving from it.

The various renditions of a citizen's reality are complicated by controversies around the relationship between citizens and the state, and citizens and civil society. Recent political debates have been concerned with citizens' obligations towards others, including a responsibility not to make demands of the state for assistance in realizing welfare rights. New Right ideologies have appropriated this critique and shifted it in alternative directions to promote social policies that emphasize individual self-sufficiency. These have increased social exclusion amongst poor people, particularly those encompassed by the term 'underclass'. These are people whom powerful elites have demonized and subjected to intensive technologies of control through the activities of welfare professionals and the custodians of the CJS (Zucchino, 1997). Growing inequalities and crime statistics expose the bankruptcy of this worldview.

Welfare rights have simultaneously been identified as key social rights in current discussions about citizenship (Bulmer and Rees, 1996). The power of these rights to eliminate existing structural inequalities, especially those related to low income and poverty, has, however, never materialized. This is partly because Marshall (1970) did not endorse economic equality. The equal (re)distribution of income amongst citizens has not been supported in British social policies. Even the Social Justice Commission set up by John Smith when Labour was in opposition rejected demands for a Citizen's Income (Bulmer and Rees, 1996). Tying income security to low wages has been associated with the reluctance of policymakers to endorse a benefit system that does not require people to work (Kaim-Caudle, 1973) or 'earn' their living, despite feminist critiques about the exclusion of women and those requiring care under present arrangements (Pascall, 1986; Dominelli, 1991b; Bulmer and Rees, 1996).

In this contested terrain, neo-liberal ideologies favouring the market have replaced those of the interventionist welfare state, which is deemed to have failed. In supporting the withdrawal of the state from the lives of citizens, New Right ideologues' emphasis on self-sufficiency has loosened the links between members of society. Fragmentation of the bonds of solidarity that tie individuals together is both a logical and practical outcome of these processes. The atomized individual was turned into a virtue and glorified in Margaret Thatcher's claim that there is 'no society, only individuals', and, it authorized a Hobbesian version of a social order in which life is 'nasty, brutish and short' (Hobbes, 1968). In a neo-liberal framework, contemporary discourses about citizenship conceptualize citizens as customers, an idea taken to its logical conclusion in the citizens' charters promoted by John Major (Taylor, 1992).

This approach to life has denied individual citizens their entitlements in the welfare arena. Neo-liberalism has left many casualties who can rightly claim a denial of citizenship rights, but they are not in a position to enforce these. This includes those who have never been waged labourers, those who have left the labour market as a result of redundancy, old age, disability, disease or caring responsibilities, and those on low wages. These citizens are not in a position to purchase their welfare needs in the welfare market and so are unable to exercise either active citizenship or active consumer rights. They are also the groups that social workers should assist in claiming their status as full participants in society by helping them mobilize in favour of non-commodified welfare.

The emphasis on the market as provider of services has also led to the creation of the workfare state as a replacement for the welfare state and reaffirmed the link between work and rights to citizenship entitlements. Although more evident in the United States, this trend is apparent to a substantial degree in Britain (Perlmutter, 1997). It has been heightened by New Labour's modernizing agenda, where the 'New Deal' has shifted discourses to a normative dimension in which waged work becomes the basis for social integration, and citizenship imposes duties on individuals rather than entitlements. Consumerism and an emphasis on individual preferences and choices go hand-in-glove with this less rights-oriented approach to welfare.

Contemporary discourses countering neo-liberal insights are opening up new terrain by focusing on a more active and holistic citizenship. This is embedded in what might be termed 'quality of life' issues, which include rights to safe and healthy physical and social environments. These include: pure food, clean air, earth and water; decent lifestyles; economic solvency for individuals; corporate accountability for commercial enterprises; leisure time; and caring services. The anti-globalization movement has taken a lead in opposing materialism based on greed and a pillage of natural resources that belong to all inhabitants of the planet for a few (Jubilee 2000, 2003), and called for a more equitable sharing of the earth's bounty. Those involved in this disparate movement led by NGOs active in civil society at both national and international levels argue for a socially responsible citizenship that recognizes the interdependent nature of human existence between and within countries. Social workers have been involved in these activities through UN summits concerned with these issues as both activists and advisers through organizations such as the IASSW, the IFSW and the International Council on Social Welfare. Practitioners can advocate for the rights of excluded people to be included in shaping a world that meets their needs.

As agency is embedded within power relations, a person exercising it has to take action to assume control over the direction of his or her life. Achieving this status means negotiating with others and compromising on difficult issues in contested terrains. Displaying agency presupposes autonomy in the capacity to act. Poor people have to negotiate degrees of constraint that hinder their ability to employ autonomy in their lives. But they remain agents of their own choices within those constraints, and they continue to be held responsible for their actions. Becoming an active citizen places the obligation of taking responsibility for one's choices and behaviour on one's own shoulders. Doing so requires agency.

Modern political and economic discourses of citizenship have, with few exceptions, ignored the 'moral' dimension. Neo-liberal ideologies have carried amorality and immorality to extremes by disregarding wasted human potential, as indicated in high indices of poverty and social exclusion. Rawls (1973) advanced universal principles of justice that were morally binding on all members of society to address this issue within an individually based ethical framework. Those arguing for social justice have attempted to include these considerations in their initiatives. But Rawls says little of relevance to the collective responsibility for both individual and group welfare. Current discourses have also been unable to steer clear of the danger of moralizing with a righteousness that brooks no counter-arguments (Webb, 1990). Social workers, with a tradition of non-judgemental approaches to people, are well placed to promote moral activities without moralizing about others' behaviour.

A citizenship of equals acknowledges 'difference' to value individual uniqueness, avoid the 'false equality trap' (Barker, 1986;
Dominelli, 2002a), and ground people in collective contexts where
individuality is forged. Achieving an egalitarian outcome requires
hard work and a commitment to redistributing power and resources
so that no one is excluded from accessing these in their daily lives.
As this entails structural changes, it is a concern for every member
of society, not just social workers. It also needs political will and
strategies for bringing it about. Social workers advocate for these.
They can also prick the public conscience with calls for action at
the political level; act as information providers who work with
those who are both included and excluded in society; and become
catalysts in the change process.

Different visions for social work

Active citizenship for all, including society's weakest members, is
central to social workers' plans for a just society. In it, the citizenship of one underpins and is underpinned by citizenship for all.
Realizing this requires a partnership between all parts of society –
the state, civil society, business, social movements seeking to end
various oppressions and more traditional organizations such as
trade unions. Each has a role in creating the wealth that provides
for the needs of citizens and each has a voice to be heard regarding
its redistribution to meet everyday needs for everybody and provide
for its constant renewal. Resource renewal requires maintaining
the sustainability of the earth's physical and social environment.
Attention to how this work is done as well as its ultimate outcome
can facilitate processes based on principles of equality and fairness.
Acting as referees, social workers can ensure that the means
whereby particular objectives are achieved are consistent with the
ends being sought.
    The rule of law has a role in regulating how citizens relate to
each other. It confers agreement and legitimacy so that laws can be
enforced to ensure that citizens interact with one another in acceptable ways. Ownership of the processes of legitimation is as crucial
as owning the goals desired. People consent to be bound by rules
that they have been actively involved in creating to an extent not
reached by those imposed upon them through the technologies of
governmentality or regulation. Equality before the law is a crucial
aspect of the rule of law. Equality in the abstract is not enough to
ensure social justice, however. Alongside process considerations,

equality is an end that has to be achieved. Achieving it requires acknowledging that people are at different starting points and that each has to be brought to the same point for a level playing field to exist. Without levelling the playing field, equality of opportunity is meaningless. Equality is realized by explicit endeavour rather than being presumed.

Formal observance of equality before the law can create situations in which some people feel disregarded by principles of fairness and equity. The *Bakke* case in California, where a white man was denied a place in medical school in favour of a less well-qualified black applicant, highlights the importance of addressing scarcity for equality to be enacted. Given that resources are not unlimited and that choices regarding their use have to be made, a key way for dealing with existing inequalities is to share resources equally amongst everyone. Sharing them equally, if determined by equal outcomes, requires different treatment in the short term to bring every person to the same starting point. The inequalities of condition and injustices that people feel pertain in a given situation have to be openly detailed and confronted if social justice is to be realized. In the *Bakke* case, the white man does not recognize that unequal conditions exist between him and the black person. Thus, he does not appreciate that the black person has to be treated differently from him to have the same equality of opportunity as he does. To reach a just outcome, their unequal starting points have to be addressed through differential treatment that is transparent to all parties and accepted as necessary for righting the privileging unfairly enjoyed by white people as a group. I say unfairly because both the black man and the white man would have been seated at and competed from the same table of opportunity were it not for racial oppression. Moreover, if the issue of scarcity had been dealt with, both men could have exercised their right to a university education, and maybe even collaborated with one another to enrich themselves individually and contribute to the broader academic community. As it is, competition embedded within oppressive racist relations needlessly consumes energies that could have been utilized for more useful and fulfilling purposes. Additionally, squandering resources on this conflict leaves festering the question of solving the scarcity problem. The idea of reciprocity between parties can point to a way forward from this impasse by facilitating the creation of a 'win-win' situation between the contesting individuals.

The previous unfair privileging has to be acknowledged and put right if reciprocity is to deal with scarcity. Reciprocity enables the gap between the position of one person and another to be bridged. If the issue of scarcity is not tackled, an individual who belongs to a privileged group but is not personally privileged will feel aggrieved, even if he or she is able to accept the unjustness of the benefits obtained earlier by others in the group. This is because 'isms' are rationing devices that do not have to be justified by those who collectively gain from their existence before being exercised. Questioning these instead of taking them for granted seems odd, inexplicable even, to those accustomed to benefiting from them. Social workers can expose these dynamics to promote the reconfiguration of social relationships between individuals in mutuality and equality. Although becoming actively involved in contesting injustice as a social worker is controversial, practitioners have no option but to find ways of transforming inegalitarian social relations if they are to remain true to their ethics and commitment to social justice.

Interdependence and solidarity

Mutuality draws on the values of interdependence and solidarity to link people to each other. These underpin citizenship and articulate one person's commitment to the well-being of another by pooling risks within a wider collective. Interdependence and solidarity are necessary for collective action to take place, usually in pursuit of a particular goal. Solidarity involves the creation or presupposition of a community of interests that brings people together. Interdependence allows the mutuality of these concerns – a dependency of one upon another – to be acknowledged. This dissolves the antagonistic binary divide that destroys mutuality and promotes dependence and independence between parties. Interdependence challenges the presumption that dependent people are unnecessary because independent people are completely self-sufficient and have the dependent one relying upon their initiatives or mercy. An active citizenship that is holistic draws on relationships of interdependence and solidarity in order to meet the needs of one and all. Facilitating their growth is part of social workers' new vision.

Reciprocity and entitlements

Reciprocity is the attribute of both receiving and giving in social interactions between individuals and groups. All those involved anticipate a social return on their endeavours, even if this is deferred to a future point. The expectation of receiving does not elapse, even if time does. Reciprocity is inclusive because it applies obligations and constraints to all those drawn into interactive relationships (Jordan, 1996). It implies agency because agreement to reciprocate makes the interaction mutual. Reciprocity also contains a commitment to improve the conditions of others alongside one's own.

Entitlements are what people expect to receive as a result of agreeing to meet certain criteria. The term is used interchangeably with rights, but unlike rights, which usually have a legally enforceable element residing in a collective agreement, entitlements are claims that may be conceded by simple agreement between participating parties: for example, poor white people living in stigmatized estates in Britain are entitled to live in decent environments. This is not a right that they can demand and expect to be met as it is not enforceable as a result of a collective agreement. They will have to establish it as a right before it can be enforced. The boundary between entitlements and rights is often blurred, and one can easily become the other. For those living on stigmatized British estates, it would be interesting to have a case taken to the European Court of Human Rights arguing that the right to full development has been denied because people living on such estates will not be lent money by large financial institutions such as banks. Thus, items that require substantial injections of cash which could improve their life chances would be beyond their reach: for example, starting off a business, purchasing homes, acquiring a university education.

Crucial to exercising one's rights, or even entitlements, is knowing what these are. Acquiring the relevant knowledge and information can be considered a capacity-building endeavour. Capacity building to secure these rights is a well-known community work activity (Putnam, Leonardi and Nanetti, 1994; Putnam, 2002). Social workers can become key players in bringing capacity-building projects to fruition. They can form alliances with others, including lawyers, to enforce people's rights to a decent lifestyle and living environment.

Modelling new directions for social work

Modern discourses about social work carry the danger of treating practice either as a monolithic whole which is of little benefit to clients (Brewer and Lait, 1980; Brindle, 2003) or as an idealistic endeavour with limited relationship to reality. Those who work in the profession know that it is complex and has elements of both. Dreams are necessary to envisage alternative practices to those that are commonplace, although it is easier to struggle against a monolithic entity than a multi-headed hydra. Fortunately, practitioners and academics can combine both idealism and realism to forge more helpful and effective forms of practice, despite tensions and setbacks along the way. Below, I describe a project that has endeavoured to work in holistic ways with people to stretch the boundaries of practice, overcome dualistic thinking and reaffirm a citizenship that acknowledges interdependence, reciprocity, solidarity and agency in creating better communities (see also Dominelli, 2002a). The narrative is based on an interview with Barbara Whittington.

Barbara is an experienced practitioner and academic with a longstanding commitment to empowering approaches to social work. These values she has put into practice in a scheme called Crossroads Community Justice (CCJ), a name chosen by its participants. The case study materials highlight the strengths and weaknesses of a citizenship-oriented social work approach to social justice. CCJ is a community-based restorative justice project that uses the process of working across boundaries to challenge the view that only professionals have the expertise necessary to address social problems. Its primary 'client' group are people who engage in anti-social behaviours that reduce levels of civility and safety in their community. These concerns are shared by many communities worldwide.

CCJ's critique of existing restorative justice schemes includes: an over-reliance on professional experts; an unhelpful divide between 'victims' and 'offenders'; the individualization of social problems; and over-emphasis on verbal dexterity in solving problems. CCJ aims to get offenders to make amends for their behaviour and for both parties to move on. It builds on people's strengths while working on inappropriate behaviours and has adapted the principles of family group conferencing to produce community conferencing. CCJ draws on the skills of a wide range of people from construction workers to lawyers. It has a code of ethics, case co-ordinators, liaison professionals and a mentorship scheme for young offenders. Its work is complex and demanding. CCJ offers a short period of training to those who participate in its activities, and does community education work. Its practice indicates that generic skills are transferable and can be made locality-specific.

Case study

CCJ is a new initiative begun by four women – Barbara, a retired probation officer, a journalist and a school counsellor. They live in the CCJ community and believe that securing justice for both individuals and the community is essential in reducing unacceptable behaviour. Their philosophy is that those living in a community are responsible for its well-being. CCJ's prime purpose is to problem-solve as a collective not an individual endeavour. The community has to 'own' problems and take 'responsibility' for tackling them.

Depicting the community as part both of the problem and of its solution confirms the feminist adage 'the personal is political' and shows commitment to cultural diversity and community inspired by First Nations teachings.

The founding group sought other participants, including the police and schools, to deal with an acknowledged community problem. This produced a range of people with diverse views about the CCJ – what it stood for, how it should work and what it should do. Easing tensions and facilitating dialogue between different groups or interests requires skill and is necessary for effective community involvement.

To avoid becoming bureaucratic and counter-participatory, CCJ has a minimalist structure – a brief constitution, chair, secretary to take minutes and treasurer. Rotating positions ensures that skills are acquired by a wide section of the community to facilitate ownership of and increase participation in CCJ activities. This structure assists in fund-raising, a nightmare for voluntary organizations. The group has limited funding from 'members', who each pay a nominal fee. This is not means-tested and so people only pay if they wish. Most do because it provides a way of contributing to the CCJ and community well-being. Building events around sharing food further encourages the flow of ideas and respect for others.

The person who has 'done wrong' and the one whom it has been 'done to' get the opportunity to talk to each other in supported, unthreatening and unstigmatizing environments. The emphasis is on making amends and securing change. People do not focus on 'shaming' the other as this is already present and not conducive to reintegrating offenders, whose behaviour has already excluded them from the community.

The language used is facilitative and asks the person to think about the other's position. People are encouraged 'to take many different points of view' without having to 'defend one to the death'. This promotes dialogue and gives more scope for exploring competing and contrasting views. People work together as part of a team rather than as adversaries. Members of a victim's family can intervene and reject 'humiliating' treatment of offenders by their families to show that matters can be handled differently and yield better results. People can work in the partnership, argue and still stay involved.

'Victims' do not come in feeling powerful, but are supported to stand up for themselves. They have a right to be there and be held accountable for the choices they make. Offenders should leave walking a little taller. Sharing information redistributes power, as everyone knows the same things. The police have admitted that CCJ provides them with a different kind of power, one not based on paperwork. There is a 'community power' that arises from doing things together and goes beyond the police. These revelations help people appreciate the limitations of institutional power.

An early point of contention concerned referrals. The founding group wanted both young people and adults referred regardless of the offence. The police rejected this approach. The crunch came when a man who had served a lengthy prison sentence for manslaughter wanted to join the group and offer mentorship. The founding group supported this; the police were vehemently opposed. Seeing the ensuing conflict, the man withdrew his offer and temporarily left CCJ. After much soul-searching and argument, CCJ accepted the police view for now, feeling it was too early in its career to fight. The issue will be reconsidered when the man returns.

Mistrust amongst the different professionals who joined the founding group was strong initially. Some wanted to focus on measurable outcomes, such as recidivism rates. Others were more interested in process and high levels of community participation. Eventually, they found enough common ground to work together in a representative structure where tasks could be shared and avoid duplication of efforts and resources, both of which are in short supply when people work in a voluntary capacity.

Participants can play unfamiliar roles: for example, a businessman whose shop was regularly raided met with a shoplifter and later employed her to catch other thieves, with great success. This act challenged the businessman's views of who could reduce shoplifting when the police were disinterested, because in an overstretched force, it was deemed a low-priority crime. The CCJ's innovative response also indicates that institutional priorities can be at variance with community ones. Moreover, these differences can become another source of tension between participants.

The police continue to participate in CCJ, and its educational work is bearing fruit. Schools are the key source of referrals. However, those referred are mainly middle-class and there is concern that working-class people are not benefiting from CCJ's potential for diversion from the court system. Class issues are being monitored and addressed through community educational programmes and mentorship initiatives.

Gender issues are problematic. The police*men* display condescending attitudes towards women volunteers, whom they see as 'do-gooders' who deal with 'easy' cases. The police are being given training to improve their attitudes and tackle institutional sexism.

Tensions surface in community forums where people are asked to participate freely, ask questions and find solutions together. This requires participants to listen carefully to others and seek compromises that will work for all. These might not be those the professionals favour. These gatherings are generating new knowledge and forms of practice. Community forum participants also form small groups to facilitate communication, handle disagreements and maximize individual contributions to decision-making processes.

Proceedings can be lengthy as participants are not encouraged to jump to conclusions, and so have to commit themselves to the time needed for discussions. This facilitates relationship building, promotes understanding and allows people to develop creative solutions to problems. Professionals cannot assume that volunteers have 'time to burn' as this is disrespectful of their contributions.

Time is also necessary in finding compromises to fundamental concerns: what restorative justice means to CCJ; why/how effectiveness will be measured and by whom; the relationship between the state and community during a time of serious cutbacks in public services; how social divisions such as class and ethnicity are played out; what difference the scheme is making and to whom; how its exclusionary potential can be curtailed; and how to increase participation without constantly having agencies usurp community agendas.

Informal community encounters contribute to CCJ's work, including: monitoring the impact of various activities; conducting informal mentoring sessions; supporting those formally referred to the scheme; and drawing people into CCJ's activities as a normal part of daily routines. This affirms key messages. Each person has a valuable and valued contribution to make to the well-being of his or her community. Crucial principles of citizenship are enacted when individual power is acknowledged and linked to the collective. Control over community activities is regained. People are recognized as knowing subjects. The offender–non-offender divide is reduced.

Finally, CCJ focuses on making people feel part of a community that is recognized as imperfect. As Barbara said, 'We are not talking about Utopia, but about being involved with each other. CCJ contributes to community building by ending isolation and exclusion.'

This case study shows how various boundaries have been transgressed and issues redefined. These include the public–private divide, inclusion–exclusion, confidentiality, community–institutional powers, volunteers–professionals. The realities to be faced may be messy, but dealing with the matters raised in a respectful and more inclusive manner is possible. The case study also demonstrates that professionals can work with community participants to produce more meaningful interventions and innovate. The benefits of CCJ encompass both individuals and community, including the wider community: for example, the local university covers CCJ work in the classroom, affecting the teaching of law and practice; businesses have rethought their attitudes to both offenders and restorative justice.

However, as Barbara acknowledges, community approaches can be abused: for example, a mentally ill person was blamed for a serious offence when incapable of understanding what was going on. Fortunately, the victim intervened to reconcile conflicting perceptions of the situation. CCJ is concerned that devolving these issues solely to the community can 'privatize justice' and enable politicians to avoid dealing with real concerns that need to be addressed, particularly resourcing these services. Having uncovered issues of poverty, and other structural problems, CCJ has been unable to address them directly. Doing so will involve other initiatives to create alliances between different groups, engage with politicians holding power and resources at one remove from the community, and use its strengths to hold them accountable.

Education and training

Social work is a distinctive profession. It is time for social work practitioners and educators to demand: a fully recognized, well-paid, high-status profession, albeit different from the others; respect and dignity of treatment for clients; services available to all at the point of need; a well-trained workforce that is respected for the work it does; and their own government department instead of being subsumed within others, including those that it has close links with such as health, education or housing, although close collaboration with these is necessary. Practitioners' remuneration should reflect the highly complex work that they do, dealing with people when others have given up hope.

Social work education and training have to change to meet the needs of practitioners working within a globalizing world. They have to respond to practitioners, desire to learn about social work and social policies in other countries to better prepare themselves for working in countries other than those in which they train (Dominelli and Khan, 2000). However, British social work education needs an even more radical overhaul if it is to respond to the challenges currently posed by the internationalization of social problems and become more citizenship- and human rights-oriented. Its value base and commitment to being a catalyst for change at both personal and structural levels has to be affirmed. It should provide the basis for a life-long career with progression in social work practice within it. This would require policymakers, practitioners and educators to work together to produce a career ladder in social work education and practice. This should encompass pre-qualifying, qualifying and post-qualifying practice and be linked to university degrees from the Bachelor's to Master's and PhD levels. It also needs to comply with European developments embodied within the Bologna Declaration if British-qualified workers' opportunities to work in the broader European Union are not to be jeopardized.

This education should address the generic–specialist divide in social work. The model of having a generic qualifying degree set at a Bachelor's honours level is a promising beginning. It could be followed with specialist training set at Master's level, and the requirement of a PhD in social work for those teaching in and administering social work departments, whether in practice or the academy.

Clients, practitioners, educators and policymakers have to work in egalitarian partnerships to devise the best forms of education and practice that meet today's needs. In the United States, Roche et al. (1999) and Van Soest and Garcia (2003) have addressed some of the issues involved in this by looking at how teachers can empower students more effectively in the classroom and use the work done within it as a basis for developing confidence in practice skills that promote diversity and social justice. They argue that social justice issues can be both practised in and supported by the pedagogic process of learning and teaching about practice. These approaches affirm the integration of theory and practice in both the academy and the field and provide insights that are relevant elsewhere, provided that they incorporate locality-specific require-ments. In other words, social work has to shed its parochialism without becoming a vehicle for neocolonialist ventures. Becoming rooted in a locally applicable but universally acknowledged form of citizenship that underpins social justice and human rights promises a fruitful way forward, and one that might appeal to a significant number of countries.

To promote citizenship, British social work education and practice have to be divorced from direct government control so that they are no longer political footballs tossed about at the whim of politicians. This means fundamental change in the British government's hand-ling of social work. Setting up a social work department with its own secretary of state would be a good start. The first task of this department would be to organize an autonomous mobile forum made up of clients, practitioners, academics, policymakers, to travel around the country asking for people's views on what a univer-sally based system of social work available to all at the point of need would look like, what it would do and how it might be funded.

The mobile forum would have to ensure that the entire diversity of the British population is reflected in its composition and amongst those consulted. New voices should be heard alongside those well known in government circles. The members of this forum should be innovative, forward-looking, progressive, and have had experi-ences of being clients, practitioners, educators or policymakers in social work. They would have to have the capacity for open-mindedness and non-judgementality in listening to the opinions of ordinary people in talking about what they want *their* caring services to look like, that is, those they would actually use. The end product of such consultations would support new legislation enshrining social work in an inclusionary human rights- and citizenship-based framework for both education and practice.

Conclusions

An active, inclusive, holistic citizenship has to underpin social relations in a socially just society. Justice is predicated on common understandings which embed citizens' commitment to equality in their relationships with each other. Citizens are agents who can create their own realities, but these are acknowledged as occurring within social relations, not externally to them. The attributes of reciprocity and mutuality whereby each person gives and receives in return are important elements of the interactions between them. Difficulties arise because resources are not shared equitably and responsibly amongst all citizens and because people draw boundaries around who is included in their distribution and who is not.

Social workers can promote discourses that challenge the inequitable distribution of resources within existing social arrangements because through their practice, they know the heavy burden of diswelfare and high costs exacted when individuals and groups cannot develop to their full potential. Practitioners cannot solve these problems on their own. They have to engage with others and form partnerships and alliances with all those who have a stake in their resolution. Transforming society has to be a shared goal.

CONCLUSIONS

Social Work, a Force for Change at Individual and Structural Levels

9

Introduction

Social work reflects the society that produces it. It is a profession that is conducted within a society riven by inequalities which are both produced and reinforced in and through social work itself. Social workers have to focus on critical reflexive practice in addressing the key question of why a profession that purports to look after people's welfare fails to do so. Its value base and commitment to taking the side of marginalized and dispossessed individuals and groups provides a way by means of which they can: critique practice and a social order that thrives on the backs of poor people; challenge the legitimacy of unequal social relations and demand the personal and structural changes required to fulfil its mandate; alleviate hardship and suffering and maintain progress over time. Deconstructing inadequate policies and practices as these are reflected in discourses about their work and how it is done will engage social workers in profound change if they are to reorient the profession to fully promote well-being.

In this chapter, I argue that social workers have a responsibility to ensure that people who are socially excluded can assume full rights of citizenship. To implement this goal in practice means making the case that entitlement to social work services is a universal social right aimed at ensuring that those who are unable to realize their human potential can do so. Being treated with dignity and accessing assistance has to become an integral part of the rights of citizenship denied to no one. In other words, unless social work can reinvent itself with a renewed mission in this direction, it will fail to meet the challenge of being a relevant professional force in the twenty-first century.

Practice is thinking and doing

Practice comprises an endless cycle of thinking and doing. Social workers constantly reflect upon what they do and what they think about what they have done. In the process of reflection, they become reflexive and engage in critical action. They also scrutinize data as these emerge from relationships they form with clients and recognize the relevance of these to the narrative they are jointly constructing in making a case for assistance. Practitioners and clients create knowledge both about each other and for each other through the work they do together. They both act reflexively and engage in a process that promotes criticality. Formal research can add to this process and can provide the data that support their demands for structural change. Mutuality of engagement in the process of criticality and reflexivity by both practitioners and clients distinguishes social work from other professions yet has been omitted from major texts on the subject, including Schon's (1983).

Knowledge is not an a priori category to be applied forcibly (White, 1997). If a social worker legitimates different ways of knowing in a relationship with clients, it can lead to different ways of acting. This way of creating knowledge is constantly open-ended and unfinished, leaving the possibility of change always there. These dynamics provide a basis for reorienting both personal behaviour and institutional practice to bring about forms of structural change that encompass both and undermine the technologies of control reaffirming the deserving–undeserving divide amongst claimants.

Social workers have a moral and ethical responsibility to promote social change. Being critical reflexive practitioners who think and do in the context of social injustice and inequality requires social workers to act as change agents at both personal and structural levels. Their action is a commitment to securing social justice and equality to provide the basis for developing a new vision for social work and innovative methods for its realization. This alternative approach is something that clients and practitioners *do together*, forming alliances with others as necessary.

Their action has to be enacted at different levels. With regards to the personal domain, change can be effected both upon the self and in and through interpersonal relations. At the structural level, change can be entertained with regards to any aspect of society.

Of particular import are the social relations that configure culture and values and the social institutions that are legitimated within and by it, for example political, economic, religious arrangements. These need to be transformed to promote human dignity, equality and well-being through mutually interdependent relationships. To achieve these changes, social workers will have to form alliances with others seeking the same end (Bishop, 1994). Allies would be amassed across the whole of society but united around a common goal. Together, they would have to deconstruct existing technologies of governmentality and replace these with discourses fostering equality.

Social workers can engage in the creation of new forms of knowledge that respond to client expectations and ambitions by forming partnerships that are permeated with a human rights- and citizenship-based equality that endorses power-sharing and legitimates different voices. In these, social workers would support clients by arguing for needs-led universal rather than stigmatized residual services. Securing these would require a public education campaign that challenges existing hegemonic discourses on this subject and convinces the public and politicians of citizenship-based welfare for all people. Demonstrating the importance of tackling both personal and structural causes of social problems will be crucial to making this case. Accumulating the evidence necessary will involve social workers in research partnerships that include clients, practitioners, policymakers, educators and researchers working together to develop capacity to examine situations holistically. Social workers can facilitate this process because they have both the data from practice that highlight the suffering and waste endured by dispossessed people and the skills in bringing people together to change this picture.

Social workers' capacity to advocate or act on behalf of dispossessed individuals and groups has been compromised by their dependency on government. Practitioners have to establish an autonomous base that is rooted in communities without losing their accountability to the general public through the democratic process. Social work also has to be democratic within its own organizational structures and practices. Developing innovative ways forward at the micro-level of practice is a task to be undertaken in partnership with those needing services rather than being imposed upon them by professionals. *Clients have a right to be involved in designing, running and using the services that will meet their requirements.* Thus, in mediating 'the social', practitioners can empower clients by providing them with the resources and knowledge they need to make decisions that they feel they own. Social workers simultaneously have to dialogue with those in government who control access to these resources and secure the legislative changes and general support necessary for transforming residual services.

Crucial to transforming social work practice in the contemporary conjuncture of neo-liberal capitalist relations is the idea of a more fluid, holistic and interactive practice that speaks to both locality-specific and global concerns. As there are no pre-determined answers, the capacity to deal with uncertainty and complexity will be a major ingredient of it. Furthermore, it will have to take as its central core the relationship between individuals and their social, political, economic, cultural and physical environments. There are a number of key principles that will help practitioners in this task. These are as follows:

- establishing relationships and working within a contextualized environment that encompasses micro-, meso- and macro-levels of intervention;
- handling uncertainty and ambiguity;
- acknowledging the negotiated and interactive nature of the client–worker relationship and the agency of both within it;
- framing the work within a human rights- and citizenship-based egalitarian empowering framework;
- understanding the multiplicity and fluidity of human identity and its social construction;
- understanding and working to undermine the dynamics of oppression;
- being able to deal with the complexities, subtleties, multi-dimensional and dialogical aspects of power;
- working to client strengths at the same time as dealing with their weaknesses
- acknowledging differences, including those applying to oneself, and celebrating diversity within a human rights- and citizenship-based egalitarian framework;
- approaching other people, including clients, as knowing subjects and knowledge creators; and
- understanding the emotional as well as intellectual repercussions of what is being said and done.

These principles have to be adapted by the practitioner to respond to the specificities of circumstances and locales. They are not a toolkit to be applied either indiscriminately or identically to similar situations. In using them thus, practitioners will decontextualize

practice and denude people and places of their meaning and complexities at the expense of the clients with whom they work. Finn
and Jacobson (2003), who are cognizant of the dangers of such an
approach, make meaning a crucial element in the development of
what they call a new paradigm for practice: 'just practice' that aims
to empower clients.

Finally, practitioners need to root their experiences in everyday
routines and practice, for it is through these that tensions between
the macro-, meso- and micro-levels are mediated to reach a
(re)solution that works for them (or not). Additionally, the quotid-
ian constitutes the terrain of what can and will be discussed (Finn
and Jacobson, 2003). These discussions will also define 'what is possible' (Cowger, 1994) and help establish the parameters for practice.
If social workers cannot engage with clients' everyday experiences,
they will increase their capacity to disempower and control the
interaction. Practitioners do so by producing silences that enable
them to stabilize middle-class power (Margolin, 1997) and use the
'technologies of governmentality' to reaffirm forms of social work
practice that produce the clients that the practitioners desire (Pease
and Fook, 1996). It is time to reorient power relations within professional client–worker relationships, as well as those involving
them as citizens in the wider social order, towards those that are
more egalitarian and life-affirming.

Conclusions

Social work is going through a turbulent time. It needs a new vision
that advances active citizenship for poor people – a citizenship of
equals which requires personal and structural changes in the existing social order. The current technologies of governmentality have
produced enormous waste in human talents and caused untold
suffering. These arrangements have to be replaced by those that
are rooted in equality between peoples who share resources, treat
one another with dignity and respect the earth's physical and social
resources as the heritage of each and every individual and community on the planet. This is the basis of social work's new empowering vision.

Social workers have to free themselves from the shackles of a
government-imposed bureau-rationality that has turned them into
bureau-technocrats unable to rise to the challenges of twenty-first-
century practice. They have to advocate alongside dispossessed
populations for the emancipation of all of the world's inhabitants,

not only those living within the borders of their particular nation-state, and minister to the needs of those residing in their specific locality. This is a challenge that educators, practitioners and policymakers inhabiting a globalizing world have to respond to. Clients will play an equal role in setting the agenda that drives the necessary developments.

NOTES

1   Words contain power relations that expose underlying worldviews, ideologies and positionalities. Clients are not a homogeneous group, and the interests of different ones may at times converge or overlap. I refer to people who access services from social workers as 'clients' because this term is most frequently associated with them in a profession recognized worldwide, and I find alternatives such as service users or consumers equally problematic.

2   The Settlement Movement endeavoured to improve housing conditions for the working classes. It began in London and spread throughout the country and later overseas, including the US, when Jane Addams opened Hull House, modelling it on Barnett House. The movement was grassroots-oriented and offered structural analyses of social problems that stood in contrast to the 'individual pathology' approach favoured by the Charity Organization Society (COS). The latter's approach to social problems, however, eventually gained the support of the government, and the COS set the mould for casework-based social work.

   The Community Development Projects (CDPs) were launched by the Labour government in the late 1960s to deal with disadvantaged people in deprived areas throughout Britain. The twelve CDPs that were initiated began with an analysis that suggested that problems could be solved through organizational adjustments that avoided duplication of services and streamlined provisions and their delivery. The government, however, was not prepared either for the radical structural analyses or for the forms of direct action in support of grassroots activities that CDP workers engaged in, and within a few years it shut the 'troublesome' projects down.

3 The IFSW began the task force on the definition of social work in the mid-1990s and invited me to join on behalf of the IASSW upon election as President in 1996 to show our commitment to having the two organizations work together more closely on behalf of the profession. Each organization separately endorsed this definition at its respective General Assembly during World Congress 2000 in Montreal. Meeting in Copenhagen in the summer of 2001, the IASSW and the IFSW announced this definition a joint one.

4 The IASSW and the IFSW agreed to work on global qualifying standards (GQS) at the Berne meeting in 1999 and formed a joint committee (GQSC) chaired by the IASSW with each organization having equal representation from all regions of the world. The GQSC initially corresponded by email and first met at the Montreal Congress with me in the chair. After the GQSC confirmed its remit and work, I appointed Vishanthie Sewpaul from South Africa, who had experience in this area, to succeed me as chair.

5 This solution to Britain's problems raises moral and ethical issues about the appropriation of educational resources in low-income countries by rich Western ones who refuse to resource training adequately at home. Not to deter labour mobility and to deal with the dilemma, countries indulging in such practices should reimburse the country of origin for training these recruits so that training for local needs can continue.

CHAPTER 2   SOCIAL WORK: A PROFESSION IN
CHANGING CONTEXTS

1 Parves Khan and I conducted a research project entitled *Globalisation, Privatisation and Social Work Practice* from 1999 to 2000 in two local authorities in southern England. In it, we administered a postal survey questionnaire to 460 social workers, of which 172 were returned, giving a response rate of 37 per cent, and we interviewed thirteen social work managers in the same areas. These findings were presented at the 'Rethinking Social Work Seminar: Focusing on Globalisation', which was held at Southampton University from 30 November to 2 December 2000.

2 The 'Orange Book' was the Bible for practice which had brought together circulars, procedures and policies to be followed in child protection cases before the 'Framework of Assessment' was adopted.

3 Women had headed small voluntary agencies in Britain prior to the Seebohm reorganization, but men assumed managerial control when these were replaced by large bureaucracies holding substantial resources (Walton, 1975; Howe, 1986; Dominelli, 1991c). This pattern raises the question of whether women are considered managerial material primarily when men are not interested.

CHAPTER 3   VALUES, ETHICS AND EMPOWERMENT

1   Adultism is the oppression of children by adults through an abuse of power that privileges adults and thereby produces adultist power relations.
2   For example, my letter to *The Observer* was never published, and I know from personal correspondence that a number of others were in the same boat.

CHAPTER 4   SOCIAL WORK INTERVENTIONS WITH CHILDREN
AND FAMILIES

1   'Indigenous' is a contested term intended to mean the original settlers of a specific piece of land. I find this problematic given the lengthy history of migration amongst human beings. In this book, I use it to mean the people who lived on particular lands prior to colonization and who are engaged in reclaiming cultural traditions that preceded capitalist-oriented ones.

CHAPTER 6   SOCIAL WORK INTERVENTIONS WITH OFFENDERS

1   Academics initiated the 'nothing works' debates during the 1980s and 1990s when research findings were failing to show significant, long-term decline in the number of offenders being reconvicted.
2   For Clunis, see p. 176 and note 4 below. Stephen Downing spent more than twenty-seven years in prison for a murder he always insisted that he did not commit. He was found guilty in 1973 on circumstantial evidence that a jury found more credible than his denials. He was eventually released in 2001 and had his conviction quashed by the Court of Appeal the following year after a long-running campaign on his behalf by his parents, relatives, friends and the editor of the *Matlock Mercury*, Don Hale (see Hale, 2001). At the time of his trial, Stephen, then 17, was alleged to have a reading age of 11. His is only one of a number of celebrated cases of people with learning difficulties being wrongly accused of and sentenced for major crimes.
3   Most offenders are men, and it is men who are most often subject to risk assessment.
4   Christopher Clunis was a mentally disordered individual with a complex history of psychiatric illness. Once discharged into the community, he did not take the requisite medication and murdered Jonathan Zito when he was waiting for a train in a London Underground station. Zito's widow, Jayne, launched a campaign critical of 'care in the community' and demanded an end to that policy because it endangered the lives of innocent citizens when mentally ill people either

forgot to take their medication or were released from psychiatric care prematurely.
5 In Lord Woolf's address he commented on his Report into the Strangeways Prison riots in 1995, and highlighted the limited progress that had been made in prison conditions during the intervening period.

CHAPTER 7   SOCIAL WORK INTERVENTIONS IN COMMUNITIES

1 The Grameen Bank provides micro-credit to poor women in a bid to help them rise out of poverty through their own initiatives. It was begun in 1976 by Professor Muhammad Yunis, Head of the Rural Economic Programme at the University of Chittagong, and became an independent bank financed primarily by its borrowers (90 per cent). Its motto is 'Discipline, Unity, Courage and Hard Work . . . in all walks of our lives'. The Desjardins movement began life as a credit union in the Province of Quebec. It has now been around for over 100 years and is a key player in its social economy. Desjardins has also become one of the major financial groups in Canada. It operates as a co-operative network committed to improving conditions for local people and funds microenterprises that are devoted to capacity building in local communities.
2 All names in this case study, as in all the others, have been altered to protect individual identities.

BIBLIOGRAPHY

Abercrombie, N., Hill, S. and Turner, B. (1994) *The Penguin Dictionary of Sociology*. Harmondsworth: Penguin.

Adams, R. (1998) *Quality Social Work*. London: Macmillan.

Ahmad, B. (1990) *Black Perspectives in Social Work*. Birmingham: Venture Press.

Ahmed, K. and Hinsliff, G. (2002) 'Race Row as Blunkett Backs "Snoopers Charter"', in *The Observer*, 20 June.

Ahmed, S. (1978) 'Asian Girls and Cultural Conflicts', in *Social Work Today*, 8, August, pp. 14–15.

Ahmed, S., Cheetham, J. and Small, J. (1986) *Social Work with Black Children and their Families*. London: Batsford.

Aldgate, J. and Tunstill, J. (2000) *Services for Children in Need: From Policy to Practice*. London: Routledge.

Aldridge, J. and Becker, S. (1993) *Children Who Care: Inside the World of Young Carers*. Loughborough: Young Carers Research Group.

Alinsky, S. (1968) *Reveille for Radicals*. New York: Vintage Books.

Anderson, B. (1999) 'Youth Crime and the Politics of Prevention', in B. Goldson (ed.) *Youth Justice: Contemporary Policy and Practice*. Aldershot: Ashgate.

Appleyard, B. (1993) 'Why Paint so Black a Picture?' in *The Independent*, 4 August.

Ariès, P. (1962) *Centuries of Childhood*. Harmondsworth: Penguin.

Armitage, A. (1996) *Aboriginal People in Australia, Canada and New Zealand*. Toronto: McClelland and Stewart.

Arnup, K. (ed.) (1995) *Lesbian Parents: Living with Pride and Prejudice*. Charlottetown: Gynergy Books.

Asante, M. (1987) *The Africentric Idea*. Philadelphia: Temple University Press.

Attlee, C.R. (1920) *The Social Worker*. London: Library of Social Service.

Audit Commission (1994) *Seen But Not Heard: Co-ordinating Community Child Health and Social Services for Children in Need*. London: HMSO.

Badgley, R. (1986) *Sexual Offences Against Children: Report of the Committee on Sexual Offences Against Children and Youths*, Vols 1 and 2. Ottawa: Minister of Supply and Services Canada.

Bagley, C. and Young, L. (1982) 'Policy Dilemmas and the Adoption of Black Children', in J. Cheetham (ed.) *Social Work Education and Ethnicity*. London: Allen and Unwin.

Bagnell, K. (2001) *The Little Immigrants: The Orphans Who Came to Canada*. Toronto: Dundurn Press.

Banks, S. (2001) *Social Work Values and Ethics*. London: Palgrave.

Barclay, L. (1982) *The Barclay Report: Social Workers, Their Roles and Tasks*. London: NISW/MacDonald and Evans.

Barker, H. (1986) 'Recapturing Sisterhood: A Critical Look at "Process" in Feminist Organisations and Community Action', in *Critical Social Policy*, 16, Summer, pp. 80–90.

Barker, R.W. (1996) 'Child Protection, Public Services and the Chimera of Market Force Efficiency', in *Children and Society*, 10, pp. 28–39.

Barlett, D.L. and Steele, J.B. (1998) 'Corporate Welfare: Special Report', in *Time*, 9 November.

Barn, R. (1993) *Black Children in the Public Care System*. London: Batsford.

Barnes, C. and Oliver, M. (1998) 'Discrimination, Disability and Welfare: From Needs to Rights', in J. Swain, V. Finkelstein, S. French and M. Oliver (eds) *Disabling Barriers – Enabling Environments*. London: Sage and Open University Press.

Barnes, M. and Maple, N. (1992) *Women and Mental Health: Challenging the Stereotypes*. Birmingham: Venture Press.

Barnett, R. (1994) *The Limits of Competence: Knowledge, Higher Education and Society*. Buckingham: SRHE/Open University Press.

Barrett, M. and McIntosh, M. (1981) *The Anti-Social Family*. London: Verso.

Barrett, M. and McIntosh, M. (1985) 'Ethnocentrism and Socialist Feminist Theory', in *Feminist Review*, 20, pp. 23–47.

Barry, M. and McIvor, G. (2000) *Diversion from Prosecution to Social Work and Other Service Agencies: Evaluation of the 100 per cent Funding Pilot Programmes*. Edinburgh: Scottish Executive Council General Research Unit.

Batty, D. (2002) 'Funding Halves Places', in *The Guardian*, 23 October.

Bauman, Z. (2000) 'Issues of Law and Order', in *British Journal of Criminology*, 40, pp. 205–21.

Beck, U. (1992) *Risk Society: Towards a New Modernity*. London: Sage.

Becker, S., Aldridge, J. and Dearden, C. (1998) *Young Carers and Their Families*. London: Carers National Association.

Begum, N. (1992) 'Disabled Women and the Feminist Agenda', in *Feminist Review*, 40, Spring, pp. 71–84.

Begum, N., Hill, M. and Stevens, A. (1993) *Reflections: The Views of Black Disabled People on Their Lives and on Community Care*. London: CCETSW.

Belenky, M.F., Clinchy, M.B., Goldberger, N.R. and Tarule, M.J. (1997) *Women's Ways of Knowing: The Development of Self, Voice and Mind*. New York: Basic Books.

Bell, C. and Newby, H. (1971) *Community Studies*. London: Allen and Unwin.

Belotti, E. (1975) *Little Girls*. London: Writers and Readers Publishing Co-operative.

Bergeron, L.R. (1999) 'Decision-Making and Adult Protective Service Workers: Identifying Critical Factors', in *Journal of Elder Abuse and Neglect*, 10, pp. 87–130.

Berridge, D. and Brodie, I. (1996) 'Residential Child Care in England and Wales: The Inquiries and After', in M. Hill and J. Aldgate (eds) *Child Welfare Services: Developments in Law, Policy and Practice*. London: Jessica Kingsley.

Bhatti-Sinclair, K. (1994) 'Asian Women and Domestic Violence from Male Partners', in C. Lupton and T. Gillespie (eds) *Working with Violence*. London: BASW/Macmillan.

Bhargava, A. (1986) 'The Bhopal Incident and Union Carbide', in *Bulletin of Concerned Asian Scholars*, 18(4), pp. 1–18.

Bhavani, K.K. (1993) 'Talking Racism and the Editing of Women's Studies', in D. Richardson and V. Robinson (eds) *Introduction to Women's Studies*. London: Macmillan.

Biesteck, F.P. (1961) *The Casework Relationship*. London: Allen and Unwin.

Biggs, S. (1993) *Understanding Ageing: Images, Attitudes and Professional Practice*. Buckingham: Open University Press.

Biggs, S. with Phillipson, C. and Kingston, P. (1995) *Elder Abuse in Perspective*. Buckingham: Open University Press.

Bignall, T. and Butt, J. (2000) 'Young, Black and Disabled'. Black Information Link. *http://www.blink.org.uk/disab/young.htm*

Bishop, A. (1994) *Becoming an Ally: Breaking the Cycle of Oppression*. Halifax: Fernwood Publishing.

Black Assessors (1994) 'DipSW Consultations a Sham', in *Community Care*, 20–6 October.

Blair, T. (1999) 'PM's 20-Year Target to End Poverty', in *The Guardian*, 19 March.

Blakemore, K. and Bonecham, M. (1994) *Age, Race and Ethnicity*. Buckingham: Open University Press.

Blom-Cooper, L. (1986) *A Child in Trust: The Report of the Panel of Inquiry into the Circumstances Surrounding the Death of Jasmine Beckford*. London Borough of Kent: Kingwood Press.

Bolen, R. (2002) *Child Sexual Abuse*. New York: Kluwer Academic/Plenum Publishers.

Bonnemaison, H. (1983) *Face à la délinquance: Prévention, répression, solidarité. Rapport au Premier Ministre de la Commission des Maines sur la Sécurité*. Paris: La Documentation Française.

Bonney, J. (2002) 'Child Poverty'. *http://www.barnardos.org.uk/whatwedo/community/poverty.jsp*

Bonny, S. (1984) *Who Cares in Southwark?* London: National Association of Carers and their Elderly Dependants.

Booth, T. (2000) 'Parents with Learning Difficulties, Child Protection and the Courts', in *Representing Children*, 13(3), pp. 175–88.

Booth, T. and Booth, W. (1998) *Growing Up with Parents Who Have Learning Difficulties*. London: Routledge.

Bornat, J., Johnson, J., Pereira, C., Pilgrim, D. and Williams, F. (eds) (1997) *Community Care: A Reader*. London: Macmillan and Open University Press.

Box, S. (1987) *Recession, Crime and Punishment*. London: Macmillan.

Boyle, J. (1977) *A Sense of Freedom*. London: Pan Books.

Bradshaw, J. (ed.) (2001) *Poverty: The Outcomes for Children*. London: Occasional Paper 26. London: Family Policy Studies Centre.

Brah, A. (1996) *Cartographies of Diaspora*. London: Routledge.

Braithwaite, J. (1995) 'Reintegrative Shaming, Republicanism and Policy', in H.D. Barlow (ed.) *Crime and Public Policy*. Oxford: Westview Press.

Brandon, M., Schofield, G. and Trinder, L., with Stone, N. (1998) *Social Work with Children*. London: Palgrave.

Brandwein, R. (1986) 'A Feminist Approach to Social Policy', in N. Van Den Bergh and L. Cooper (eds) *Feminist Visions for Social Work*. Silver Spring, MD: NASW.

Brewer, C. and Lait, J. (1980) *Can Social Work Survive?* London: Temple Smith.

Brindle, D. (2001) 'Counting the Losses', in *The Guardian*, 18 April.

Brindle, D. (2003) 'Social Workers Trail Behind in Survey on Role Importance', in *The Guardian*, 19 March.

British Association of Social Workers (BASW) (1996) *A Code of Ethics for Social Work*. Birmingham: BASW.

British Medical Association (BMA) (1986) *All Our Tomorrows: Growing Old in Britain*. London: BMA.

Broadbent, J. and Laughlin, R. (1990) *Recent Financial and Administrative Changes in the NHS: A Critical Theory*. Sheffield: Sheffield University Management School Series.

Brooks, D. (ed.) (1996) *Backward and Upward: The New Conservative Writing*. New York: Random House.

Bruyere, G. (2001) 'First Nations Approaches to Social Work', in L. Dominelli, W. Lorenz and H. Soydan (eds) *Beyond Racial Divides: Ethnicities in Social Work*. Aldershot: Ashgate.

Bryant, B., Dadzie, S. and Scafe, S. (1985) *The Heart of the Race: Black Women's Lives in Britain*. London: Virago.

Bulmer, M. and Rees, M.A. (eds) (1996) *Citizenship Today: The Contemporary Relevance of T.H. Marshall*. London: University College London Press.

Burchard, J.D., Burchard, S.N. and Farrington, D.P. (1989) 'Prevention of Delinquent Behaviour', in *Contemporary Psychology*, 34(7), pp. 674–94.

Burkett, I. (2002) 'Globalized Microfinance: Economic Empowerment or Just Debt?' Paper given at the Rethinking Social Work Seminar, Southampton University, 28 November–2 December.

Butler-Schloss, E. (1988) *Report of the Inquiry into Child Abuse in Cleveland*. London: HMSO.

Butrym, Z. (1976) *The Nature of Social Work*. London: Macmillan.

Callahan, M., Strega, S., Ruttman, D. and Dominelli, L. (2000) *Looking Promising*.

Campbell, B. (1998a) *Stolen Voices*. London: Women's Press.

Campbell, B. (1998b) *Unofficial Secrets: The Child Abuse Scandal in Cleveland Revisited*. London: Virago. First published in 1988.

Campbell, M. (1983) *Half-Breed*. Halifax: Formac Publishing Company Limited. (First published in 1973.)

Canadian Business (1997) 'Corporate Welfare: High Tech, Low Returns', 70(7), June, pp. 150–5.

Cannan, C. (1992) *Changing Families, Changing Welfare: Family Centres and the Welfare State*. Hemel Hampstead: Harvester Wheatsheaf.

Cannan, C. and Warren, C. (1997) *Social Action with Children and Families: A Community Development Approach to Children and Families*. London: Routledge.

Carers National Association (1997) *Still Battling? The Carers Act One Year On*. London: Carers National Association.

Carlebach, J. (1970) *Caring for Children in Trouble*. London: Routledge and Kegan Paul.

Carlen, P. and Worrall, A. (eds) (1987) *Gender, Crime and Justice*. Milton Keynes: Open University Press.

Carlile, L. (1994) *Carlile Review: Child Protection in the NHS*. London: HMSO.

Carvel, J. (2001) 'UNISON Calls Social Workers Strike', in *The Guardian*, 27 October.

Carver, B. (2002) *Anatomy of Greed: The Unshredded Truth from an Enron Insider*. New York: Carroll and Graf Publishers.

Cassidy, F. (ed.) (1992) *Aboriginal Title in British Columbia: Delgamuukw v. The Queen*. Montreal: Oolichan Books.

Castel, R. (1991) 'From Dangerousness to Risk', in G. Burchell, C. Gordon and P. Miller (eds) *The Foucault Effect: Studies in Governmentality*. Hemel Hempstead: Harvester Wheatsheaf.

Cedersund, E. (1999) 'Using Narratives in Social Work Interaction', in A. Jokinen, K. Juhila and T. Poso (eds) *Constructing Social Work Practices*. Aldershot: Ashgate.

Central Council for Education and Training in Social Work (CCETSW) (1976) *Values in Social Work*. London: CCETSW.

Central Council for Education and Training in Social Work (CCETSW) (1989) *Requirements and Regulations for the Diploma in Social Work. Paper 30*. London: CCETSW. (Revised in 1991 and 1995.)

Chambon, A., Irving, A. and Epstein, C. (eds) (1999) *Reading Foucault for Social Work*. New York: Columbia University Press.

Chaplin, J. (1988) *Feminist Counselling in Action*. London: Sage.

Cheetham, J., Fuller, R., McIvor, G. and Petch, A. (1992) *Evaluating Social Work Effectiveness*. Buckingham: Open University Press.

Christie, A. (2001) *Men and Social Work: Theories and Practices*. London: Macmillan.

Churchill, W. (1998) *A Little Matter of Genocide*. Winnipeg: Arbeiter Ring Publishing.

Clarke, J. and Newman, J. (1997) *The Managerialist State*. London: Sage.

Cleaver, E. (1971) *Soul on Ice*. New York: Pan Books.

Clegg, S.R. (1989) *Frameworks of Power*. London: Sage.

Clifford, D. (1998) *Social Assessment Theory and Practice*. Aldershot: Ashgate.

Clinton, H.R. (1996) *It Takes a Village: And Other Lessons Children Teach Us*. New York: Touchstone Books.

Cohen, S. (1980) *Folk Devils and Moral Panics* (2nd edn). Oxford: Martin Robinson.

Colley, H. and Hodkinson, P. (2001) 'Problems with Bridging the Gap: The Reversal of Structure and Agency in Addressing Social Exclusion', in *Critical Social Policy*, 21(3), pp. 335–59.

Collins, P.H. (1991) *Black Feminist Thought: Knowledge, Consciousness and the Politics of Empowerment*. London: Routledge.

Comer, J.P. and Poussaint, A.P. (1975) *Black Child Care*. New York: Pocket Books.

Compton, B. and Galaway, B. (1975) *Social Work Processes*. Homewood, IL: The Dorsey Press.

Connell, R.W. (1995) *Masculinities*. Cambridge: Polity.

Cook, D. and Hudson, B. (1993) *Racism and Criminology*. London: Sage.

Cork, D. (1998) *The Pig and the Python: How to Prosper from the Aging Baby Boomers*. New York: Prima Publishing.

Corrigan, P. and Leonard, P. (1978) *Social Work under Capitalism*. London: Macmillan.

Cowburn, M. and Dominelli, L. (2001) 'Masking Hegemonic Masculinity: Deconstructing the Paedophile as the Dangerous Stronger', in *British Journal of Social Work*, 31(3), pp. 399–415.

Cowger, C. (1994) 'Assessing Client Strengths: Clinical Assessment for Clinical Empowerment', in *Social Work*, 39, pp. 262–68.

Cowgill, D.O. and Holmes, L. (1972) *Aging and Modernization*. New York: Appleton-Century-Crofts.

Cox, R.W. (1981) 'Social Forces, States and World Orders: Beyond International Relations Theory', in *Millennium*, 10(2), pp. 146–57.

Craig, G. (2001) 'Social Exclusion: Is Labour Working?' in *Community Care*, 27 September–3 October.

Craig, G. and Mayo, M. (1995) *Community Empowerment: A Reader in Participation and Development*. London: Zed Books.

Cross, W.E. (1978) 'The Thomas and Cross Models of Psychological Nigrescence', in *The Journal of Black Psychology*, 5(1), pp. 13–27.

Culpitt, I. (1992) *Welfare and Citizenship: Beyond the Crisis of the Welfare State*. London: Sage.

Currey, L., Wequin, J. and Associates (1993) *Educating Professionals: Responding to the New Expectations for Competence and Accountability*. San Francisco: Jossey Bass.

Currie, E. (1988) 'Two Visions of Community Crime Prevention', in T. Hope and M. Shaw (eds) *Communities and Crime Reduction*. London: HMSO.

Dale, J. and Foster, P. (1986) *Feminists and State Welfare*. London: Routledge and Kegan Paul.

Davies, M. (1974) *Social Work in the Environment*. London: HMSO.

Davies, M. (1985) *The Essential Social Worker*. Aldershot: Gower.

De Haan, A. (1998) 'Social Exclusion: An Alternative Concept for the Study of Deprivation?' in A. De Haan and S. Maxwell (eds) *Poverty and Social Exclusion in North and South, IDS Bulletin*, 29(1), January, pp. 10–19.

Dearden, C. and Becker, S. (1998) *Young Carers in the United Kingdom*. London: Carers National Association.

Department for Education and Employment (DfEE) (2002) *Working Together: Connexions and Social Services.* http://www.dfee.gov.uk/careerpubs/uploads/cp workingtogether.pdf

Department for Education and Skills (DfES) (2003) *Every Child Matters*. Norwich: The Stationery Office.

Department of Health (DoH) (2001) *Crossing Bridges: A Training Resource for Working with Mentally Ill Parents and Their Children*. London: Stationery Office.

Department of Health (DoH) (2002) *Guidance on Child Protection*. London: DoH.

Department of Health (DoH), Department for Education and Employment (DfEE) and the Home Office (2000) *Framework for the Assessment of Children in Need and their Families*. London: Stationery Office.

Department of Health and Social Security (DHSS) (DoH) (1995) *Child Protection: Messages from Research*. London: HMSO.

Department of Trade and Industry (DTI) (2001) *The Maxwell Inquiry*. London: DTI.

Devlin, A. (1995) *Criminal Classes*. Winchester: Waterside Press.

Dews, V. and Watts, J. (1994) *Review of Probation Officer Recruitment and Qualifying Training*. London: Home Office.

Dominelli, L. (1983) *Women in Focus: Community Service Orders and Female Offenders*. Coventry: University of Warwick.

Dominelli, L. (1986) 'The Power of the Powerless: Prostitution and the Reinforcement of Submissive Femininity', *Sociological Review*, Spring, pp. 65–92.

Dominelli, L. (1988) *Anti-Racist Social Work*. London: Macmillan. (2nd edn published in 1997.)

Dominelli, L. (1989) 'Betrayal of Trust: A Feminist Analysis of Power Relationships in Incest Abuse and Its Relevance for Social Work Practice', *British Journal of Social Work*, 19, pp. 291–307.

Dominelli, L. (1990) *Women and Community Action*. Birmingham: Venture Press.

Dominelli, L. (1991a) *Gender, Sex Offenders and Probation Practice*. Norwich: Novata Press.

Dominelli, L. (1991b) *Women across Continents: Feminist Comparative Social Policy*. Hemel Hempstead: Harvester Wheatsheaf.

Dominelli, L. (1991c) '"Race", Gender and Social Work', in M. Davies (ed.) *The Sociology of Social Work*. London: Routledge.

Dominelli, L. (1996) 'Deprofessionalising Social Work: Equal Opportunities, Competence and Postmodernism', in *British Journal of Social Work*, 26, pp. 153–75.

Dominelli, L. (1997) *Sociology for Social Work*. London: Macmillan.

Dominelli, L. (1998a) 'Anti-Oppressive Practice in Context', in R. Adams, L. Dominelli and M. Payne (eds) *Social Work: Themes, Issues, and Critical Debates*. London: Macmillan.

Dominelli, L. (1998b) 'Globalisation and Gender Relations in Social Work', in B. Lesnick (ed.) *Countering Discrimination in Social Work*. Aldershot: Ashgate.

Dominelli, L. (ed.) (1999) *Community Approaches to Child Welfare: International Perspectives*. Aldershot: Avebury.

Dominelli, L. (2000) 'Empowerment: Help or Hindrance in Professional Relationships?' in D. Ford and P. Stepney (eds) *Social Work Models, Methods and Theories: A Framework for Practice*. Lyme Regis: Russell House Publishing.

Dominelli, L. (2001) 'Globalization: A Myth or Reality for Social Workers?' translated as 'Globalizacija: mit ili stvarnost za socijalne radnike?' in *Revija za Socijalnu Politiku*, 3–4, pp. 259–66.

Dominelli, L. (2002a) *Anti-Oppressive Social Work Theory and Practice*. London: Palgrave.

Dominelli, L. (2002b) *Feminist Social Work Theory and Practice*. London: Palgrave.

Dominelli, L. (2002c) '"Glassed-in": Women's Reproductive Rights', in R. Adams, L. Dominelli and M. Payne (eds) *Critical Practice in Social Work*. London: Palgrave.

Dominelli, L. (2002d) *Sure Start Rowner: Baseline Report*. Southampton: Southampton University.

Dominelli, L. and Gollins, T. (1997) 'Men, Power and Caring Relationships', in *Sociological Review*, 45(3), August, pp. 396–415.

Dominelli, L. and Hoogvelt, A. (1996a) 'Globalisation, Contract Government and the Taylorisation of Intellectual Labour', in *Studies in Political Economy*, 49, pp. 71–100.

Dominelli, L. and Hoogvelt, A. (1996b) 'Globalisation and the Technocratisation of Social Work', in *Critical Social Policy*, 16(2), pp. 45–62.

Dominelli, L. and Khan, P. (2000) 'Globalisation, Privatisation and Social Work Practice'. Paper presented at the Rethinking Social Work Seminar: Focusing on Globalization, 30 November–2 December, Southampton University.

Dominelli, L. and McLeod, E. (1989) *Feminist Social Work*. London: Macmillan.

Dominelli, L. and Thomas Bernard, W. (eds) (2003) *Broadening Horizons: International Exchanges in Social Work*. Aldershot: Ashgate.

Dominelli, L., Jeffers, L., Jones, G., Sibanda, S. and Williams, B. (1995) *Anti-Racist Probation Practice*. Aldershot: Avebury.

Dominelli, L., Callahan, M., Rutman, D. and Strega, S. (forthcoming) 'Endangered Children: The State as Parent and Grandparent', in *British Journal of Social Work*.

Donzelot, J. (1980) *The Policing of Families: Welfare versus the State*. London: Hutchinson.

Doress, P.B. and Siegal, D.L. (1987) *Ourselves Growing Older*. New York: Simon and Schuster.

Downes, D. and Morgan, R. (1994) 'Hostages to Fortune: The Politics of Law and Order in Post-War Britain', in M. Maguire, R. Morgan and R. Reiner (eds) *The Oxford Handbook of Criminology*. Oxford: Clarendon Press.

Duffy, K. (1995) *Social Exclusion and Human Dignity in Europe*. Report for the Council of Europe. Brussels: CDPS.

Duncan, S. and Edwards, R. (1996) 'Rational Economic Man or Lone Mothers in Context? The Uptake of Paid Work', in S. Burtolara (ed.) *Good Enough Mothering: Feminist Perspectives on Lone Motherhood*. London: Routledge.

Duncan, S. and Edwards, R. (1997) 'Single Mothers in Britain: Unsupported Workers or Mothers?' in S. Duncan (ed.) *Single Mothers in an International Context: Mothers or Workers?* London: University College London Press.

Durkheim, É. (1957) *Anomie: A Study in Sociology*. Glencoe, IL: Free Press. (Originally published in 1897.)

Egan, G. (1998) *The Skilled Helper: A Problem Management Approach to Helping*. Pacific Grove, CA: Brooks/Cole Publishing Company.

Eichler, M. (1983) *Families in Canada*. Toronto: Gage.

Erickson, E.H. (1959) 'Identity and the Life Cycle', in *Psychological Issues*, 1(1), pp. 151–71.

Estes, C.L. (1989) 'Ageing, Health and Social Policy: Crisis and Crossroads', in *Journal of Aging and Social Policy*, 1(1/2), pp. 17–32.

European Foundation for the Improvement of Living and Working Conditions (1995) *Public Welfare Services and Social Exclusion: The Development of Consumer-Oriented Initiatives in the European Union*. Dublin: EFILWC.

Eysenck, H. (1997) 'Obituary of H.J. Eysenck', in *The Guardian*, 13 September.

Fariman Fariman, S. (1996) *Social Work as Social Development: A Case History*. Manchester: Manchester Metropolitan University/IASSW.

Farrington, D. (1990) 'Implications of Criminal Career Research for the Prevention of Offending', in *Journal of Adolescence*, 13(2), pp. 93–113.

Farrington, D., Gallagher, B., Morley, L., St Ledger, R. and West, D. (1986) 'Unemployment, School Leaving and Crime', in *British Journal of Criminology*, 26, pp. 335–56.

Field, S. (1990) *Trends in Crime and their Interpretation*. Home Office Research Study, 119. London: HMSO.

Findlay, J., Bright, J. and Gill, K. (1990) *Youth Crime Prevention: A Handbook of Good Practice*. Swindon: Crime Concern.

Finn, D. (1985) *The Community Programme*. London: Centre for the Unemployed.

Finn, J. and Jacobson, M. (2003) *Just Practice: A Social Justice Approach to Social Work*. Peosta, IA: Eddie Bowers.

Fisher, M. (1997) 'Man-Made Care: Community Care and Older Male Carers', in *British Journal of Social Work*, 24, pp. 659–80.

Flexner, A. (1915) 'Is Social Work a Profession?' in *Studies in Social Work*, No. 4. New York: New York School of Philanthropy.

Fook, J. (1993) *Radical Casework: A Theory of Practice*. London: Allen and Unwin.

Foucault, M. (1977) *Discipline and Punish*. London: Allen Lane.

Foucault, M. (1979a) *The History of Sexuality: An Introduction*, Vol. 1. London: Allen Lane/Penguin.

Foucault, M. (1979b) 'Truth and Power', in M. Morris and P. Patton (eds) *Michel Foucault: Power, Truth, Strategy*. Sydney: Feral Publications.

Foucault, M. (1980) *Power/Knowledge: Selected Interviews and Other Writings, 1972–77*. New York: Pantheon Books.

Foucault, M. (1983) 'The Subject and Power', Afterword to H. Dreyfus and P. Rabinow (eds) *Michel Foucault: Beyond Structuralism and Hermeneutics*. Chicago: University of Chicago Press.

Foucault, M. (1991) 'Governmentality', in G. Burchell, C. Gordon and P. Miller (eds) *The Foucault Effect: Studies in Governmentality*. Hemel Hempstead: Harvester Wheatsheaf.

Fox-Harding, L. (1991) 'The Children's Act in Context: Four Perspectives in Child Care Law and Policy', in *Journal of Social Welfare and Family Law*, 3, pp. 179–93.

Frank, R. (1995) *Hegemonic Masculinity*. London: Sage.

Frankenburg, R. (1997) *Displacing Whiteness: Essays in Social and Cultural Criticism*. London: Duke University Press.

Franklin, A. and Franklin, B. (1996) 'Growing Pains: The Developing Children's Rights Movement in the UK', in J. Pilcher and S. Wagg (eds) *Thatcher's Children? Politics, Childhood and Society in the 1980s and 1990s*. London: Falmer Press.

Franklin, B. (ed.) (1995) *The Handbook of Children's Rights: Comparative Policy and Practice*. London: Routledge.

Fraser, N. (1989) *Unruly Practices: Power, Discourse and Gender in Contemporary Theory*. Minneapolis: University of Minneapolis Press.

Freire, P. (1972) *The Pedagogy of the Oppressed*. Harmondsworth: Penguin.

French, M. (1985) *The Power of Women*. Harmondsworth: Penguin.

Friedan, B. (1993) *The Fountain of Age*. New York: Simon and Schuster.

Furniss, E. (1995) *Victims of Benevolence: The Dark Legacy of the Williams Lake Residential School*. Vancouver: Arsenal Pulp Press.

Gaffney, D. (2002) 'Capital of Child Poverty', in *The Guardian*, 22 November.

Garber, R. (2000) 'World Census of Social Work and Social Development Education: Interim Report', in *Social Work and Globalization, Special Issue*, July, pp. 198–214.

Garrett, L. (1992) *Leaving Care and After*. London: National Children's Bureau.

Geraghty, J. (1991) *Probation Practice in Crime Prevention*. Crime Prevention Unit, Paper 24. London: Home Office.

Gibbons, J., Gallagher, B., Bell, C. and Gordon, D. (1995) 'Development after Physical Abuse in Early Childhood: A Follow-Up Study of Children on Protection Registers', in Department of Health, *Child Protection: Messages from Research*. London: HMSO.

Giddens, A. (1990) *The Consequences of Modernity*. Cambridge: Polity.

Giddens, A. (1993) *Modernity and Self-Identity: Self and Society in the Late Modern Age*. Cambridge: Polity.

Giddens, A. (1998a) 'Risk Society: The Context of British Politics', in J. Franklin (ed.) *The Politics of Risk Society*. Cambridge: Polity.

Giddens, A. (1998b) *The Third Way: The Renewal of Social Democracy*. Cambridge: Polity.

Gilbert, M. and Russell, S. (2002) 'Social Control of Transnational Corporations: The Age of Marketocracy', in *International Journal of the Sociology of Law*, 30(1), pp. 33–50.

Gilbert, S. (2001) 'Social Work with Indigenous Australians', in M. Alston and J. McKinnon (eds) *Social Work: Fields of Practice*. Victoria, Australia: Oxford University Press.

Gilder, G. (1981) *Wealth and Poverty*. New York: Bell Books.

Gillan, A. (2002) 'Prison Worked, Says Truants' Mother', in *The Guardian*, 27 May.

Gillen, S. (2001a) 'Report into Lauren Wright's Death Puts Spotlight on Role of Health Staff', in *Community Care*, 4–10 April.

Gillen, S. (2001b) 'Shock at Foster Care Abuse Survey', in *Community Care*, 24–30 April.

Gillen, S. (2002) 'Charities Accuse Statutory Agencies of Failing Child Prostitutes', in *Community Care*, 10–16 December.

Gilligan, C. (1982) *In A Different Voice*. Cambridge, MA: Harvard University Press.

Gilroy, J. (1999) 'Lessons from the Field', in L. Dominelli (ed.) *Community Approaches to Child Welfare: International Perspectives*. Aldershot: Ashgate.

Gilroy, P. (1987) *There Ain't No Black in the Union Jack*. London: Hutchinson.

Gilroy, P. (1995) *The Black Atlantic: Modernity and Double Consciousness*. Cambridge, MA: Harvard University Press.

Gingerbread (2000) 'Lone Parent Families: Routes to Social Inclusion'. *http://gingerbread.org.uk/prtsi.html*

Graef, R. (1992) *Living Dangerously: Young Offenders in Their Own Words*. London: HarperCollins.

Graham, H. (1983) 'Caring: Labour of Love', in J. Finch and D. Groves (eds) *Labour of Love: Women, Work and Caring*. London: Routledge and Kegan Paul.

Graham, M. (2002) *Social Work and African-Centred Worldviews*. Birmingham: Venture Press.

Greenhorn, M. (1996) *Cautions, Court Proceedings and Sentencing, England and Wales, 1995. Home Office Statistical Bulletin, 16*. London: Home Office.

Greer, P. (1994) *Transforming Central Government: The Next Steps Initiatives*. London: Open University Press.

Griffiths, R. (1988) *Community Care: Agenda for Action, The Griffiths Report*. London: HMSO.

Grimwood, C. and Popplestone, R. (1993) *Women in Management*. London: BASW/Macmillan.

Gutierrez, L. and Lewis, E. (1999) *Empowering Women of Color*. New York: Columbia University Press.

Haig-Brown, C. (1988) *Resistance and Renewal: Surviving the Indian Residential School*. Vancouver: Tillicum Library/Arsenal Pulp Press.

Haines, K. and Drakeford, M. (1998) *Young People and Youth Justice*. London: Macmillan.

Haines, K., Jones, R. and Isles, E. (1999) *Promoting Positive Behaviour in Schools*. Report submitted to the Wales Office of Research and Development.

Hall, C. (1997) *Social Work as Narratives: Storytelling and Persuasion in Professional Texts*. Aldershot: Ashgate.

Hall, S. (1992) 'The Question of Cultural Identity', in S. Hall, D. Held and T. McGrew (eds) *Modernity and Its Futures*. Cambridge: Polity.

Hall, S., Critchen, C., Jefferson, T., Clarke, J. and Roberts, B. (1978) *Policing the Crisis: Mugging, the State and Law and Order*. London: Macmillan.

Hanmer, J. and Statham, D. (1988) *Women and Social Work: Towards a Woman-Centred Practice*. London: Macmillan.

Hanscombe, G. and Forster, J. (1982) *Rocking the Cradle: Lesbian Mothers*. London: Sheba Feminist Publishing.

Haraway, D. (1991) *Simians, Cyborgs, and Women: The Reinvention of Nature*. London: Routledge.

Harvey, L. (2002) 'Is Dryden Road the Worst Street in Sheffield?' in *The Star*, 14 June.

Harvey, L., Burnham, R., Kendall, K. and Pease, K. (1992) 'Gender Differences in Criminal Justice: An International Comparison', in *British Journal of Criminology*, 32, pp. 209–17.

Healy, L. (2001) *International Social Work: Professional Action in an Interdependent World*. Oxford: Oxford University Press.

Hencke, D. (2001) 'Private Jail Makes Huge Profit', in *The Guardian*, 4 July.

Hester, M., Pearson, C. and Harwin, N. (2000) *Making an Impact: Children and Domestic Violence – A Reader*. London: Department of Health.

Hill, A. (2000) 'First Nations Child Welfare', in M. Callahan, S. Hessle and S. Strega (eds) *Valuing the Field: Child Welfare in International Perspectives*. Aldershot: Ashgate.

Hills, J. (1995) *Joseph Rowntree Foundation Inquiry into Income and Wealth: A Summary of the Evidence*. York: JRF.

Hirst, P. (1981) 'The Genesis of the Social', in *Politics and Power*, 3, pp. 67–82. Routledge and Kegan Paul.

Hobbes, T. (1968) *Leviathan*. Harmondsworth: Penguin.

Hollway, W. (1989) *Subjectivity and Method in Psychology: Gender, Meaning and Science*. London: Sage.

Holman, R. (1988) *Putting Families First*. London: Macmillan.

Home Office (1990) *Partnership in Dealing with Offenders in the Community*. London: Home Office.

Home Office (1992) *National Standards for the Supervision of Offenders in the Community*. London: Home Office. (Revised in 1995 and 2000.)

Home Office (1994) *The Ethnic Origins of Prisoners. Home Office Statistical Bulletin*, 21(94). London: HMSO.

Home Office (1997) *Race and the Criminal Justice System: A Home Office Publication Under Section 95 of the Criminal Justice Act, 1991*. December. London: HMSO.

Home Office (1998) *Probation and Community Sentences*. London: Home Office.

Home Office (2002) *Statistics on Women and the Criminal Justice System, 2002: A Home Office Publication Under Section 95 of the Criminal Justice Act, 1991*. London: Home Office.

hooks, b. (1984) *Feminist Theory: From Margins to Centre*. Boston: South End Press.

hooks, b. (1990) *Yearning: Race, Gender and Cultural Politics*. Boston: South End Press.

hooks, b. (2000) *Where We Stand: Class Matters*. London: Routledge.

Hope, M. and Chapman, T. (1998) *Evidence-Based Practice: A Guide to Effective Practice*. London: Home Office.

Hopkins, N. (2002) 'Petty Offences, Borough's Big Problem', in *The Guardian*, 27 May.

Hough, M. (2002) *The British Crime Survey 2001*. London: Home Office.

Howarth, C., Kenway, P., Palmer, G. and Miorelli, R. (1999) *Monitoring Poverty and Social Exclusion*. York: Joseph Rowntree Foundation.

Howe, D. (1986) 'The Segregation of Women and Their Work in the Personal Social Services', in *Critical Social Policy*, 15, pp. 21–35.

Hudson, A. (1990) 'Elusive Subjects: Researching Young Women in Trouble', in L. Gelsthorpe and A. Morris (eds) *Feminist Perspectives in Criminology*. Buckingham: Open University Press.

Hughes, B. (1995) *Older People and Community Care: Critical Theory and Practice*. Buckingham: Open University Press.

Humphries, S. (1997) *The Lost Children*. Sydney: Hale and Iremonger.

Hunter, D. (1994) 'To Market! To Market! A New Dawn for Community Care?' in *Health and Social Care*, 1, pp. 3–10.

Ife, J. (2001) *Human Rights and Social Work*. Oxford: Oxford University Press.

Ingleby, D. (1985) 'Professions as Socializers: The "Psy" Complex', in A. Scull and S. Spitzer (eds) *Research in Law, Deviance and Social Control* 7. New York: JAI Press.

International Association of Schools of Social Work (IASSW) and International Federation of Social Workers (2001) International Definition of Social Work. *http://www.iassw.soton.ac.uk*

Jack, G. (2000) 'Ecological Influences on Parenting and Child Development', in *British Journal of Social Work*, 30(3), pp. 703–20.

Jackson, D. (1995) *Destroying the Baby in Themselves*. Nottingham: Mushroom Publishing.

Jackson, S. and Nixon, P. (1999) 'Family Group Conferences: A Challenge to the Old Order?' in L. Dominelli (ed.) *Community Approaches to Child Welfare: International Perspectives*. Aldershot: Ashgate.

Jaikumar, R. and Upton, M.D. (1993) 'The Co-ordination of Global Manufacturing', in S.P. Bradley, J.A. Hausman and R.I. Nolan (eds) *Globalization, Technology, Competition: The Fusion of Computers and Telecommunications in the 1990s*. Cambridge, MA: Harvard Business School Press.

Jaques, E. (1975) 'Social Analysis and the Glacier Project', in W. Brown and J.E. Brown (eds) *The Glacier Project Papers*. London: Heinemann.

Jaques, E. (1977) *A General Theory of Bureaucracy*. London: Heinemann.

John-Baptiste, A. (2001) 'Africentric Social Work', in L. Dominelli, W. Lorenz and H. Soydan (eds) *Beyond Racial Divides: Ethnicities in Social Work*. Aldershot: Ashgate.

Jones, C. (1996) 'Anti-Intellectualism and the Peculiarities of British Social Work', in N. Parton (ed.) *Social Theory, Social Change and Social Work*. London: Routledge.

Jones, C. (1998) 'Social Work and Society', in R. Adams, L. Dominelli and M. Payne (eds) *Social Work: Themes, Issues and Critical Debates*. London: Palgrave. (2nd edn published in 2002.)

Jordan, B. (1996) *A Theory of Poverty and Social Exclusion*. Cambridge: Polity.

Jordan, B. (2000) *Social Work and the Third Way: Tough Love as Social Policy*. London: Sage.

Jubilee 2000 (2003) From the website: *http://www.jubilee2000uk.org*

Kaim-Caudle, P.R. (1973) *Comparative Social Policy and Social Security: A Ten-Country Study*. London: Martin Robinson.

Kaseke, E. (1994) 'Social Work and Social Development in Zimbabwe'. Paper presented at IASSW Seminar, Sheffield University, 28 February.

Kaseke, E. (2001) 'Social Development in Africa'. Paper given at the IASSW Board Seminar in Durban, South Africa, 20–3 January.

Kaufman, A., Zacherias, L. and Karson, M. (1995) *Managers vs Owners: The Struggle for Corporate Control in American Democracy*. Oxford: Oxford University Press.

Keida, R.P. (1994) *Black on Black Crime: Facing Facts, Challenging Fiction*. New York: Wyndham Hall Press.

Kelly, L. (1988) *Surviving Sexual Violence*. Cambridge: Polity.

Kemshall, H. and Pritchard, J. (eds) (1996) *Good Practice in Risk Assessment and Risk Management*. London: Jessica Kingsley.

Kendall, K. (1991) *IASSW – The First Fifty Years, 1928–1978*. Washington, DC: IASSW/CSWE.

Kendall, K.A. (2000) *Social Work Education: Its Origins in Europe*. Alexandria, VA: Council for Social Work Education.

Kendall, K.A. (2002) *Council on Social Work Education: Its Antecedents and First Twenty Years*. Alexandria, VA: Council for Social Work Education.

Khan, P. (2001) 'The Feminisation of Care: The Impact of Globalisation on Women in their Roles as Providers, Service Users and Social Work Professionals', in C. Brina, C. Britton and A. Assiter (eds) *Millennial Visions: Feminisms into the 21st Century*. Cardiff: Cardiff Academic Press.

Khan, P. and Dominelli, L. (2000) 'The Impact of Globalisation on Social Work Practice in the UK', in *European Journal of Social Work*, 3(2), pp. 95–108.

Kilkey, M. (2000) *Lone Mothers between Paid Work and Care: The Policy Regime in Twenty Countries*. Aldershot: Ashgate.

Kincaid, J. (1973) *Poverty and Inequality in Britain*. Harmondsworth: Penguin.

King's Fund (2001) *Future Imperfect?* London: King's Fund.

Kinsella, W. (1998) *The Web of Hate: The Far Right Network in Canada*. Toronto: HarperCollins.

Knijn, T. and Ungerson, C. (1997) 'Introduction: Care Work and Gender in Welfare Regimes', in *Social Politics*, Fall, pp. 323–7.

Konstantin, P. (2002) *The Day in North American Indian History*. New York: Da Capo Press.

Kuhn, M. (1991) *No Stone Unturned: The Life and Times of Maggie Kuhn*. New York: Ballantine Books.

Kwo, E.M. (1984) 'Community Education and Community Development in Cameroon: The British Colonial Experience, 1922–1961', in *The Community Development Journal*, 19(4), pp. 204–13.

La Rossa, R. (1995) 'Fatherhood and Social Change', in E. Nelson and B. Robinson (eds) *Gender in the 1990s: Images, Realities and Issues*. Toronto: Nelson Canada.

Laclau, E. and Mouffe, C. (1985) *Hegemony and Socialist Strategy*. London: Verso.

Laming, H. (2003) *The Inquiry into Victoria Climbié*. London: Stationery Office.

Lappin, B. (1965) *Stages in the Development of Community Organization Work as a Social Work Method*. PhD thesis, University of Toronto.

Lawrence, H. (2002) 'Legalize Sale of Cannabis', in *The Star*, 14 June.

Leason, K. (2001) 'Health Visitor Struck Off Register for Ignoring Warnings of Child Abuse', in *Community Care*, 4–10 April.

Le Grand, J. and Bartlett, W. (eds) (1993) *Quasi-Markets and Social Policy*. London: Macmillan.

Lee, S. with Wiley, R. (1993) *By Any Means Necessary: The Trials and Tribulations of the Making of Malcolm X*. London: Vintage.

Leonard, D. and Speakman, M.A. (1986) 'Women in the Family: Companions or Caretakers?' in V. Beechey and E. Whitelegg (eds) *Women in Britain Today*. Buckingham: Open University Press.

Levitas, R. (ed.) (1986) *The Ideology of the New Right*. Cambridge: Polity.

Levitas, R. (1997) 'The Concept of Social Exclusion and the New Durkheimian Hegemony', in *Critical Social Policy*, 16(1), pp. 5–20.

Levy, A. and Kahan, B. (1996) *Who Do We Trust? The Abuse of Children Living Away from Home*. London: HMSO.

Limandri, B.J. and Sheridan, D.J. (1995) 'Prediction of Interpersonal Violence: An Introduction', in J.C. Campbell (ed.) *Assessing Dangerousness: Violence by Sexual Offenders, Batterers, and Child Abusers*. London: Sage.

Lindsay, M. (1992) *An Introduction to Children's Rights*. Highlight No. 113. London: National Children's Bureau.

Lister, R. (1997) *Citizenship: Feminist Perspectives*. London: Macmillan.

Loney, M. (1983) *Community against Government: The British Community Development Project 1968–1978: A Study of Government Incompetence*. London: Heinemann.

Loney, M. (1986) *The Politics of Greed: The New Right and the Welfare State*. London: Pluto Press.

Lorenz, W. (1994) *Social Work in a Changing Europe*. London: Routledge.

Lukes, S. (1974) *Power: A Radical View*. London: Macmillan.

Lum, D. (2000) *Culturally Competent Practice: A Framework for Growth and Action*. San Francisco: Wadsworth Publishing Co.

Lundquist, A. and Jackson, S. (2000) 'Case Study: An Aboriginal Nation's Efforts to Address Substance Abuse during Pregnancy', in D. Rutman, M. Callahan, A. Lundquist, S. Jackson and B. Field (eds) *Substance Use and Pregnancy: Conceiving Women in the Policy-Making Process*. Ottawa: Status of Women Canada.

Lupton, D. (ed.) (1999) *Risk and Sociocultural Theory: New Directions and Perspectives*. Cambridge: Cambridge University Press.

McDowall, A. (2002) 'Mistreatment of Disabled Children is Routinely Ignored', speech to National Deaf Children's Society, 2 December.

McGuire, J. (1995) *What Works: Reducing Reoffending – Guidelines from Research and Practice*. Chichester: Wiley.

McGuire, J. (2000) *Cognitive Behavioural Approaches: An Introduction to Theory and Research*. London: Home Office.

McIvor, G. (1990) *Sanctions for Serious or Persistent Offenders: A Review of the Literature*. Stirling: University of Stirling Social Work Research Centre.

McIvor, G. (2000) *Evaluation of the Airborne Initiative*. Edinburgh: Scottish Executive Central Research Unit.

McKinnon, J. (2001) 'Community Development and Micro-enterprises'. Paper given at 'Revitalising Communities through Partnerships amongst Business, Government, Universities, Practitioners and Local Communities' at Southampton University, 20–3 September.

MacPherson, C.B. (1962) *The Political Theory of Possessive Individualism: Hobbes to Locke*. Oxford: Oxford University Press.

Macpherson, W. (1998) *Report of the Inquiry into the Murder of Stephen Lawrence: The Macpherson Report*. London: HMSO.

Maguire, K. (2002) 'Unison Rejects Privatization Plan', in *The Guardian*, 19 June.

Malcolm, X. (1989) *The Autobiography of Malcolm X*. New York: Random House.

Mama, A. (1989) *Hidden Struggle: Statutory and Voluntary Responses to Violence Against Black Women in the Home*. London: Race and Housing Unit.

Mandelson, P. (1997) 'Labour's Next Steps: Tackling Social Inclusion'. Lecture given to the Fabian Society, 14 August.

Mandelstam, M. and Schewr, B. (1995) *Community Care Practice and the Law*. London: Jessica Kingsley.

Maracle, L. (1993) *Ravensong*. Vancouver: Press Gang Publishers.

Maracle, L. (2002) *Daughters are Forever*. Vancouver: Press Gang Publishers.

Margolin, L. (1997) *Under the Cover of Kindness: The Invention of Social Work*. Charlottesville, VA: University of Virginia Press.

Marsden, D. and Oakley, P. (1982) 'Radical Community Development in the Third World', in G. Craig, N. Derricourt and M. Loney (eds) *Community Work and the State: Towards a Radical Practice*. London: Routledge and Kegan Paul.

Marshall, T.H. (1970) *Social Policy in the Twentieth Century*. London: Hutchinson.

Martinson, R. (1974) '"What Works?" Questions and Answers about Prison Reform', in *The Public Interest*, 35, pp. 22–54.

Mathiesen, T. (1990) *Prison on Trial: A Critical Assessment*. London: Sage.

Maxime, J. (1986) 'Some Psychological Models of Black Self-Concept', in S. Ahmed, J. Cheetham and J. Small (eds) *Social Work with Black Children and Their Families*. London: Batsford.

Mayo, M. (1977) *Women in the Community*. London: Routledge and Kegan Paul.

Mayo, M. and Jones, D. (1974) *Community Work One*. London: Routledge and Kegan Paul.

Mendelsohn, A. (1980) *The Work of Social Work*. London: New Viewpoints.

Miller, J. and Ridge, T. (2001) *Families, Poverty, Work and Care: A Review of the Literature on Lone Parents and Low-Income Couple Families with Children*. Leeds: Department of Work and Pensions/HMSO.

Miller, J.B. (1978) *Towards a New Psychology of Women*. Harmondsworth: Penguin.

Miller, P. (1987) *Domination and Power*. London: Routledge and Kegan Paul.

Miller, P. and Rose, N. (1988) 'The Tavistock Programme: The Government of Subjectivity and Social Life', in *Sociology*, 22(2), pp. 171–92.

Mills, C.W. (1970) *The Sociological Imagination*. London: Pelican Books.

Mirrlees-Black, C., Mayhew, P. and Percy, A. (1996) *The 1996 British Crime Survey: England and Wales*. Home Office Statistical Bulletin, 19. London: Home Office.

Mishna, F. and Muskat, B. (2001) 'Social Group Work for Young Offenders', in *Social Work with Groups*, 24(3/4), pp. 11–32.

Moosa-Mitha, M. (2002) *Rights Discourses and Child Sex Trade Workers*. PhD paper, Southampton University.

Morgan, D.H.J. (1983) *Social Theory and the Family*. London: Routledge.

Morris, J. (1991) *Pride against Prejudice: Transforming Attitudes to Disability*. London: Women's Press.

Morris, L. (1995) *Dangerous Classes: The Underclass and Social Citizenship*. London: Routledge.

Mullaly, R. (1993) *Structural Social Work*. Toronto: McClelland and Stewart.

Mullender, A. and Morley, R. (eds) (1994) *Children Living with Domestic Violence: Putting Men's Abuse of Women on the Child Care Agenda*. London: Whiting and Birch.

Murray, C. (1984) *Losing Ground: American Social Policy*. New York: Basic Books.

Murray, C. (1990) *The Emerging British Underclass*. London: Institute of Economic Affairs.

Murray, C. (1994) *Underclass: The Crisis Deepens*. London: Institute of Economic Affairs.

Naples, N.A. (ed.) (1997) *Community Activism and Feminist Politics: Organizing Across Race, Class and Gender*. London: Routledge.

National Association for the Care and Rehabilitation of Offenders (NACRO) (1994) *Statistics on Black People within the Criminal Justice System*. London: NACRO.

Neary, M. (1992) 'Some Academic Freedom', in *Probation Journal*, 39, pp. 200–2.

Nolan, M., Grant, G. and Keady, J. (1996) *Understanding Family Care: A Multidimensional Model of Caring and Coping*. Buckingham: Open University Press.

O'Connell, W. (1983) 'Where Next: Family Dilemmas?', in *Community Care*, 4–10 April.

Ohri, A., Manning, B. and Curno, P. (1982) *Community Work and Racism*. London: Routledge.

Oliver, M. (1990) *The Politics of Disablement*. London: Macmillan.

Osberg, L. (2002) *Redistribution of Income between Rich and Poor*. London: Institute for Social and Economic Research.

Packman, J. (1994) '"Who Needs to Care?" Social Work Decisions about Children', in *Child Abuse and Neglect*, 18, pp. 913–21.

Pahl, J. (1980) 'Patterns of Money Management within Marriage', in *Journal of Social Policy*, 9, pp. 326–39.

Pahl, J. (1985) *Private Violence and Public Policy*. London: Routledge and Kegan Paul.

Panet-Raymond, J. (1991) *Partnership or Paternalism?* Montreal: University of Montreal Publication.

Parker, G. and Lawton, D. (1994) *Different Types of Care, Different Types of Carer: Evidence from the General Household Survey*. York: Social Policy Research Unit.

Parry, N., Rustin, M. and Satymurti, C. (1979) *Social Work, Welfare, and the State*. London: Edward Arnold.

Parsons, T. (1957) *Essays in Sociological Theory*. New York: Free Press.

Parton, N. (1985) 'The Politics of Child Abuse', in K. Browne and S. Saqi (eds) *Early Prediction and Prevention of Child Abuse*. Chichester: John Wiley and Sons.

Parton, N. (1996) 'The New Politics of Child Protection', in J. Pilcher and S. Wagg (eds) *Thatcher's Children: Politics, Childhood and Society in the 1980s and 1990s*. London: Falmer Press.

Parton, N. (1998) 'Risk, Advanced Liberalism and Child Welfare: The Need to Rediscover Uncertainty and Ambiguity', in *British Journal of Social Work*, 28(1), pp. 5–27.

Pascall, G. (1986) *Social Policy: A Feminist Analysis*. London: Tavistock.

Patel, N. (1990) *Race against Time: Ethnic Elders*. London: Runnymede Trust.

Pattison, G. (2002) *Connecting Communities: The Single Regeneration Budget and Community Participation*. Southampton: Southampton University.

Pease, B. and Fook, J. (eds) (1999) *Transforming Social Work Practice: Postmodern Critical Perspectives*. London: Routledge.

Perlmutter, F. (1997) *From Welfare to Work: Corporate Initiatives and Welfare Reform*. Oxford: Oxford University Press.

Peters, M. (1997) '"Social Exclusion" in Contemporary European Social Policy: Some Critical Comments', in G. Lavery, J. Pender and M. Peters (eds) *Exclusion and Inclusion: Minorities in Europe*. ISPRU Occasional Papers in Social Studies. Leeds: Leeds Metropolitan University.

Phillips, M. (1993) 'An Oppressive Urge to End Oppression', in *The Observer*, 1 August.

Phillips, M. (1994) 'Illiberal Liberalism', in S. Dunant (ed.) *The War of the Word: The Political Correctness Debate*. London: Virago.

Phillipson, C. (1982) *Capitalism and the Construction of Old Age*. London: Macmillan.

Phillipson, C. (1998) *Reconstructing Old Age: New Agendas in Social Theory and Practice*. London: Sage.

Philp, M. (1979) 'Notes on the Form of Knowledge in Social Work', in *Sociological Review*, 27(1), pp. 83–111.

Philp, M. (1985) 'Michel Foucault', in Q. Skinner (ed.) *The Return of Grand Theory in Human Sciences*. Cambridge: Cambridge University Press.

Philpot, T. and Ward, L. (eds) (1995) *Values and Visions: Changing Ideas in Services for People with Learning Difficulties*. Oxford: Butterworth-Heinemann.

Pinker, R. (1993) 'A Lethal Kind of Looniness', in *Times Higher Educational Supplement*, 10 September.

Pitcairn, T. and Waterhouse, L. (1996) 'Evaluating Parenting in Child Abuse', in L. Waterhouse (ed.) *Child Abuse and Child Abusers: Protection and Prevention* (2nd edn). London: Jessica Kingsley.

Pittaway, E. (1995) *Services for Older Canadians*. Victoria, BC: Ministry of Health/Ministry Responsible for Seniors.

Pitts, J. (2000) 'The New Youth Justice and the Politics of Electoral Anxiety', in B. Goldson (ed.) *The New Youth Justice*. Lyme Regis: Russell House Publishing.

Pitts, J. and Hope, T. (1998) 'The Local Politics of Inclusion: The State and Community Safety', in C. Finer and M. Nellis (eds) *Crime and Social Exclusion*. Oxford: Blackwell.

Piven, F. and Cloward, R. (1977) *Regulating the Poor*. London: Tavistock.

Piven, F. and Cloward, R. (1982) *The New Class War*. New York: Pantheon Books.

Power, M. (1994) 'The Audit Society', in A.G. Hopwood and P. Miller (eds) *Accounting as Social and Institutional Practice*. Cambridge: Cambridge University Press.

Pratley, N. and Treanor, J. (2002) 'Xerox in $2 bn Scandal', in *The Guardian*, 29 June.

Pratt, H.J. (1993) *Gray Agendas: Interest Groups and Public Pensions in Canada, Britain and the United States*. Ann Arbor: University of Michigan Press.

Preston, P. (2001) 'The Scandal of Feltham', in *The Guardian*, 6 August.

Priestley, M. (1999) *Disability Politics and Community Care*. London: Jessica Kingsley.

Prigoff, A. (2000) *Economics for Social Workers: Social Outcomes of Economic Globalization with Strategies for Community Action*. Stamford, CT: Wadsworth Publishing.

Pringle, K. (1994) 'The Problem of Men Revisited', in *Working with Men*, 2, pp. 5–8.

Pringle, K. (1995) *Men, Masculinities and Social Welfare*. London: University College London.

Pringle, K. and Harder, M. (1997) *Protecting Children in Europe: Towards a New Millennium*. Aalburg: Aalburg University Press.

Prior, P. (1999) *Gender and Mental Health*. London: Macmillan.

Pritchard, C. (2001a) *Sex Offenders: Profiles and Containment Strategies*. London: Home Office.

Pritchard, C. (2001b) *Teenage Suicides: Reducing Rates in Detention Centres*. London: Home Office.

Pritchard, J. (1992) *The Abuse of Elderly People: A Handbook for Professionals*. London: Jessica Kingsley.

Pugh, G. and De'Ath, E. (1984) *Working towards Partnership in the Early Years*. London: National Children's Bureau.

Putnam, R. (2002) *Democracies in Flux: The Evolution of Social Capital in Contemporary Society*. Oxford: Oxford University Press.

Putnam, R., Leonardi, R. and Nanetti, R.Y. (1994) *Making Democracy Work*. Princeton: Princeton University Press.

Quinsey, V.L. (1995) 'Predicting Sexual Offences: Assessing Dangerousness', in J.C. Campbell (ed.) *Violence by Sexual Offenders, Batterers and Child Abusers*. London: Sage.

Ralph, D., Regimbald, A. and St-Amand, N. (1997) *Open for Business: Closed to People*. Halifax: Fernwood Publishing.

Rawls, J. (1973) *A Theory of Justice*. Oxford: Oxford University Press.

Raynor, P., Smith, D. and Vanstone, M. (1994) *Effective Probation Practice*. London: Macmillan.

Raynor, P. and Vanstone, M. (1996) 'Reasoning and Rehabilitation in Britain: The Results of the Straight Thinking on Probation (STOP) Programme', in *International Journal of Offender Therapy and Comparative Criminology*, 40(4), pp. 272–84.

Reitzer, J. (2000) *The McDonaldisation of Society*. London: Allen and Unwin.

Rhone, S. (2001) 'NHS Accused of Racism', in *Precious Magazine* and available from *http://www.preciousonline.co.uk*

Richards, A. (2001) *Second Time Around: A Survey of Grandparents Raising their Grandchildren*. London: Family Rights Group.

Roberts, Y. (2002) 'We Are All Deserving, Including the Lazy', in *Community Care*, 2–8 May.

Robinson, L. (1995) *Psychology for Social Workers: Black Perspectives*. London: Routledge.

Robinson, L. (1998) *'Race': Communication and the Caring Professions*. Buckingham: Open University Press.

Roche, S.E., Dewees, M., Trailweaver, R., Alexander, S., Cuddy, C. and Handy, M. (1999) *Contesting Boundaries in Social Work Education: A Liberatory Approach to Cooperative Learning and Teaching*. Alexandria, VA: Council for Social Work Education.

Rock, P. (1990) *Help for Victims of Crime*. London: Clarendon Press.

Rose, D. (2002) 'Criminals Go Free in Legal Crisis', in *The Observer*, 23 June 2002.

Rose, N. (1985) *The Psychological Complex: Psychology, Politics, and Society in England, 1869–1939*. London: Routledge and Kegan Paul.

Rose, N. (1996) 'The Death of the Social? Refiguring the Territory of Government', in *Economy and Society*, 25(3), pp. 327–50.

Rose, N. and Miller, P. (1992) 'Political Power beyond the State: Problematics of Government', in *British Journal of Sociology*, 43(2), pp. 172–205.

Rose, S. (2000) 'Reflections on Empowerment-Based Practice', in *Social Work*, 45(5), pp. 403–12.

Rosenbaum, D. (1988) 'A Critical Eye on Neighbourhood Watch: Does it Reduce Crime and Fear?' in T. Hope and M. Shaw (eds) *Communities and Crime Reduction*. London: HMSO.

Rosenberg, H. (1995) 'Motherwork, Stress and Depression: The Costs of Privatized Social Reproduction', in E. Nelson and B. Robinson (eds) *Gender in the 1990s: Images, Realities and Issues*. Toronto: Nelson Canada.

Ross, R., Fabiano, E. and Ewles, C. (1988) 'Reasoning and Rehabilitation', in *International Journal in Offender Therapy and Comparative Criminology*, 32, pp. 29–35.

Rothman, J. (1970) 'Three Models of Community Organization Practice', in F. Cox, J. Erlich, J. Rothman and J. Tropman (eds) *Strategies of Community Organization*. Itaska, IL: Peacock Publishing.

Russell, D.E. (1984) *Sexual Exploitation*. London: Sage.

Russell, G. and Radojevic, M. (1992) 'The Changing Role of Fathers? Current Understandings and Future Directions for Research and Practice', in *Infant Mental Health Journal*, 13(4), Winter, pp. 296–311.

Russell, K.C. and Phillips-Miller, D. (2002) 'Perspectives on the Wilderness Therapy Process and its Relation to Outcomes', in *Community Forum*, 31(6), pp. 415–37.

Rutman, D., Callahan, M., Lundquist, A., Jackson, S. and Field, B. (eds) (2000) *Substance Use and Pregnancy: Conceiving Women in the Policy-Making Process*. Ottawa: Status of Women Canada.

Ruwhiu, L. (1998) *Te Puawaitango o te ihi me te wehi. The Politics of Maori Social Policy Development*. PhD submission, Massey University.

Saraceno, B. and Barbui, C. (1997) 'Poverty and Mental Illness', in *Canadian Journal of Psychiatry*, 42, pp. 288–90.

Saunders, L. and Broad, B. (1997) *The Health Needs of Young People Leaving Care*. Leicester: De Montfort University.

Schmidt, G., Westhuies, A., Lafrance, J. and Knowles, A. (2001) 'Social Work in Canada: Results from the National Sector Study', in *Canadian Social Work*, 3(2), Winter, pp. 83–92.

Schofield, J. (1998) *Men, Sexuality and Gender*. London: Sage.

Schon, D. (1983) *The Reflective Practitioner: How Practitioners Think in Practice*. New York: Basic Books.

Schorr, A. (1992) *The Personal Social Services: An Outsider's View*. York: Joseph Rowntree Foundation.

Scourfield, J. (2001) *Gender and Child Protection*. London: Palgrave.

Scrutton, S. (1989) *Counselling Older People: A Creative Response to Ageing*. London: Edward Arnold.

Segal, L. (1983) *What is to be Done about the Family?* Harmondsworth: Penguin Books.

Sevenhuijsen, S. (1998) *Citizenship and the Ethics of Care: Feminist Considerations on Justice, Morality and Politics*. London: Routledge.

Sewpaul, V. (2002) *Global Qualifying Standards*. Paper presented at the IASSW Conference in Montpellier, France, 15–18 July.

Sewpaul, V. (2003) 'Reframing Epistemologies and Practice through International Exchanges: Global and Local Discourses in the Development of Critical Consciousness', in L. Dominelli and W. Thomas Bernard (eds) *Broadening Horizons: International Exchanges in Social Work*. Aldershot: Ashgate.

Shah, R. and Hatton, C. (1999) *Caring Alone: Young Carers in South Asian Communities*. London: Barnado's.

Shapland, J., Willmore, J. and Duff, P. (1985) *Victims in the Criminal Justice System*. Aldershot: Ashgate.

Sheldon, B. (2000) *Evidence-Based Practice*. Lyme Regis: Russell House Publishing.

Shragge, E. and Fontane, J. (eds) (2000) *Social Economy: International Debates and Perspectives*. Montreal: Black Rose Books.

Siegal, R. (1995) 'Massachusetts Dispute over Aversion Therapy for Autism' in *E-Library*. Article available from *http://www.ask.elibrary.com*

Simpkin, M. (1979) *Trapped within Welfare: Surviving Social Work*. London: Macmillan.

Simpkin, M. (2001) *Practice in the New Millennium*. London: Sage.

Simpson, B. (2002) *Social Work in Informal Settlements in the Durban Metro Region*. PhD submission, University of Natal.

Skogan, K. (2001) *The Child Within*. London: Sage.

Skogan, W.G. (1990) *The Police and the Public in England and Wales: A British Crime Survey Report*. Home Office Research Study No. 117. London: HMSO.

Small, J. (1984) 'The Crisis in Adoption', in *International Journal of Psychiatry*, 30, Spring, pp. 129–41.

Smart, C. (1976) *Women, Crime and Criminology: A Feminist Critique*. London: Routledge.

Smith, D. (1995) *Criminology for Social Work*. London: BASW/Macmillan.

Smith, D. (1998) 'Social Work with Offenders', in R. Adams, L. Dominelli and M. Payne (eds) *Social Work: Themes, Issues and Critical Debates*. London: Macmillan.

Smith, D., Blagg, H. and Derricourt, N. (1988) 'Mediation in South Yorkshire', in *British Journal of Criminology*, 28(3), pp. 378–95.

Smithers, R. (2002) 'Truancy Sweep Catches 12,000', in *The Guardian*, 19 June.

Sone, K. (1995) 'Get Tough', in *Community Care*, 16 March.

Stack, C. (1975) *All Our Kin: Strategies for Survival in a Black Community*. New York: Harper and Row.

Staples, R. (1988) *Black Masculinity: The Black Male's Role in American Society*. San Francisco: Black Scholar Press.

Status of Women (2001) *Women's Economic Independence and Security: A Federal/Provincial/Territorial Strategic Framework from the Ministers Responsible for the Status of Women*. Ottawa: Status of Women.

Steele, M. (2002) 'Tide of Anger in a Sleepy Seaside Town', in *The Guardian*, 23 March 2002.

Stogdon, J. (2000) *An Account of My Journey to the United States of America to Explore the Role of Grandparents and Kinship Care*. Report prepared for the Winston Churchill Memorial Trust. London: WCMT.

Strega, S. (2001) 'The Case of the Missing Perpetrator'. Paper given at the SWS Research Seminar, Southampton University, 20 May.

Strega, S., Callahan, M., Dominelli, L. and Rutman, D. (2002) 'Undeserving Mothers: Social Policy and Disadvantaged Mothers', in *Canadian Review of Social Policy/Revue Canadienne de Politique Sociale*, 49–50, Spring/Fall, pp. 175–98.

Sullivan, P. and Knutson, J. (2000) *Maltreatment and Disabilities: A Population-Based Epidemiological Study*. London: National Working Group on Child Abuse and Disability.

Summerskill, B. (2002) 'Pensioners Worse Off', in *The Observer*, 20 June.

Sure Start (2002) 'About Sure Start'. *http://www.surestart.gov.uk/aboutFaq.cfm/section*

Tait-Rolleston, W. and Pehi-Barlow, S. (2001) 'A Maori Social Work Construct', in L. Dominelli, W. Lorenz and H. Soydan (eds) *Beyond Racial Divides: Ethnicities in Social Work Practice*. Aldershot: Ashgate.

Tapley, J. (2002) *Victims' Rights: A Critical Examination of the British Criminal Justice System from Victims' Perspectives*. PhD, Southampton University.

Tatchell, P. (1996) 'Aversion Therapy Exposed', in *THUD*, 2 August.

Taylor, D. (1992) 'A Big Idea for the Nineties? The Rise of Citizens Charters', *Critical Social Policy*, 33, pp. 87–94.

Taylor, M. (1999) 'Co-ordinators in FGC', in L. Dominelli (ed.) *Community Approaches to Child Welfare: International Perspectives*. Aldershot: Ashgate.

Teeple, G. (1995) *Globalization and the Decline of Social Reform*. Toronto: Garamond Press.

Thompson, E. (1994) *Fair Enough: Egalitarianism in Australia*. Sydney: University of New South Wales Press.

Toennies, F. (1957) *Community and Association*. Michigan: Michigan State University Press.

Towle, C. (1965) *Common Human Need*. Washington, DC: NASW.

Townsend, P., Davidson, N. and Whitehead, M. (1992) *Inequalities in Health: The Black Report and the Health Divide*. Harmondsworth: Penguin.

Toynbee, P. (2002) 'The Myth of Women's Lib', in *The Guardian*, G2, 6 June.

Toynbee, P. (2003) *Hard Work*. London: Bloomsbury.

Travis, A. (2001) 'Number of Boys Held on Remand Doubles', in *The Guardian*, 2 January.

Travis, A. (2002) 'Blunkett Hits at Police Handling of Crime Figures', in *The Guardian*, 14 May.

Travis, A. and Hopkins, N. (2002) 'Criminal Justice System Ineffectual, Says Blair', in *The Guardian*, 19 June.

Travis, A. and White, M. (2002) 'Former Prisoners Blamed for Almost a Fifth of Rising Crime', in *The Guardian*, 18 June.

Trinder, L. (2000) *Evidence-Based Practice: A Critical Appraisal*. Oxford: Blackwell.

Twigg, J. and Atkin, K. (1994) *Carers Perceived: Policy and Practice in Informal Care*. Buckingham: Open University Press.

Undergown, A. (2002) ' "I'm Growing Up Too Fast": Messages from Young Carers', in *Children and Society*, 16, pp. 57–60.

United Nations Development Programme (UNDP) (1996) *The 1996 Report on Human Social Development*. New York: UNDP.

United Nations Development Programme (UNDP) (2000) *Overcoming Human Poverty*. New York: UNDP.

United Nations Human Rights Commission (UNHRC) (2002) *Report of the Committee on the Rights of the Child, Review of the United Kingdom*. Geneva: UNHRC.

Van Soest, D. and Garcia, B. (2003) *Diversity Education for Social Justice: Mastering Teaching Skills*. Alexandria, VA: Council for Social Work Education.

Vass, A. and Weston, A. (1990) 'Probation Centres as an Alternative to Custody: A "Trojan Horse" Examined', in *British Journal of Criminology*, 30(2), pp. 190–206.

Walby, S. (ed.) (1997) *New Agendas for Women*. London: Palgrave.

Walker, A. (1990) 'The "Economic" Burden of Ageing and the Prospect of Intergenerational Conflict', in *Ageing and Society*, 10, pp. 377–96.

Walker, D. (2002) 'Can they Deliver on . . . Crime?' in *The Guardian*, 27 May.

Walton, R. (1975) *Women in Social Work*. London: Routledge and Kegan Paul.

Ward, D. (1998) 'Groupwork', in R. Adams, L. Dominelli and M. Payne (eds) *Social Work: Issues, Themes and Dilemmas*. London: Palgrave.

Ward, L. (2002) 'High Risk of Baby Deaths Among Teen Mothers' in *Guardian Unlimited*. http://www.guardian.co.uk/society/exclusion/story (14 May).

Waterhouse, R. (2000) *Lost in Care: The Report of the Tribunal of Inquiry into the Abuse of Children in Care in the Former County Council Area of Gwynedd and Clwyd since 1974*. London: Stationery Office.

Webb, D. (1990) 'Puritans and Paradigms: A Speculation of the New Moralities in Social Work', in *Social Work and Social Sciences Review*, 2(2), pp. 236–41.

Weber, M. (1978) *Selections from Max Weber*. Berkeley: University of California Press.

Wendell, S. (1996) *The Rejected Body: Feminist Philosophical Reflections on Disability*. London: Routledge.

White, S. (1997) 'Beyond Retroduction? Hermeneutics, Reflexivity and Social Work Practice', in *British Journal of Social Work*, 27(3), pp. 739–753.

Whitehouse, P. (1986) 'Race and the Criminal Justice System', in V. Coombe and A. Little (eds) *Race and Social Work*. London: Tavistock.

Whitton, C. (1931) *Report on the Operation of Mothers' Pensions in British Columbia, 1920–1 to 1930–1*. Victoria, BC: Province of British Columbia.

Wichterich, C. (2000) *The Globalized Woman: Reports from a Future of Inequality*. London: Zed Books.

Wiebe, R. and Johnson, Y. (1998) *Stolen Life: The Journey of a Cree Woman*. Toronto: First Vintage Canada.

Williams, F. (1989) *Social Policy: A Critical Introduction – Race, Gender and Class*. Cambridge: Polity.

Willis, A. (1985) 'Alternatives to Imprisonment: An Elusive Paradise', in J. Pointing (ed.) *Alternatives to Custody*. Oxford: Basil Blackwell.

Wilmot, P. and Young, M. (1968) *Family and Kinship in East London*. London: Pelican. (First published in 1957.)

Wilson, E. (1977) *Women and the Welfare State*. London: Tavistock.

Wilson, M. (1993) *Crossing the Boundary: Black Women Survive Incest*. London: Virago.

Wilson, R. (1997) *Bringing Them Home: The Stolen Children Report*. Canberra: Australian Government Publishing Service.

Wintour, P. (2002) 'Get Tough and Tender on Youth Crime, Says Tory', in *The Guardian*, 20 June.

Woolf Report (2001) 'The Woolf Report: A Decade of Change?' Address given by Lord Woolf to the Prison Reform Trust, London, 31 January.

Worall, A. (1990) *Women Offending: Female Lawbreakers and the Criminal Justice System*. London: Routledge.

Wyre, R. (1986) 'A Treatment Programme and a Study of the Serious Sex Offender'. Paper presented for HMP Albany, Isle of Wight.

Young, J. (1999) *The Exclusive Society*. London: Sage.

Younghusband, E. (1978) *Social Work in Britain, 1950–1975*. London: Allen and Unwin.

Zucchino, D. (1997) *Myth of the Welfare Queen*. New York: Touchstone Books.

GLOSSARY

Authoritarian populism: The view that offenders should be punished and warehoused rather than rehabilitated, which is spreading to all aspects of the 'law and order' debate.

Beveridge Report, 1948: The key document that established the British welfare state.

Contract government: The use of contracts to regulate private providers of services paid for by the state.

Instruments of governmentality: Measures that are used to guide behaviour in directions endorsed by the state or ruling elite. Professionals use these in their practice to legitimate particular ways of working. Individuals use them to regulate their own behaviour, when these become self-regulation.

'Law and order' debate: The controversies about the causes of crime and how to deal with offenders.

Modernizing agenda: New Labour's programme for shifting public services in more market-oriented directions. Key planks include: a specific 'New Deal' each for disabled people, lone parents, people over 50, unemployed people and young people; community regeneration programmes; child poverty alleviation schemes; and measures to promote social cohesion.

Neo-liberal approaches to welfare: Policies that promote market-driven welfare provisions. These are usually provided by commercial and voluntary agencies rather than the welfare state and charge users for their services. The state is involved as purchaser of services and sets the regulatory frameworks.

New managerialism: The management tool rooted in market-driven ideas and philosophies that has been used to change the service ethic in the public sector to a more market-oriented one, favouring monitoring and surveillance of workers and users.

Philanthropic gaze: The casting of service provision to target the most needy people in charitable terms that legitimate the privileging of professional voices over clients'.

Poverty reduction strategies: Policies that aim to reduce poverty nationally and globally. Eliminating child poverty is a key aim of the United Nations.

Privatization: The sale of state-owned assets, including housing, transport, water, residential homes, prisons, railways.

Punitive welfarism: Policies and practices that undermine entitlement to benefits by linking these to paid work. Workfare is a classic example.

Purchaser–provider split: The division of welfare service delivery into agencies, usually in the private or voluntary sectors, that provide the services (providers) and the state, which purchases or buys them (purchaser).

Regimes of control: A coherent set of policies and frameworks used to promote particular lifestyles, usually approved by the state.

Residual welfare: Welfare provisions that target only the neediest of those in need and are provided on a means-tested or charitable basis.

Social cohesion: The state reached when people have been integrated into mainstream society.

Social exclusion: Being left out of mainstream society through lack of access to social resources.

Social inclusion: Being brought into mainstream society, usually through opportunities that allow individuals to improve themselves.

Sure Start: A scheme that prepares 0- to 4-year-olds living in poor families for school, aimed at giving them a better start in life.

UNISON: The largest public sector union in Britain. It covers social work.

Universal welfare: Publicly funded welfare provisions that are provided to all as a right when needed.

Welfare consensus: Agreement on what welfare provisions citizens are entitled to. In the post-war period, two models have dominated: universal provisions paid for through general taxation and provided by the welfare state; and market-driven provisions purchased by the user.

Welfare legislation: The legal framework that specifies entitlement to benefits.

Welfare provisions: Social services that provide care and other forms of support.

Workfare: The philosophy of removing people from welfare rolls by linking access to benefits to taking up (low-paid) work.

AUTHOR INDEX

GENERAL INDEX